Marriage and Its Alternatives

Marriage and Its Alternatives

Lucile Duberman

PRAEGER PUBLISHERS
New York · Washington

Published in the United States of America in 1974
by Praeger Publishers, Inc.
111 Fourth Avenue, New York, N.Y. 10003

© 1974 by Praeger Publishers, Inc.

Library of Congress Cataloging in Publication Data

Duberman, Lucile, 1926–
  Marriage and its alternatives.

  (New viewpoints in sociology)
  Bibliography: p. 217.
  1: Family—United States. 2. Marriage—United
States. I. Title.
  HQ536.D8   301.42′0973   72-90660

Printed in the United States of America

Affectionately dedicated to my mother,
Josephine Duberman,
and, in loving memory,
to my father,
Joseph Duberman

Contents

Editor's Foreword

by Jerry Rose

VIEWPOINTS IN SOCIOLOGY is intended to make available to the beginning student of sociology a series of provocative treatises in the several areas of sociological study. One purpose of the series is to demonstrate the fallacy of the aphorism "Short writing makes long reading." Authors were given the difficult task of covering the major areas of their topic succinctly, but without producing an overly terse treatment. This could be accomplished only through the exercise of a keen sense of the sociologically relevant—an ability to separate the quick from the dead and the essential from the trivial. The model is analogous to that of the successful classroom lecturer who is faced with the need to present a seemingly infinite amount of material in a decidedly finite amount of time. It is, then, not coincidental that the authors in this series are gifted teachers as well as scholars.

Within the broad mandate outlined above, each author was encouraged to give his or her essay whatever individual slant was considered appropriate to the subject. Completely detached analysis is not one of the goals of the series. If the writers sometimes display passion and commitment, this is because sociology is itself a variety of human behavior.

In this volume Dr. Duberman has successfully consolidated and presented an immense amount of research and theory in the area of the family. It is one of the few books in this field to give scholarly attention to variant forms of male-female relationships. Considering the frequency, well documented in this book, of nonmarital sexual arrangements, divorce, remarriage, and step-relationships, to mention a few items, it is surprising that these topics are treated so lightly in most of the textbooks in the field.

Willard Waller once sarcastically remarked, "According to Victorian ideology, all husbands and wives live together in perfect amity; all children love the parents to whom they are indebted for the gift of life; and if these things were not true, they should be, and even if one knew these things were not true, he ought not to mention it."* Thus, the implicit model of family behavior among sociologists and laymen alike runs somewhat as follows: Virgin male meets virgin female. They fall in love and marry. He works and exercises ultimate authority; she keeps house and raises kids. They remain sexually faithful to each other throughout the marriage. Ultimately, the children leave home and the couple is presented with grandchildren—the joy of their old age. The grandfather dies and the grandmother remains a widow for some ten years, maintaining perfect loyalty to the memory of her lost mate.

Today few people follow, or even pretend to follow, this ideal, romantic, role-differentiated script. We all know families in which the wife is the dominant partner or ones in which a child never leaves the parental home or ones in which the husband and/or the wife is involved in extramarital sexual relations. Students of sociology are invariably going to raise hard questions about the discrepancy between the traditional sociological model and some of the families they know. Lucile Duberman treats these questions realistically. Her "futurological" focus encourages questions and arguments about changes in some forms of intimate and family behavior. One may not always agree with her projections of family trends, but the challenge will be invigorating for most students.

* Willard Waller, *The Family: A Dynamic Interpretation* (New York: Gordon Co., 1938), p. 13.

Acknowledgments

No one ever writes a book alone, and for that I am very thankful. Without the help and advice of my friends and colleagues, many obstacles could not have been overcome. My thanks go first to my trusted friend and adviser the late Erwin O. Smigel for suggesting the book in the first place. I wish to thank Arthur Vidich and Jerry Rose for their careful readings of the entire manuscript and their invaluable suggestions and criticisms. I also would like to thank my friend and attorney, Herman Taub, for commenting on the legal references. Special appreciation goes to my friend and editor, Gladys Topkis, who surely has no peer. Finally, my thanks go to my husband, Ralph Kaminsky, just for being there.

Introduction

There are two broad principles on which sociologists are in agreement. One is that man cannot live in isolation. That is, it is only through interaction and association with other human beings that man develops his personality and his humanness. Second, sociologists are agreed that social life is natural and that it is neither haphazard, random, nor accidental. Social life is intrinsically patterned, orderly, and regular, and, therefore, predictable. At the same time, sociology is a way of looking at a constantly changing social order. The concern of sociologists is to discover, describe, and explain the regularity and the irregularity (which in itself is orderly) of social life.

It is in the context of the family that man first interacts with others and learns the recurrent, predictable patterns of his social world. The family is the traditional culture-bearer. It transmits the society's values, goals, attitudes, and norms to succeeding generations. Furthermore, the family possesses the ability to alter the culture if change becomes necessary or desirable for society. The family is probably the most basic and pervasive of all human institutions. Everyone is born into some form of the family, and almost everyone helps to establish a new family during his lifetime. The family, then, is the most relevant institution to the greatest number of people.

And yet, sociologists did not begin to study the family systematically until the latter part of the nineteenth century. Like most social-science investigation, the study of the family was at first dominated by Social Darwinism. Charles Darwin first conceived of evolution as an explanation for change in the plant and animal worlds. Over time, sociologists like Herbert Spencer applied this theory by analogy to the development of society, from the primitive to the advanced. Spencer believed that social life is governed by laws of competition and conflict, that social evolution is a unilinear development, and that, by natural selection, the fittest societies and the fittest members of those societies will survive and the weakest will be eliminated. Those who held such a philosophy made little attempt at empirical verification; their interest focused on the evolution of the family. How did it begin? Where is it going? The answers supplied to such questions were more philosophical and wish-fulfilling than sociological.

During the early part of the twentieth century there was great concern throughout the world, especially in the United States, with social evils and social reform. Sociologists turned away from their focus on evolution and became advocates of social change, regarding the family as the best agent for such change. Once philosophers, they became ameliorists.

After World War I, however, sociologists began the scientific study of the family. Ernest Burgess, of the University of Chicago, led this movement as he urged sociology to abandon its interest in the origins of the family and its focus on the family as a vehicle for societal change. By viewing the family instead as a "unity of interacting personalities," he focused on the social factors that influence the family.[1] How do we select a mate? What are the forms of interaction among family members? What are the social factors in divorce? More than any other sociologist, Burgess is responsible for moving the study of the family out of the realms of speculation, of social reform, of psychology, and under the umbrella of sociology.

The most recent era in the history of the sociological study of the family began about 1950 and has been called the period of theory-building.[2] Family sociology is now considered to have emerged into maturity because of improved research methods, an interest in theory development, and a new willingness among members of the general population to discuss their personal lives. All this has enabled us to collect more reliable data, which, in turn, have helped to disperse the "sacred" aura surrounding the family. Now we can more easily penetrate the taboos surrounding husband-wife relationships, sexual behavior, courtship patterns, and so on. Family sociologists are no longer armchair speculators, musing over the mist-covered origins of family life. We are no longer do-gooders, concerned with reforming society through the offices of the family. We now have the tools, the theory, and the cooperation needed to discover and understand the patterns of the intimate interactions between men and women, children and adults in family life.

There are many textbooks on the sociology of the family. Most of them have chapters or sections on certain traditional areas, such as kinship, socialization, dating, mate selection, marriage, children, sex behavior and attitudes, marital dissolution, and remarriage. This book is not intended to offer yet another presentation of these traditional subjects but to supplement the more conventional works by focusing especially on predicting the probable direction each area will take in the near future. I will address myself to all the topics that should be and generally are covered in a course on the family, but then I will speculate on the trends that I believe are likely to emerge by the end of the century. I will consider such questions as: What will be the dominant form of the family? How will our dating patterns change? On what basis will we select our mates? Will our sexual attitudes and behaviors become more or less permissive? Are the divorce and remarriage rates likely to increase or decline?

Prediction is, at best, hazardous. The past is knowable; the future, always uncertain. "If we are faced with two conflicting opinions regarding a past event, we try to determine which is true; if we are faced with two conflicting opinions regarding a future event, we try to determine which one is more plausible. For, in the latter case, we have no way of arriving at certainty."[3]

In traditional societies, which are governed by custom, prediction of the future is relatively simple. Men live by rote; they can be sure that any given behavior will produce a given reaction. Unlike most traditional societies, ours is rapidly changing. Yet we still have the need to anticipate and understand others' reactions. Thus, we must take the known data and try to use them to prepare for the future.

There are several other reasons that this book focuses on prediction. One is human curiosity. This may sound like an idle reason, but why shouldn't we be curious? Without curiosity we would make few discoveries or inventions. So curiosity in and of itself has an important place in the human scheme of things. Another reason to speculate about the future is that it gives us greater understanding of the present. If we examine the future effects of a current phenomenon, we are likely to get insights into what is occurring right now. Finally, prediction is indispensable for formulating social policy. Changes in family life and interpersonal mores must be anticipated because issues and problems will inevitably arise with which our society and government must be prepared to cope. The educational system, housing administration, social welfare system, health care services, and so on, all must be ready to serve the needs of the coming generations.[4]

Hill identifies four ways to approach the amorphous area of prediction.[5] We can (1) extrapolate from current family trends, (2) draw inferences from studies of three generations of families, (3) speculate on the effects of technology on family life, or (4) assess the effects that family "experts" have on the family. Hill says that the first method—extrapolation from current trends—is dangerous but exciting. For one thing, trends have the unfortunate habit of occasionally reversing themselves. Many trends are short term, such as those of marriage, birth, and divorce rates. And trends are often unstable. Nevertheless, this is the method of choice in this book because the other methods are even less feasible.

We cannot use the method of drawing inferences from studies of three generations of families, because such studies are not available in all the areas covered. Evaluating the impact of technology on the family is, in my opinion, too narrow. Certainly it is true, as Ogburn and Nimkoff have eloquently pointed out, that technology has had a tremendous effect on the American family in terms of saving time and changing leisure-time patterns, but there are other factors, of equal strength, that affect the family.[6] The fourth method has been rejected because it is based on what I regard as an unlikely premise —that families are strongly influenced by the advice and suggestions of "experts." I do not feel that scientists as yet wield very much power for change in American social life.

I have chosen the method of trend extrapolation in order to speculate about the future of the American family and the relationships between men and women, between parents and children, and among siblings. I can hardly promise complete accuracy; indeed, I cannot be certain of any degree of accuracy. I can only use the available information as logically as possible in order to make the most reasonable statements I can in answer to the most important question faced by people everywhere, today as in all previous generations: What are we in our society doing today that will influence it for the generations that will follow us?

NOTES

1. Ernest W. Burgess, "The Family as a Unity of Interacting Personalities," *The Family* 7 (March):3-6 (1926).
2. Harold T. Christensen, ed., *Handbook of Marriage and the Family* (Chicago: Rand McNally, 1964), p. 10.
3. Bertrand de Jouvenel, *The Art of Conjecture,* trans. Nikita Lary (New York: Basic Books, 1967), p. 5.
4. Marvin B. Sussman, "Changing Families in a Changing Society," *Report of Forum 14: 1970 White House Conference on Children* (Washington, D.C.: Government Printing Office, 1971); Marvin B. Sussman, "Family Systems in the 1970's: Analysis, Politics, Programs," *Annals of American Academy of Political and Social Science* 396 (1971): 40–56; Marvin B. Sussman, "A Family Policy" (Paper presented at Groves Conference of Marriage and the Family, Winston-Salem, N.C., 1970); and Betty E. Cogswell and Marvin B. Sussman, "Changing Family and Marriage Forms: Complications for Human Service Systems," *Family Coordinator* 21:4 (1972):505–516.
5. Reuben Hill, "The American Family of the Future," *Journal of Marriage and the Family* 26 (1964):20–28.
6. W. F. Ogburn and M. F. Nimkoff, *Technology and the Changing Family* (Boston: Houghton Mifflin, 1955).

Marriage
and Its
Alternatives

1 What Is a Family?

Almost all Americans grow up in some form of the family, and therefore we tend to have an almost instinctive understanding of what the word *family* means. We have interacted daily with parents and siblings. We have planned and worked with them as a unit. We have been involved in disputes, sometimes serious and even destructive. Most people, then, think they have a complete understanding of what a family is, what occurs within it, what can be expected of its members.

This understanding is derived from living in families, and the feeling is that there is nothing else to know beyond that. After all, the phenomenon has been intimately experienced. But this is an egocentric view and limits our knowledge to the one or two families in which we have participated. Actually, the term *family* has as many different meanings as there are types of societies. In order to understand the family fully, we would need to take into account at least the areas of psychology, political science, history, biology, physiology, economics, and law. However, in this book we are bounded by sociology and we will therefore restrict our inquiry to the family as a social institution.

How can we define the family? What is its structure? What are its functions? Is it universal? If we confine ourselves to American society, it seems easy to define the family. We could use the model of the ideal family, the conjugal nuclear-family type, consisting of the husband, who is the breadwinner, the wife, who is the homemaker, and their biological offspring.* But we can readily see that there are innumerable exceptions to this model. There are one-parent families, headed by men as well as women. There are married couples without children. There are group marriages. There are unmarried couples living together with or without children. Should these be considered families also?

If we extend our vision beyond Western societies, we see many other structures. There are polygamous families of several types. One is called polyandrous and consists of one woman married to several men at the same time. In polygyny, the most common type, a man has several wives concomitantly. In cenogamy, a rare form, several men are married to several women simultaneously. If all these and more are legitimate forms of the family, then we must indeed define the term more cautiously. Let us examine how one of the major theoretical schools in sociology has addressed the question.

Structural-functional theorists, as exemplified by Talcott Parsons, analyze social phenomena in terms of the structure of the society and the functional relations of its parts. The approach takes as its basic assumption that social units are in interaction and that interaction is mutually influential—each part adjusts to the others. Through social processes, such as cooperation, conflict, accommodation, and competition, these social units form a relatively unified social system. Action, then, is conceived of as reciprocal, and the strain is toward equilibrium. The functionalist sees the social system as having a structure (a pattern of interrelated roles and statuses) and interdependent, cooperative parts that function harmoniously in order to maintain the society in balance.

Functionalists do not examine the institution of the family in isolation. Because they believe that all the parts of a social system

* At the present time most American family sociologists address themselves to what they call the conjugal nuclear family, defined as a type of family organization containing a husband, wife, and their unmarried offspring, with the primary focus on the marital relationship, as opposed to the extended family. The extended family is generally defined as one that includes at least three generations: parents, their married and unmarried children, and their grandchildren. There is a popularly held belief that this was the dominant form of the American family until the mid-nineteenth century; however, Reiss claims that this is untrue. (Ira L. Reiss, *The Family System in America* [New York: Holt, Rinehart, and Winston, 1971], p. 50.)

are interdependent, they study the family in relation to economic, religious, political, and other institutions.

If we look at the family in terms of this theory, we would say that the structure of the nuclear family is functional in an industrial society because it helps to maintain the social system. It is self-contained and isolated from the larger extended family, and it has the mobility required in an urbanized society. Conversely, functional theorists believe that industrialization is functional for the conjugal family because it permits the family to separate itself economically from the extended family. In other words, industrialization and the nuclear family are at the same time reciprocal functions of each other.

Talcott Parsons linked the family to the economic system in Western society in order to explain what he believed was its isolated character.[1] He wrote that one of the primary features of our occupational system is its stress on functional achievement. This means that people must compete for jobs, prestige, financial rewards, and the like. In order to compete effectively they must be available and mobile. They cannot be committed to the family farm or business. Our economic system requires a small family unit that can move anywhere in the world on short notice.

We can see, then, that there is a reciprocal relationship between our occupational institution and the nuclear family. Just as a certain type of economic system requires a certain type of family system, a given family system also requires a certain type of economic system. Parsons tried to show that the small, mobile family developed because a family farm or small family business can support only a limited number of adult children. As each son marries, he needs to find a way to earn a living away from the family farm or business. Thus, an economic system evolved capable of supporting nuclear families because several such families could not subsist on the land. The family and the economic institution thus interact and influence each other. Changes in either system will produce changes in the other; their cooperation helps to maintain equilibrium in the larger social system.

George Peter Murdock is another structural-functionalist who has studied the family. His definition of the family has caused a great deal of controversy:

The family is a social group characterized by common residence, economic cooperation and reproduction. It includes adults of both sexes, at least two of whom maintain a socially approved sexual relationship, and one or more children, own or adopted, of the sexually cohabiting adults.[2]

Murdock classifies three types of family. The nuclear family, as we have already noted, consists of the married couple and their children. The polygamous family is composed of at least one male or one female who is married to two or more spouses and has children by at least two of them. The third type is the extended family, consisting of two or more nuclear families, usually a married couple and their married sons and daughters with children of their own. Murdock refers to the last two types as composite families, but, he says, the nuclear family is basic and is found in all known societies. He does not claim that the nuclear family is the numerically dominant form in every society. Often it is deeply embedded in the polygamous and extended forms. However, the nuclear unit can be found and is functional in all cultures.

Murdock also discusses the functions of the family. He argues that the nuclear family is always associated with four basic functions—reproduction, socialization (see Chapter 2), economic cooperation, and sexual regulation—and that these functions must be performed by this family in any society in order for the society to survive. Therefore, the nuclear family structure is necessary for a society's existence. In this way, Murdock tries to prove that the nuclear family structure is everywhere and at all times universal, however deeply it may be hidden within other, sometimes seemingly different structures.

Since Murdock first presented his views in 1944, research has uncovered contradictory data. Murdock's four functions are certainly essential to the survival of a society and are therefore universal in the sense that they are performed in every ongoing society. However, it has by no means been established that these functions must be performed by the nuclear family. A 1955 study by Gough offers ethnographic information that seriously challenges Murdock's position.[3]

Gough's study is concerned with the Nayars, members of a military caste in India during the period before the nineteenth century. As military men, Nayars more often than not were away from home. Socialization was therefore carried out by the matrilinear *taravad,* which consisted of hundreds of people, divided into local residential groups called *tavaris,* each headed by a woman.

The Nayars practiced two kinds of marriage. The first occurred prior to puberty and was a ritual marriage called *tali.* A Nayar girl was married to a group of men in her own caste, represented by one as the *tali* husband. This marriage legitimized the girl as a sexually mature woman, capable of having children. The usual custom was for the *tali* husband to spend four nights with his bride. After that he might or might not continue to have sexual relations with her. Nevertheless, her children by any man in her caste were legitimate because the *tali* husband was considered the father.

The second marriage was called *sambandham,* meaning visiting husband. A woman in Nayar society was free to have as many such husbands as she wished, provided that they were in the same or a higher caste. Any child born to her by a lower-caste man was considered illegitimate.

The frequent absence of the Nayar men had a heavy impact on socialization practices. A woman lived with her mother and sisters and their children, and the responsibility for the socialization of her offspring fell on her and her female relatives. The father, at best an infrequent visitor, was not expected to participate in socializing her children. Furthermore, two other "universal" functions, reproduction and sexual regulation, were not charged to this family in the sense that they are to Western families. Sexual relations were almost completely without regulation except for the rule that they should not occur between a woman and a lower-caste man. Reproduction could be the result of any union between a woman and one of her *sambandham* husbands and was not confined to relations between one man and one woman.

Furthermore, economic cooperation, which Murdock also claimed was a function of all nuclear families, was not typical between Nayar spouses. Instead, it was the obligation of the matrilinear clan, the *taravad.* The mother's brother or oldest male relative supported the family. Nayar marriage, then, did not involve nuclear families. Rather, it was a form of group marriage. Understanding the Nayar practices forces us to question Murdock's assertion of the universality of the nuclear family, defined as a functioning unit of father, mother, and children, all residing together.

Another study that brings Murdock's contention into question is the work of Spiro on the Israeli kibbutzim.[4] Kibbutzim are usually small farming communities in Israel. Most of the people who founded these settlements came originally from Western European ghettoes, where they belonged to patriarchal (father-headed) families. Such people had generally not been allowed to hold property in their country of origin. Therefore, there was great hunger for land, and they set about reclaiming the desert as they attempted to unite the Jews in Palestine.

As members of extended families, the early kibbutz settlers were able to include entire communities, often numbering as many as a thousand people. A kibbutz might contain three-generational families, but they did not live as independent, self-sufficient socializing and economic units. The members did not reside together. That is, married couples lived together, but their children lived communally with their age peers, who became the most important socializing agents. This is not to say that the nuclear family did not exist on the kibbutz, or that it was functionless, as was once believed. Instead, we now understand that there was a minimal nuclear structure; in many ways the married couple and their children did function as a unit. However, this structure was absorbed within the larger community, which was responsible for socializing the children and for economic cooperation. The stress was on peer relationships, not on those that result from blood and marriage. The community, not the nuclear family, was the focus for economic cooperation and socialization, with the family playing a minor role.

The family life style just described was more characteristic of the kibbutz before 1948, when Israel became a state, than it is today. Nevertheless, the nuclear family in Israel is still very different from the American concept. Both the Nayar and the kibbutzim demonstrate that societies can and do live together without dependence on the nuclear family form.

DEFINITION OF THE FAMILY

Zelditch[5] argues that in order to define the family adequately and precisely we need to discover some norm* always and every-

* A "norm" may be defined as an accepted standard of behavior that is shared by the members of a society.

where associated with some group that can be called the family. The norm he selected was Malinowski's Principle of Legitimacy, which states that a family can exist only if some person performs the role of father.[6] The functions of that person (the pater, or social father) are twofold: (1) The status of the pater determines the status, rights, and obligations of the child, and (2) the pater has responsibility for the behavior of the child.

Zelditch noted that anyone, male or female, or any group of people, such as the members of a kibbutz, can be the social father. Such a person or group need not socialize the child; he need only assume responsibility for the child's conduct and for his status placement. This notion stresses the primacy of the social over the biological role of the father. If we define a family as a group that legitimates the child as a legal, recognized member of the society, we can incorporate many seemingly disparate family forms into our definition, provided that the paternal role is institutionalized in some way.

Ira L. Reiss has attempted to modify Murdock's and others' definitions of the family. He claims that there is only one universal function, not four, and that function is nurturance of the young. This definition, he asserts, is applicable to any family structure. Thus, Reiss defines the universal aspect of the family as follows: "The family institution is a small kinship-structured group with the key function of nurturant socialization of the newborn."[7] By "kinship-structured group" Reiss is referring to a social meaning instead of a biological one for the determination of kin members. Thus people who are related by blood can be less kinsmen, in the social sense of providing warmth, love, interest, and obligation, than people who are close to each other emotionally.[8]

Kinship, then, whether defined by blood, bond, or both, is the closest social tie found in any society. It involves special rights and obligations. It is easy to see that, if this is so, the structure of kinship groups can vary enormously. The point Reiss makes is that whoever performs the nurturant function for the infant is the core member of the kin group. It may be the biological mother, the grandmother, the nurse in the kibbutz, the biological or social father. One need not be the biological mother—indeed, one need not even be female—to be the nurturer, the social mother, of the newborn. Every society has such a small kinship-group system, defined in many ways, which socializes the child and provides him with emotional and physical support.

We can now define the family as an institution, found in several variant forms, that provides the child with a legitimate position in society and with the nurturance that will enable him to function as a fully developed member of that society.

THE FAMILY IN THE FUTURE

Structure

I have thus far demonstrated that from a worldwide perspective the structure of the family shows great variation. There are matrilinear families in which fathers, biological or social, are nearly invisible. There are patrilinear families in which mothers play almost no role. There are forms that stress the extended kin group, in which relatives other than parents are most important. Finally, there are societies that emphasize the larger community, in which the major socializers are age peers or other people who do not share a relationship based on either blood or marriage.

The most common form in the United States, however, is still the nuclear family. What will be the future structure of this family? Many alternatives are now available, and these alternatives have been increasing in number and acceptance in recent years. I can predict that this trend will continue so that structures will be more varied in the future than they have been.

In a series of articles, Cogswell and Sussman have pointed out the proliferation of variant family forms during the past decade.[9] They feel that this is in part the result of people's constant struggle for self-fulfillment and their search for means to that end. Cogswell and Sussman note that adaptation is an important function of the family because as a socializing agent it must mediate between the society and the individual. Its job, then, is to reflect in its socialization procedures the social changes that are occurring in the wider society. At the present time our society is changing rapidly, and the family must transmit and mitigate such changes in order to equip the neophyte to live in the world outside the family. The family's ability to adapt, Cogswell and Sussman tell us, can be seen in the creation of variant family forms. Each new form means recognition of a need for new role socialization and modification of individual and societal perspectives.

We now know that there are many types of families. Many sociologists are urging popular and professional recognition of these variant structures. Sussman and Cogswell write that the family "is not immune or impervious to social innovations and it is [able] in different settings and situations to influence as well as be influenced by sources and structures of change. In this decade the pluralism which heretofore was limited to descriptions of ethnic and class differentiations is now recognized as applying to the family."[10] These authors consider such variations to be "harbingers of the future."

In a special issue of *The Family Coordinator* dealing with experimental and variant marriage and family forms, almost all the contributors state explicitly or imply that the traditional nuclear family is inadequate today.[11] Most of them want to see this form at least modified, on the ground that the institution of the family as it is currently structured is oppressive, dull, and not productive of personal fulfillment. Some of these authors favor non-marriage. Others, such as Joy and Howard Osofsky, believe that equality can emerge in heterosexual relationships if our society alters its stereotypes of man's and woman's work.[12] Some, like Olson, believe that marriage will change in an evolutionary way, not radically, despite the experiments of our young people.[13]

The point I am trying to make is that there are and always have been many forms of the family other than the traditional nuclear family. What is new is that their existence is being discussed more often by social scientists today and is now being recognized, albeit not necessarily approved, by more members of our society. Let us now consider some of these forms and try to predict what will become of them by the beginning of the twenty-first century.

Group marriage means that several men and women are married to one another and cohabit indiscriminately within the group. The children are communal children, with several mothers and fathers, without regard to biological relationship. The ideology is one of sharing income, tasks, relationships, and every resource in a network of reciprocal exchange, based on availability of time, competence, and inclination, in the interests of the welfare of the entire "family."

I do not believe that this form of marriage is likely to become widespread, because at the present time most human beings, especially Americans, are socialized to be jealous and possessive of their mates. A radical change in emotional attitude would be essential for this form of the family to become common in the foreseeable future.

Communal families include several monogamous couples and their children who share everything except sexual relations. All tasks and income are communal. The family jointly owns a home, cars, furniture, and the like. Children are reared by the extended family, although the biological relationships are acknowledged.

Such systems are as old as recorded history. Their success in today's world is doubtful because of the intricacies of our economic system. It takes an enormous amount of trust to surrender all one's economic resources to a group. However, we cannot completely write off this form of the family, because there is a great deal of evidence that young people today, and some older people too, are experiencing a growing need for community. Many feel that in our impersonal, bureaucratic society there is much too little sharing, and they actively seek a sense of belonging. If the need for community becomes stronger than the need for individual economic "success," this form of the family will gain many adherents.

Several social scientists advocate *polygyny,* an arrangement in which two or more women are married to one man, particularly for the older members of our society, because of the high ratio of aged women to aged men.[14] Polygyny seems realistic because it offers widowed older women, who would normally be isolated, a chance to belong to a meaningful family group. Our small modern apartments and streamlined suburban homes preclude widowed parents from living with married children and finding family with them. There is simply not enough room. Furthermore, our ideology does not encourage three-generational families because of supposed conflicts in child-rearing practices and life styles. Grandparents can no longer play the meaningful role they once did in the traditional family. Polygyny would offer a viable alternative.

Another reason for endorsing polygyny among people over sixty is based on practical considerations. Many of our senior citizens have limited incomes. Two can live almost as cheaply as one, and three can live even more cheaply together than individually. If older people pooled their resources, diets and living conditions would improve because income could stretch farther, housework could be shared, and sex would be available to women who are widowed as young as sixty and who might otherwise remain chaste because they accept our societal norm against unmarried sex.

There are also emotional reasons. Older widows need not endure the loneliness and isolation that befall so many. Depression, caused by feelings of uselessness and alienation, could be avoided. In short, there are many good reasons for over-sixty polygyny.

However, I doubt that this structure of the family will make many gains in popularity during this century. For one thing, children might object because they fear the loss of inheritance or baby-sitting services. Secondly, major changes would be required in our laws on marriage and inheritance, which would be a long time coming given the tenacity of our present values.

In *homosexual marriage* members of the same sex could form legally recognized unions and have the legal right to adopt children. Some women feel that they can never attain equality in marriage to a man, that it can only result in attenuated desires and capabilities. In marriage between women, they contend, there is no subjugation, inhibition, or constraint and consequently mutual trust, openness, understanding, and honesty are possible.[15]

We cannot predict great advances for this form of the family, although certainly within the decade of the 1970s we will see much greater acceptance of homosexual alliances. For both male and female couples, there will be many legal problems, especially involving adoption of children. Furthermore, the present life style of male homosexuals does not encourage formalized relationships or the establishment of permanent homes.[16]

Unmarried marriage involves people who prefer to remain single but live conjugally, often, but not necessarily, sharing financial arrangements. This form already accounts for a sizable group among upper-middle-class and intellectual people, either during college and early post-college years or after the childbearing years. I believe that premarital and postmarital sexual involvement will increase; that is, more and more unmarried people will feel free to have sexual relations without seeing themselves as "in love" or as planning to marry. I believe that, as a result, the custom of living together without marriage will be adopted by more people over time. However, it probably will not replace marriage for the younger people. Johnson found that most of the subjects in his study of "courtship and commitment" who were living together were firmly committed to each other.[17] Reiss interprets this to mean that "living together may simply be an alternative form of courtship and not a sign of the ultimate breakdown of the marital system."[18] It appears to me that such couples will marry when they decide they want to have children, because they value the continuity of their relationship and are probably too well socialized to have families "without benefit of clergy."

Those who are past the age of childbearing and who prefer living together will probably tend not to legalize their relationships, especially if the woman is financially independent. For people of this age, there will probably be less need to marry.

In sum, then, I predict that living together will continue to be a form of courtship for most young people and that the practice will spread down through the class hierarchy, as many customs, fads, and fashions do. However, the desire to have children will probably induce them to marry eventually. Older people, who are financially independent, who cannot or do not wish to have children, and who are mature enough to withstand social pressures may, however, institutionalize unmarried marriage.

The *dual-career family without children* is a category that includes married couples who neither have nor plan to have children, perhaps because of the increasing cost of childbearing and rearing, the growing concern with an expanding worldwide population, the increase in knowledge about and availability of contraceptive information and devices, or the decline in the norm of having children.* In the recent past, nearly all people who married expected to have children, and if a year or two passed without evidence that

---

* However, the birth rate in the United States has steadily declined since 1955. In fact, the National Center for Health Statistics reported that, during the last nine months of 1972, the birth rate dropped below replacement level. (*New York Times,* 5 December 1972, p. 1.)

they were starting a family the young couple themselves and their parents were likely to be worried. Today many young women seriously doubt the value of motherhood. Journalist Gail Greene expresses this position clearly as she explains her decision not to have children:

> I don't want to have any children. Motherhood is only a part of marriage, and I am unwilling to sacrifice the other equally important feminine roles upon the overexalted altar of parenthood. Instead of condemning myself to the common syndrome of the unhappy creature who is mother first, wife second, woman third, and human being last, I champion the wondrously satisfying love of a woman and her husband, two adults enjoying the independence, accepting responsibility, yet independent and free.[19]

I predict that, for all the reasons given above—cost, concern with overpopulation, increasing availability of contraception, and decline in norm strength—more and more married couples will not produce children. An even more significant reason will be the growing awareness on the part of young women, partly as a result of the efforts of the women's liberation movement, that they can be more than mothers and that they have full equal rights with men to pursue meaningful, full-time careers without guilt. In such women there will be a diminished drive to "fulfill" themselves in the only way that was once open to them—motherhood.

The *dual-career family with children* is a form of the family including two adults, each with a full-time career, both contributing to the household in money and tasks, yet neither willing to sacrifice the pleasures of having children for a career. This family has two "heads," equally responsible to and for the household. This form of the family, although still represented by only a very small minority* in our society, demonstrates by its structure and in its expressed values what we can expect to see in the post-industrial society. Values are emerging that stress self-expression, individual achievement, and personal development for all human beings, especially for women. Sex roles are becoming more and more egalitarian. The

---

* Women comprised only 10 per cent of all professional workers in the United States in 1971. (Athena Theodore, ed., *The Professional Woman* [Cambridge, Mass.: Schenkman, 1971], p. 3.)

trend has been uneven, it is true, but nevertheless, there is a marked change in some segments of our society from the traditionally hierarchical family to one in which both parents participate jointly in all areas of family life.

Rapoport and Rapoport, reporting on a study of the relationship between work and family life, note that dual-career parents suffer from "role overloads," but that most couples have been able to come to terms with such problems because they benefit so vastly from the increased income, the personal development of the wife, and the closeness between father and children that result. These authors claim that "the trend toward cultural norms which are compatible with the dual career family seems to be well under way."[20] They regard the stresses expressed by their subjects as transitory and predict that they will disappear as society becomes more accepting of this type of family structure.

The *one-parent family* consisting of a parent whose spouse has died and one or more minor children has always been present in all societies. I predict that it will decrease numerically, both because there will be fewer deaths among young parents as a result of improved health and work conditions, and because remarriage is becoming more prevalent, so that young widowed people will remarry more often in the future than they have in earlier times.

The one-parent family consisting of a parent who is divorced from his/her spouse and one or more minor children will probably become more common as divorce becomes more acceptable. Our society's negative views of divorce are a reflection of our positive views of traditional marriage, but such values are less and less applicable to post-industrial society. Only a few decades ago the marital relationship was secondary to the larger familial unit. Today, however, we stress the ego needs of individuals, and divorce is considered an acceptable path if these needs are not met. I predict, therefore, that for many reasons divorce will become more frequent and that more people will be rearing their children singlehandedly.

The one-parent family may also consist of children and a parent who was not married at the time of their birth and is not currently married. The children are not necessarily biological children, and not all such families are woman-headed. At the moment there seem to be three very slight trends visible. One is for unmarried men to adopt children; another is for career women who do not plan to marry to adopt children; and the third is for such women to give birth to children. These phenomena reflect the growing recognition that many people who want to have children do not want to be married.

I do not, however, believe that unmarried single parents will comprise an appreciably large percentage of our population. One deterrent is our deeply embedded norm that a child needs two parents in order to develop in a healthy way. Another is that the cost, both financial and emotional, is very high for the single parent. The trend is more likely to be in the direction of childlessness.

A *reconstituted family* contains a man and a woman, at least one of whom has been married before, and one or more children from the previous marriage of either or both spouses. I believe that this structure is most likely to compete numerically with the traditional nuclear family in the future. One reason is the rapid acceleration of our divorce rate. Statistics indicate that about one third of the divorcing husbands and two fifths of the wives are in their twenties at the time of the divorce. With people divorcing at younger ages after shorter marriages, it may be that they will be increasingly likely to marry more than once during their lifetimes. Finally, the number of minor children involved in divorce has increased rapidly even as the birth rate has continued to decline. This increase in the number of divorcing couples with children indicates that children are becoming less and less of a deterrent to divorce.

Although the divorce rate is rising, the remarriage rate is rising even more rapidly. Actually, there are statistically very few single divorced people in our population. A survey made in 1962 showed that there was approximately one single divorcée in America for every 29 married people, making a total of about 3 million single divorcées.

I believe that remarriage may become one of the dominant forms in the future. Two major factors combine to make this assumption reasonable. One is our lengthened life span. The other is the rising divorce rate. We shall discuss these factors in greater detail in Chapters 7 and 8. Already nearly one of every four marriages contains a remarried person. There is every reason to expect that, if the rates continue to increase as they have during the past two decades, remarriage will numerically outdistance marriage in our society. Sociologists have already talked about "serial monogamy," the practice of repeated marriage, divorce, and remarriage. In fact, some segments of our society are already practicing this pattern.

It seems likely, then, that traditional marriage will lose adherents to all of the structures we have mentioned. The family will continue to exist, but in more forms than in the past. Probably the most prevalent form will be the reconstituted family. Americans are beginning to realize that the permanent, monogamous, traditional nuclear family is far from the only possible structure in which men and women can live together, achieve satisfaction for themselves, and raise healthy children.

Functions

The concept of function may have several different meanings. We can talk about the ways in which the family is functional for society, that is, beneficial or helpful to it. We can talk about how the functions of the family have changed in that the tasks performed within the setting of the family today are not the same as the tasks performed in the past. Finally, we can discuss the manner in which the family functions for itself—the ways in which it operates. We noted that many sociologists have discussed what they called the "universal family functions," and that Murdock has identified four: reproduction, economic cooperation, control of sexual relations, and socialization, while Reiss has claimed that there is only one universal function—the nurturance of the infant.

William J. Goode believes there are three universal functions: reproduction, or the replacement function; status placement, or the integrative function; and socialization, or the social-control function.[21] Goode, however, warns that these functions are not constant but vary in that not all societies have family systems that perform these functions to the same degree or in the same way. For example, the status-placement function is performed more rigorously in a caste society like India's than in an open-class society like ours. On the kibbutz in Israel the peer group has more responsibility for socialization than in the United States. Goode cautions us to take these variations into account when we attempt to compare societies.

Bernard Farber has contributed an important criticism in this regard.[22] Even when the family is carrying out its functions, he points out, it may be that it is not contributing to the well-being of the society. Perhaps reproduction is detrimental to the society in a time of population growth. Perhaps socialization to conform is harmful in a period when a society needs innovators. It is important to bear in mind that, when we speak of universal functions, we are not evaluating the worth of the performance.

Before we consider these functions of the family in the light of our present society and try to predict the future, let us summarize the work of two other sociologists who have discussed how the family has been changing since Colonial times.

Ogburn and Tibbitts advance the thesis that technology removed the traditional functions from the American family.[23] They feel that in pre-modern times the family performed six major functions, which it now performs either minimally or not at all. These were economic, protective, religious, recreational, and educational functions and status placement.

During the Colonial era, the family produced almost everything its members needed. Husband, wife, and children all worked together. Gradually, however, the family began to purchase what it needed as goods began to be manufactured by outside agencies. With these changes, the nature of the family changed also. Because people no longer needed single dwellings that could also serve as factories, multifamily dwellings increased. Men began to work outside the home; wives began to lose their economic importance; children became economic liabilities rather than assets. Thus, according to Ogburn and Tibbitts, industrialization caused the family to lose its function as an economic producing unit. This function has decidedly disappeared today. The family purchases almost everything it needs. Instead of being a producing unit, the family today is a consuming one.

Formerly the family was charged with guarding the members from harm by outsiders and with providing them with economic security during childhood, illness, periods of unemployment, and old age. Today, protection against outsiders is provided by the police and the military. Hospitals and medical practitioners safeguard our health. Insurance, social welfare, and various forms of compensation provide for us during unemployment and old age.

As bureaucracy and socialism increase, this function is likely to diminish still more.

In earlier times the family also performed a religious function. Prayers were read and services conducted in the home, with the father acting as the minister. Families said grace before meals, read the Bible together, and sang hymns together. Today few families pray together in their homes; the function has been taken over by the organized church. Children are sent to church and Sunday school to learn ethical and moral codes rather than taught at home. I predict, therefore, that the religious function also will disappear from the province of the family.

When most Americans lived on isolated farms or in small towns, recreation had to be sought around the family hearth. Often the parents read aloud in the evenings or the family enjoyed taffy-pulls, corn-popping, or group singing. Today we have commercial recreation. People jam our arenas for spectator sports, such as baseball and ice hockey. People participate in public places, playing golf or tennis, and go to concert halls, theaters, movie-houses, museums, nightclubs, and restaurants. Rarely do families go to these places together. Even television viewing, which is still done in the home, is no longer a family activity, as children, teenagers, and adults each watch different programs on different sets in different rooms of the house. The family as a recreational group is soon to be a thing of the past.

In Colonial times learning was rudimentary. Schools were frequently great distances from the home, and the three R's were taught by parents. Today, in our credentials-conscious society, children often enter nursery school at three and do not complete graduate school until they are close to thirty. Education is compulsory and has gone well beyond the basics. The classroom offers much more than formal education; it has begun to teach social behavior, morals, ethics—many of the lessons formerly taught at home. I estimate that, as day-care centers multiply and more post-secondary programs are offered, the function of formal education will vanish from the home almost completely.

The last function Ogburn and Tibbitts discuss is status placement. Membership in a family placed the individual in the social hierarchy. John Smith's son knew quite well how far he would go in school, what work he would do, whom he could marry, where he would live, and so on. This function also is disappearing and will probably continue to do so. People become anonymous in a large city. Children compete freely in a universalistic system. The rich man's son no longer automatically inherits the family business, and the poor man's son is no longer automatically relegated to a menial job.

With the decline of its institutional functions, Ogburn and Tibbitts believe that certain subtle functions of the family are becoming more conspicuous and important. In the past women were expected to be good housekeepers and mothers; men, to be good providers; children, to be obedient and industrious. Nobody thought about personal fulfillment or emotional satisfaction. Nobody worried about being "happy" or "well adjusted." But now, with the loss of its original functions, the family has become a setting for developing interpersonal relationships, seeking individual growth, cultivating social life. Thus, Ogburn and Tibbitts believe, the family has fewer and less mundane functions, but it is discharging them as well as it did the older functions of the past.

We might say that the family today has two major functions. One is affective. The family provides a setting in which the individual can freely express his personality and expect to receive understanding, consideration, and love. The ability of any given family unit to provide this service is a key determinant of its success. The second major function is that of consumer. Our economy demands that the family purchase the goods produced by our industry. If it fails to do this, our economic system is greatly endangered. Thus, there is a powerful economic impetus for people to marry, create homes, and have children, so that they will purchase those things that are necessary for the maintenance of society.

What functions will the family perform in the future? Certainly the six functions noted by Ogburn and Tibbitts will be almost totally taken over by other institutions. What will become of the affective and consumption functions?

I believe that the family will continue to act as consumer. The stress on material possessions is growing even stronger in our society, and that stress, combined with our tendency to build obsolescence into our products, will probably develop our consumer habits to an even greater degree. I also believe that people will continue to seek affective ties within the structure of the family, in the sense of trust, confidence, and security.

Will the family of the future continue to function as the setting in which to develop one's personality or satisfy one's emotional needs? I would guess that the answer is negative. A new ideology is growing in this country and it exalts the individual. It impels us to reach more into ourselves and to rely on ourselves. It urges us to withdraw from dependence on others, to avoid entanglements, and to keep our relationships temporary and tentative. Individualism, reliance on oneself, is becoming the supreme ethic. Our struggle is to free ourselves from involvement with all others, including the family, and to recognize that others do not really understand who we are, what we want, why we do as we do, or what we hope to become. The key is oneself—nobody else, not even one's family, can ultimately be considered trustworthy. Therefore, I predict that people in the families of the future will turn inward for self-satisfaction and will regard the family as a place where one lives in temporary peace, not where one seeks to develop his personality or find fulfillment.

In conclusion, I feel that the family of the future will be a reconstituted family. People will practice serial monogamy and children will take the presence of stepkin for granted. The family will continue to perform most of the older functions, but in a greatly attenuated form. It will continue to be a consuming unit and a dispenser of non-sexual love. People will turn inward for personal satisfaction and growth.

I have reserved discussion of the function of socialization for a separate chapter because it has always been considered the most important function the family is required to perform.

Notes

1. Talcott Parsons, "The Social Structure of the Family," in *The Family: Its Function and Destiny,* ed. Ruth N. Anschen (New York: Harper, 1959), pp. 241–274.
2. George P. Murdock, *Social Structure* (New York: Free Press, 1949), p. 1.
3. E. Kathleen Gough, "The Nayars and the Definition of Marriage,"

Journal of the Royal Anthropological Institute 85 (1955): 45–80. See also Joan P. Mencher, "The Nayars of South Malabar," in *Comparative Social Systems*, ed. M. F. Nimkoff (Boston: Houghton Mifflin, 1965), pp. 163–191.

4. M. E. Spiro, "Is the Family Universal?" *American Anthropologist* 56 (1954): 839–846; and M. E. Spiro, *Children of the Kibbutz* (Cambridge, Mass.: Harvard University Press, 1958).

5. Morris Zelditch, "Family, Marriage, and Kinship," in *Handbook of Modern Sociology*, ed. R. E. L. Faris (Chicago: Rand McNally, 1964), p. 681.

6. Bronislaw Malinowski, "The Principle of Legitimacy," in *The Family: Its Structure and Functions*, ed. Rose L. Coser (New York: St. Martin's Press, 1964), pp. 3–19.

7. Ira L. Reiss, *The Family System in America* (New York: Holt, Rinehart, and Winston, 1971), ch. 2.

8. David M. Schneider, *American Kinship: A Cultural Account* (Englewood Cliffs, N.J.: Prentice-Hall, 1968).

9. Marvin B. Sussman, "Changing Families in a Changing Society," *Report of Forum 14: 1970 White House Conference on Children* (Washington, D.C., Government Printing Office, 1971); Betty E. Cogswell and Marvin R. Sussman, "Changing Family and Marriage Forms: Complications for Human Service Systems," *Family Coordinator* 21:4 (1972): 505–516; Marvin B. Sussman and Betty E. Cogswell, "The Meaning of Variant and Experimental Marriage Styles and Family Forms in the 1970's," *Family Coordinator* 21:4 (1972): 375–381; Marvin B. Sussman, "Family Systems in the 1970's: Analysis, Politics, Programs," *Annals of American Academy of Political and Social Science* 396 (1971): 40–56; and Marvin B. Sussman, "A Family Policy" (Paper presented at Groves Conference of Marriage and the Family, April 1970, Winston-Salem, N.C.).

10. Sussman and Cogswell, *op. cit.*

11. *Family Coordinator* 21:4 (1972).

12. Joy Osofsky and Howard Osofsky, "Androgyny as a Life Style," *Family Coordinator* 21:4 (1972): 411–418.

13. David H. Olson, "Marriage of the Future: Revolutionary or Evolutionary Change?" *Family Coordinator* 21:4 (1972): 383–393.

14. For example, Victor Kassel, "Polygyny After Sixty," *Geriatrics* 21 (1966).

15. Janis Kelly, "Sisterlove: An Exploration of the Need for Homosexual Experience," *Family Cordinator* 21:4 (1972): 473–475.

16. For a discussion of the possible mutual exclusivity of homosexuality and traditional family life, *see* Carl Wittman, "A Gay Manifesto," in *Intimate Life Styles*, eds. Joann S. DeLora and Jack R. DeLora (Pacific Palisades, Calif.: Goodyear, 1972), pp. 255–265.

17. Michael P. Johnson, "Courtship and Commitment: A Study of Cohabitation on a University Campus" (Master's thesis, University of Iowa, 1969).

18. Reiss, *op. cit.*, p. 398.

19. Gail Greene, "A Vote Against Motherhood: A Wife Challenges the Importance of Childbearing," in *Toward a Sociology of Women*, ed. Constantina Safilios-Rothschild (Lexington, Mass.: Xerox College Publishing, 1972), pp. 112–115.

20. Rhona Rapoport and R. N. Rapoport, "Work and Family in Contemporary Society," *American Sociological Review* 30 (1965): 393.
21. William J. Goode, "The Sociology of the Family," in *Sociology Today,* eds. Robert K. Merton, Leonard Broom, and Leonard J. Cottrell (New York: Basic Books, 1959), ch. 7.
22. Bernard Farber, *Family: Organization and Interaction* (San Francisco: Chandler, 1964), pp. 23–28.
23. William F. Ogburn and Clark Tibbitts, "The Family and Its Functions," Report of the President's Research Committee on Social Trends, in *Recent Social Trends in the United States* (New York: McGraw-Hill, 1934), pp. 661–708.

2 Socialization

From the beginning of life each of us occupies a number of social statuses, positions in the social structure of the society that are related to other positions. Some statuses are consecutive: First we are infants, then school children, then college students, husbands and wives, parents, and finally grandparents or great-grandparents. We also occupy statuses concomitantly: A man can be a son, a husband, a lawyer, a brother, and a middle-aged person all at the same time.

Each status is expressed in terms of a role, a pattern of behavior structured around specific prestige, rights, and obligations within a group. We define a person's role by the set of expectations for his behavior held by others and by the person himself. When we occupy a social position (a status) and perform the role appropriate to that status, we are responding to the normative expectations of others and at the same time we are stating our own normative expectations of ourselves and those with whom we are interacting.

In order to learn his various statuses and the accompanying roles, a man must associate with other men. In so doing, he develops his personality and his humanness, and he establishes his place in society. This is accomplished by means of the process called socialization, which Brim defines as the "process by which individuals acquire the knowledge, skills, and dispositions that enable them to participate as more or less effective members of groups and the society."[1] Socialization is social learning and it occurs in a social setting. The learner is always part of that setting, and he responds to cues from others in the environment, just as they respond to him. Thus, the individual is at the same time a socializer and a socializee. Both the individual and the society are dependent on the process of socialization because they create each other. The infant must be molded into a social being, and the society must pass its culture on to the coming generation. Each helps to shape and change the other; neither can exist without the other.

Socialization is a lifetime process. Throughout the life cycle, as we enter new statuses, we have to learn new roles. The most important time for socialization is during childhood, and it is within the family, the most important primary group, that the most significant socialization occurs. Although there are always other socializing agents, such as teachers, peers, and the mass media, the family is the first such agent, and it has the most profound and long-lasting effects.

Here I must digress in order to elaborate on the important concept *primary group*. American sociology has followed the formulation of Charles Horton Cooley, in 1909:

> By primary groups I mean those characterized by intimate face-to-face association and cooperation. They are primary in several senses, but chiefly in that they are fundamental in forming the social nature and ideals of the individual. The result of intimate association . . . is a certain fusion of individualities in a common whole, so that one's very self, for many purposes at least, is the common life and purpose of the group. Perhaps the simplest way of describing this wholeness is by saying that it is a "we"; it involves the sort of sympathy and mutual identification for which "we" is the natural expression.[2]

Cooley's description of the primary group is best exemplified by the ideal-type family. The family is in face-to-face association; that is, there is frequent close physical proximity among the members. The family is always a relatively small, long-lasting group, both characteristics being necessary for the close association to be meaningful. Further, a primary relationship implies that the association is an end in itself, a good in its own right; the relationship is spontaneous, sentimental, personal, and inclusive. We regard other members of our primary group in a nonspecialized way; we are concerned with the whole person. We value them as people rather than as means to some end. The family, then, is the prototype of the primary group. Other primary groups, according to Cooley, are children's play groups and neighborhood groups. It is chiefly in such groups that socialization takes place.

George Herbert Mead described how the process of socialization works.[3] He began by assuming that no man can become human unless he interacts with other men. Studies have shown Mead to have been correct. Davis described cases of "isolated children," children who were reared with only minimal communication and contact with other human beings.[4] When found, they seemed to be mentally retarded and deaf and dumb. These children did not respond when spoken to. They had not developed into human beings, because they had not interacted with others, although they had the biological attributes that would have made such development possible.

Mead recognized, of course, that a social environment is not sufficient for humanness to occur. There must first be the necessary biological equipment, because man is the product of both his hereditary system and his social system. Obviously, *whether or not* a man learns is the product of his genes and chromosomes—his biological inheritance. *What* he learns is the product of his social system. The two modes are interdependent; both are necessary for the development of the full human being.

We are concerned here with the development of the individual from the point of view of his social world. For our purposes we will assume that the biological equipment is intact. How, then, does the social process work? Actually, our dependence on the social environment starts before we are born. Our parents have already been socialized. They have met, courted, married, and performed the sexual act in socially prescribed ways. They are, then, already prepared and predisposed to socialize their children in approved ways. At birth direct socialization begins, and the long, slow, gradual development of the self starts. This self emerges out of contact and communication with others.

Mead spoke of role-taking, a process in the course of which we put ourselves in another's place in order to understand the other's reactions. By imagining ourselves as that person, we can anticipate his behavior and—the most important aspect—we begin to see ourselves through the eyes of others. Mead noted that the self has a reflexive quality; man can be both subject and object to himself. We are capable of reflecting on ourselves. How is this possible? We become self-conscious by guessing how we appear to others and how others judge us. What we really do, then, is adopt the attitudes we think others have toward us and we behave in accordance with that evaluation. Without this role-taking, there can be no interaction and no communication. There would be no socialization, which means that society would disappear and man would not be human. Socialization, then, is a means of learning about our social setting: how to live in it effectively, how to behave in order to gain acceptance, how to evaluate ourselves, how to predict and control our lives. Unless we understand the attitudes of others and internalize* the values, goals, attitudes, and behaviors of others, society cannot continue and we cannot grow into social beings.

When two people hold a conversation they are role-taking. If one doesn't pay attention, the meaning of the other's remarks is lost. There is no communication, because the person being addressed is not role-taking. A similar situation occurs if, while reading, the reader allows his mind to wander. He ceases to role-take with the author, and the meaning of the words is lost.

Mead, we can see, stressed interpersonal interactions. He showed that people relate to each other in a social setting. One person acts and the other reacts, thus engaging in social acts. Meaning is attached to these social acts by the use of symbols, the most important of which constitute language. Of course we have other symbols, such as gestures, ways of holding and moving our bodies, manners of speech and dress. These are all symbols that we use every day to convey our messages to each other. They are ways of expressing who we are, what we feel, what we want, what we expect of each other.

These are the basic assumptions of symbolic-interaction theory (also referred to as interactional theory or role theory), which tries to explain the social-psychological processes of personality develop-

---

* As the term is used by role theorists, to *internalize* means to accept as part of oneself the norms of the group. It means that the individual adopts the standards of his society as part of his self-image, so that the attitudes and behaviors of the group come to feel "natural," as if there were no possible alternatives.

ment and socialization. The theory addresses itself to the problem of the relationship between the individual and his society. How is the personality organized? How do we develop persistent, recurrent behavior patterns? How do we acquire ways of behaving, attitudes, and norms?

In attacking these problems, role theory makes certain basic assumptions: (1) It assumes that man is different from other animals because his behavior derives from social interaction; therefore, nothing is to be gained from studying non-human beings. (2) Because man is born into a structure of interacting individuals, the best way to study his social behavior is to study his society. (3) A newborn child is asocial, neither antisocial nor social. He is not yet "human" but has the equipment for humanness to develop, which is most likely to occur within a family setting. (4) Man is both actor and reactor. That is, he not only responds to stimuli from his environment but also produces stimuli for other people and for himself. Further, say the interactionists, man not only responds to a given physical environment but also mediates that environment by creating symbols. He selects out of the external world and then interprets and reacts to his own selections. Thus, men stimulate themselves and respond to these self-generated products. The interactionist, knowing this, always tries to incorporate man's subjective point of view into his research. Therefore, role theory addresses itself especially to the family because it is within the framework of the family that the processes of personality development and socialization are most likely to occur.

Role theorists define the self in terms of social interaction. Society is dependent on the individual, and individuals cannot exist outside of society. The self, then, is a social product, and it is in primary groups that the self evolves. The child's early years within the family are significant because it is then and there that he learns what is important, what to strive for, how to attain his goals, what to value, believe in, and trust.

Symbolic interaction depicts the family as a system of interdependent roles. Every society institutionalizes these roles, but the actors may be interchangeable. Thus in certain matrilinear societies the social father is frequently the mother's brother. In our society the social father and the biological father are almost always the same person. Burgess, Locke, and Thomas have given us a classical definition of the family from the point of view of role theory:

> The family may . . . be defined as a group of persons united by ties of marriage, blood, or adoption; constituting a single household; interacting and communicating with each other in their respective roles of husband and wife, mother and father, son and daughter, brother and sister; and creating and maintaining a common culture.[5]

Role theorists, then, emphasize the operation of the family in terms of interrelated roles that are defined by the society. They assume that the significant variables are the roles, not the individuals who occupy the statuses.

We role-take with many different people all through our lives, and in the process we develop a well-integrated set of attitudes, which Mead defined as the social self. Now, although many of our attitudes are shared with others, as we grow older we learn to select certain attitudes and to reject others. Mead had a special name for this practice of selection. He said that the people who strongly influence our lives and our attitudes from the time of birth until death are "significant others." In infancy and childhood, significant others are parents, siblings, and perhaps grandparents. As we go out into the world, the group broadens to include peers, teachers, famous people, and so on—all those with whom we come into contact who are important to us, either negatively or positively. A significant other can be someone we admire and wish to emulate or someone we dislike and make an effort to avoid imitating. If he influences our concept of ourselves in any way, he is a significant other. Thus, the social self develops through a process of selection, and the result is that people develop differently as they select differently, until each evolves into a unique human being.

One function of socialization, then, is to teach the individual how to be a bona fide member of his society. Another is to enable him to develop a sense of himself as a social being. Yet another is to help him learn how to anticipate the reactions of other people, which makes it possible for him to interact with confidence. Finally, becoming socialized means learning the expected roles attached to a status we will occupy in the future. This is called anticipatory socialization.[6] One such status is sex.

LEARNING SEX ROLES

At birth a child's sex is a very obvious physiological fact that for almost everyone will remain constant throughout life. All human beings, with rare exceptions, are members of one of two classes—male or female. Sex, then, is an ascribed status—one we inherit at birth and in ordinary circumstances cannot change. Sex status is used in every known society as a basis for differentially assigning tasks and prestige. We tend to believe in inherent dissimilarity. Unfortunately, societies often go too far in assuming that certain differences in talents, attitudes, and other characteristics can be attributed to the physical differences between men and women, when they are in fact either nonexistent or products of differential socialization.

I have explained how people learn their statuses and roles in society through the process of socialization. Let us move from this general description to a specific analysis of how children learn the roles associated with being masculine or feminine. We learn our sex roles just as we learn how to be sons, mothers, teachers, and doctors—by role-taking. Within a social setting, usually the family, using symbols to communicate and express meanings, children learn to become masculine and feminine. We are born into an ascribed status, either male or female, but we are socialized into achieved statuses—masculinity or femininity according to societal definitions. Children learn the dress, body movements, attitudes, and goals appropriate for their own sex. Generally, they imitate the parent of the same sex, gradually internalizing all the proper attributes for that sex. Each sex learns the rights, obligations, and prestige attached to its sex status. At the same time, the child learns the reciprocal role. Girl children role-take with their fathers as well as their mothers, because they cannot become feminine unless they understand the rules that apply to their role partners.

Research by Kagan and others has shown that children as young as three years are aware of our cultural definitions of masculinity and femininity.[7] They are able to tell us that little girls should be cute and pretty while little boys should be big and strong. They indicate that daddies are aggressive while mommies are nurturant and passive. They know that girls are allowed to be more dependent and conforming than boys. What is of special interest here is that there are social-class differences in these attitudes.[8] Lower-class children, for example, make sharper sex-role distinctions. Lower-class women are seen by their children as more passive, nurturant, dependent, and so on than are middle-class women by their children. If it is true that parents are the models for the males and females the children are describing, then we can assume that different classes must have different attitudes toward sex roles. This is important because it indicates that the obvious biological differences between men and women need not be rigidly interpreted. Much of the "proper" behavior for each sex is socially determined.

Most researchers agree that a child is more likely to develop clear, traditional behavioral and attitudinal sex postures if he achieves strong identification with the same-sex parent, especially if the parent behaves in traditional ways.[9] That is, the little girl who helps her mother in the kitchen and the little boy who follows his father into the workshop are apt to be more "feminine" and more "masculine," respectively, than those who do not. The significant point here is that, as children learn their sex roles, they are encouraged to inhibit or display certain attitudes and behaviors, which they come to regard as masculine or feminine because they are so defined by the society. It well may be that there is little that is biological or innate about most of these stances, that the young-sters are instead responding to cultural pressures to which they will probably continue to respond for life.

In summary, we learn sex roles just as we learn any other role suited for a status we occupy. Small children observe those around them and, by internalizing what they observe, come to see themselves in a status. Gradually the role behavior comes to feel "natural," so that little girls "instinctively" prefer dolls to baseball bats and little boys "innately" prefer trucks to paper dolls. However, these are culturally, not biologically, induced characteristics, and they need not represent maleness and femaleness if we do not allow them to dominate our thinking.

SEX STEREOTYPING

Stereotyping and the process of socialization interact and reinforce one another, and nowhere is this interaction more dramatic than in the case of sex stereotyping. According to the traditional stereotype, women are and should be passive, unthinking, emotional, subjective, intuitive, practical, self-sacrificing, narcissistic, inconsistent, helpless, and dependent. Men, on the other hand, are and should be strong, unemotional, brave, dependable, rational, coherent, and intelligent.

As parents want their sons to become masculine and their daughters feminine, they socialize their children to believe in, and act according to, these models. And the more successful the socializing process is, the more powerful and "valid" the stereotype becomes.

To illustrate: We observe that, if Jane's parents accept the notion that it is feminine to be passive, intuitive, and subjective rather than assertive, rational, and logical, they will socialize Jane to act accordingly. The more successful they are, the more they will be convinced of the validity of the stereotype and the propriety of their actions. The final confirmation will come when Jane shows that she has internalized the stereotype by repeating the process with her own daughter, demonstrating that she has been socialized to socialize her daughter appropriately. Any doubts that either Jane or her parents may have had will be readily dispelled by the vast numbers in the society who share these ideas and act accordingly. Thus, the stereotype gains strength from two sources. On the one hand, it has the character of a self-fulfilling prophecy, and, on the other, it receives almost universal acceptance.

In the language of sociology, the term *stereotype** is reserved to describe a phenomenon that has detrimental results. The results are detrimental in large part because the stereotyped person himself accepts the stereotype as valid, either consciously or unconsciously. A particularly interesting experiment was carried out by Goldberg, who tried to discover how women regarded their own sex.[10] Did they consider women inferior?

Goldberg reasoned that, in addition to the obvious physical differences there are real differences between men and women that he believed were socially determined and induced. What concerned him was whether women perceive their own sex not only as different but as inferior. He felt that, like any prejudice, anti-feminism distorts

---

* *Stereotype* may be defined as a set of biased generalizations about a given group of people, almost always exaggerated and oversimplified.

perception. If women see themselves as deficient vis-à-vis men, they will tend to see feminine accomplishments as inferior. To an anti-feminist, what is feminine is inferior and what is inferior is feminine.

Goldberg asked 140 college girls to sex-type a list of fifty occupations. On the basis of their ratings, he determined that law and city planning were identified as male occupations and elementary school teaching and dietetics were considered female, whereas linguistics and art history emerged as sex-neutral. Goldberg then selected one article from the professional literature on each of these six fields and "prepared" them for review by each of these 140 girls. The preparation consisted of assigning fictitious authorship, so that for each article seventy copies were "written" by a man, the other seventy by a woman. Each subject was then handed a package of six articles, one from each field, the packages prepared in such a way that each girl received three articles "written" by men and three articles "written" by women. No special mention was made of the authors, although their names were clearly printed on the title page.

The girls were asked to rate the articles for value, persuasiveness, and profundity and to rate the authors for style, competence, and ability to sway the reader. The researchers expected that the male "authors" would rate higher both in the "men's" fields and in the neutral fields and that women would rate higher in the "women's" fields. Instead, the men "authors" were rated higher in all six fields.

Goldberg interpreted these findings to mean that women tend to downgrade the work of other women, even professionals, and even in traditionally female fields. Clearly there was distortion in their perception, because the ratings depended not on the content of the articles but, rather, on whether their "authors" were men or women.

SOCIALIZATION IN THE FUTURE

In order to talk about changes in socialization patterns, we must first examine changes in family structures and functions. Prior to the 1930s, family life in America was shaped predominantly by tradition. Ritual and discipline were embodied in an unquestioned hierarchy of power, from father through mother to children. In the traditional family there were clearly defined sex-differentiated role specifications firmly based in custom. The husband's role was held to be instrumental; the wife's, expressive-integrative.*

By the 1940s, however, a new form—the companionship family —began to emerge, deriving its meaning less from community pressures and tradition and more from interpersonal relations and feelings of sympathy, understanding, and comradeship. The so-called companionship marriage, which is still largely a middle-class form, emphasizes the affective aspects of the male-female relationship. Role specifications are taken for granted, and the emphasis is on personal interaction, love, companionship, sexual pleasure, and that little-understood but highly touted value—communication.

This heightened concern for each other's personal happiness and for "togetherness" spread rapidly after World War II. Children acquired more freedom to make choices, moved closer to their parents, and participated in decision-making in a parent-guided democracy. The family turned gradually into an emotional depot, with members more openly expressing the whole gamut of loving hostility toward one another. Not only husband and wife but children as well became "intimate enemies."[11] Hostility, of course, is no less prevalent than in the traditional family. The difference is that in the companionship family the expression of conflict is not only sanctioned but encouraged.

A critical change also occurred in the relations between the family and other sectors of the society. The family participated less as a family in established religious and cultural centers. Mobility increased greatly, so that fewer marriages matured in the midst of long-lasting friendships or frequently encountered kinfolk. Relationships with neighbors became more superficial. This trend resulted in two phenomena: (1) fewer informal groups that included the nuclear family and its extended kin group and (2) a preoccupation with achievement in work, career, and school.

* The instrumental role includes responsibility for major decisions, discipline of the children, and solutions of family problems. The expressive-integrative role is said to be responsible for the management of tension, for emotional care, and for support and affection.

The companionship family, however, carries the seeds of its own destruction. Society's definition of the wife as a loving, subordinate companion, secreted in suburbia with *Kinder und Kuche,* television, and ladies' home journals as her chief sources of self-fulfillment, is being challenged by women's growing demands for equality. In many cases the husband's work has become so specialized that he cannot talk coherently about it with his wife. The growing isolation of the family unit from strong community bonds means that independence eventually has to be replaced by freedom to choose alternative cultural styles and social goals. Thus, companionship families are beginning to founder and to turn inward—each home becoming a well-fortified citadel.

This, then, is the deteriorating middle-class companionship family. The ideal of "togetherness" is disappearing under the forced recognition that men and women, children and parents are not "natural" associates in a closed corporation with shared values and goals. It is becoming clear that each sex and each age group have distinct needs and different ways of attaining them, that dependence can be the catalyst for hatred and anger.

Upper-middle-class and intellectual American families, then, are moving toward a third form—the existential family.* "Existential" refers to the fundamental right assumed by the individual to question the meaning of every authority, every relationship, including the family. To question the role of the family in one's life is to challenge, to deny, and ultimately to choose one's own interests over family loyalty and feeling. A meaningful difference between the new form and its precursors has to do with time and space perception. The existentialist is concerned with the present, not with the past or future. His own lifetime is an end in itself; the value stresses the "now"—the effort to find oneself and live one's own life fully, today.

It must be made clear that this new form of the family at present can be found only among the upper middle class and the intellectual class in the United States. However, it is not inconceivable that it will eventually trickle down the social hierarchy and become the dominant form.

---

* This term was first described to me by Howard Polsky, whose definition and explanation of it are used in this book.

This "liberated" way of life will see each family member granting a charter of independence to the others, with the expectation of satisfaction attached mainly to activities carried on independently. There will be a marked tendency toward segregation of the generations, with adolescents finding their way apart from their parents. Existentialists will not take the support of the family for granted. More and more we will find individuals asking first and most frequently, "What's in it for me?" The popularity of "doing one's thing" will impel people to rely more and more on themselves.

These changes in the structure of the family and in the interaction among family members will have a marked effect on the family's function of socialization. Parents, in their pursuit of self, will be much less concerned to see that their children receive the "proper" values and attitudes. They will be more likely to allow the children to find their own way, with a minimum of guidance and direction. Children, especially very young children, will turn to peers, siblings, and teachers for the socialization they will not be aware they are seeking. Teachers, however, being human adults, will most likely share the ideology of the parents and therefore will be of little help as trainers of the young. Without another salient choice, then, children will turn to their siblings and age peers.

Although there has been little empirical research in the area of sibling relationships, several authors have suggested that the ties among siblings are second in strength only to those between parent and child; "sibling solidarity" may be the fundamental kinship bond in bilateral systems.[12]

Many authors have noted the important functions the sibling relationship performs.[13] Having a sibling contributes to early socialization process by providing peer role models and training in cooperation, accommodation, and conflict management. The relationship evokes the idea of fair play and provides an early concept of social reality. Furthermore, siblings offer one another companionship, emotional security, and love. Having a sib means that one learns early how to share privileges and obligations.

We can see, then, that, if given the opportunity, socialization by age cohorts can be an extremely effective force in shaping personality. It can also leave marked effects on sex-role development. Brim, as well as Sutton-Smith and Rosenberg, believes that children in the same family tend to become like one another.[14] That is, a boy will acquire feminine characteristics if he has a sister and masculine characteristics if he has a brother. The findings of Leventhal do not support this "imitation" hypothesis.[15] Leventhal discovered that men with sisters displayed a more masculine response pattern than men with brothers. He suggests that a younger male child will tend to adopt traits that are opposite those of his older sibling, a theory he calls the "contrast" hypothesis.

A series of follow-up studies by Leventhal led him to the conclusion that both hypotheses are correct. That is, the imitation theory holds for some characteristics while the contrast hypothesis holds for others. Leventhal used culturally approved modes of behavior and interest to test his hypothesis. He found that men with sisters tended to be more interested in outdoor and athletic activities and to have higher motor-fitness scores and greater athletic competence than men with brothers. Furthermore, men with female siblings were more likely to choose a "masculine" occupation, such as engineering, and to be interested in belonging to fraternities than men with male siblings. Leventhal found that, in these areas, which are thought of as being more "male" than "female," the contrast hypothesis was more likely to obtain: Men with sisters appeared to have more "masculine" interests than men with brothers.

In terms of emotional behavior, however, Leventhal found that men with sisters displayed more "feminine" traits, such as greater anxiety and emotional reactivity, than men with brothers. Finally, in the area of interpersonal behavior, the findings indicate that men with sisters were likely to be less dominant and assertive than men with brothers. The last two groups of findings are consistent with the imitation hypothesis.

Research in this area is incomplete, but I believe that further study will support the imitation hypothesis: Cross-sex siblings adopt each other's traits. If that is so, we can speculate that, as more socialization is carried out by siblings and peer-group members, there will be a general tendency for male and female children to become more alike than if they were to continue to be socialized by adults. Although we cannot expect this to be true for every characteristic, the ideals of the women's liberation movement and the change in attitude in the mass media, with the current stress on equality of the sexes, should support this convergence of sex-role learning.

What would be the result of less specific and less rigid sex-role socialization? Girls, for example, might be expected to become more interested in careers and activities other than marriage and motherhood. They will be less likely to try to "prove" their femininity in traditional ways and more likely to assert their personal ambitions outside the areas traditionally assigned to females. Boys, on the other hand, are likely to feel freer to express emotions, to cry, to display an interest in homemaking and child-rearing activities. In short, I predict that the ties that have bound both girls and boys into sex roles that did not always fit their personalities will be loosened and that both sexes will gain a measure of freedom. Girls will be able to pursue careers, to refuse to marry for security alone, to put off having children, perhaps forever. Boys will be able to display weakness without fear of loss of "masculinity." They will be able to indulge the gentler side of their natures without ridicule. We may see a reversal of roles in many instances. Some men may stay home to care for the house and the children while their wives are out working to support the family. If such role reversal is suitable for certain couples, this could be a liberating factor of great value to our society.

In short, I predict that the family is likely to become more existential. That is, its members are likely to be less dependent on each other and more concerned with themselves. It follows that parents will minimize their function of socialization, which will be taken over by peers and siblings. The result will be a decline in sex-specific socialization.

Notes

1. O. G. Brim, Jr., "Socialization Through the Life Cycle" in *Socialization After Childhood*, eds. O. G. Brim, Jr., and S. Wheeler (New York: John Wiley, 1966).
2. C. H. Cooley, *Social Organization* (New York: Charles Scribner's Sons, 1909), p. 25.
3. George H. Mead, *Mind, Self, and Society* (Chicago: University of Chicago Press, 1934).
4. Kingsley Davis, *Human Society* (New York: Macmillan, 1949), pp. 204–208.

5. Ernest W. Burgess, Harvey J. Locke, and Mary Margaret Thomas, *The Family: From Institution to Companionship,* 3d ed. (New York: American Book, 1963), p. 2.
6. Robert K. Merton, *Social Theory and Social Structure* (New York: Free Press, 1957).
7. Jerome Kagan, "Acquisition and Significance of Sex Typing and Sex Role Identity," in *Review of Child Development Research,* vol. I, eds. Martin L. Hoffman and Lois W. Hoffman (New York: Russell Sage Foundation, 1964), pp. 137–196.
8. Melvin L. Kohn, *Class and Conformity* (Homewood, Ill.: Dorsey, 1969).
9. David B. Lynn and William L. Sawrey, "The Effects of Father-Absence on Norwegian Boys and Girls," *Journal of Abnormal and Social Psychology* 59 (1958): 258–262.
10. Philip Goldberg, "Are Women Prejudiced Against Women?" in *Toward a Sociology of Women,* ed. Constantina Safilios-Rothschild (Lexington, Mass.: Xerox College Publishing, 1972), pp. 10–13.
11. George R. Bach and Peter Wyden, *The Intimate Enemy* (New York: William Morrow, 1969).
12. R. Pherson, "Bilateral Kin Groups as a Structural Type," *University of Manila, Journal of East Asiatic Studies* 3 (1954): 199–202.
13. Clifford Kirkpatrick, *The Family as Process and Institution* (New York: Ronald Press, 1963), pp. 247–253.
14. O. G. Brim, Jr., "Family Structure and Sex Role Learning by Children: A Further Analysis of Helen Koch's Data," *Sociometry* 21 (1958): pp. 1–16; and B. Sutton-Smith and B. G. Rosenberg, "Age Changes in the Effects of Ordinal Position on Sex-Role Identification," *Journal of Genetic Psychology* 107 (1965), pp. 61–73.
15. Gerald S. Leventhal, "Influence of Brothers and Sisters on Sex-Role Behavior," *Journal of Personality and Social Psychology* 16:3 (1970), pp. 452–465.

3 Sexual Attitudes and Behavior

In this chapter I will discuss American attitudes toward sexual matters, before, within, and outside marriage. Then we will examine how those attitudes conform to actual behavior.

Most sociologists agree that an attitude is learned, emotionally colored, and relatively persistent. An attitude involves a negative or a positive evaluation and generally evokes a predictable and characteristic response.[1] For example, parental attitudes toward premarital sexual intercourse are generally negative. Parents learn these attitudes from their own parents during their adolescence, and the attitudes are reinforced by society when their own children are growing up. Furthermore, parents are likely to hold these negative feelings strongly and are unlikely to change them except perhaps to intensify them. Finally, when they are faced with any evidence that their child has violated this norm, the parental reaction is predictably and characteristically negative.

Behavior has been defined as the reaction or response of an individual to stimuli—bodily movements or verbal statements of others and internal experiences. Behavior is similar to action, but it is a broader term because it is used to apply to everything a person does, thinks, says, or feels, even if it seems meaningless to that person.

Given these definitions of attitude and behavior, we are tempted to say that a behavior is merely the overt manifestation of an attitude. Parents disapprove of premarital intercourse—that is the attitude—and they express it by insisting that their children come home from a date at a given time, or by demanding to know their teenagers' whereabouts, or by restricting the use of a car or money—these are behaviors. We have all experienced such direct behavioral expressions of attitudes.

Research indicates, however, that one-to-one relationships between attitudes and behaviors do not always exist. Many studies have demonstrated an inconsistency between attitude and behavior.[2] But others have shown a consistency between attitude and behavior.[3] Most data indicate that both consistency and inconsistency exist. We can probably say that it is possible to predict behavior from attitude, but without much precision.

Let us see how consistent our attitudes and behaviors are in the area of premarital sexual relations. What are the norms of our society regarding premarital intercourse? What is the actual behavior among our unmarried population in this area?

Premarital Sex: Attitudes

Every society exerts some sort of social control over the sexual activity of its members, although there is great variation in the methods used and in the behavior considered to need control. When it comes to premarital sexual behavior, there are usually very specific institutions that provide opportunities for young people to meet and to get to know one another. America is a very unusual society in the extent of privacy we allow our young men and women and the relatively great amount of information about sex we dispense to them while at the same time prohibiting premarital intercourse. In most societies that restrict sexual activity, there is a concomitant restriction on the amount of knowledge that is circulated, there is segregation of the sexes, and there is strict chaperonage. But our young people are allowed almost limitless opportunities to learn about sexual techniques and can spend endless hours alone together. Yet we advocate celibacy before marriage, especially for women.

It should be noted, however, that no society has ever existed that was able completely to prevent coitus from occurring among its unmarried population. Premarital sex has never been completely obliterated, sublimated, denied, or destroyed. Thus, in our discussion of American attitudes, we must bear in mind that humans are innately sexual creatures, and that no controls will ever totally succeed in preventing them from having sex. Let us also remember that the peculiar American creed is contradictory and probably confusing to young people. On the one hand, we say that there must be no premarital activity; on the other, we permit an enormous amount of opportunity for it to occur.

Most of the research on premarital sexual attitudes has been conducted during the last three decades. Unfortunately, the focus of most studies is on the white, better-educated groups in American life. Recognizing this, our discussion is general, centering on traditional attitudes. But we must bear in mind that there are innumerable exceptions.

The early American family was patriarchal: that is, the father was the ruling power with absolute and final authority in the family. When the father is seen as dominant, having differential prestige in a family, he is usually also seen as having stronger sex drives and needs than his wife. During the early part of our history, men were viewed as being "animalistic"; that is, it was accepted that they had powerful, even uncontrollable sex needs that had to be satisfied. Women, on the other hand, were supposedly indifferent to sex and indulged in it only in order to have children and to satisfy their husbands' needs and demands.

In a patriarchal society women are frequently viewed as property, and marriages are arranged along economic lines. The important thing is to ensure the legitimate succession of the male line. A man needs to know without doubt that any son born to his wife is his child. Therefore, premarital virginity is an important commodity, and the value of a woman is greatly reduced if she is not virgin at the time of her marriage. Beyond that, since women were assumed to be disinterested in sex, non-virginity hinted that she might be promiscuous, sexually available to any man. This, of course, threatened her image as an object that had sexual purity, a virtue desirable in a wife.

This view of femininity caused confusion for men. On the one hand, a man was supposed to have uncontrollable sex drives and therefore needed a woman for satisfaction. On the other hand, society demanded that he look for a wife who cared nothing about sex. The result was that men saw women as either "good" or "bad." One married a "good" woman and had minimal sexual contact with her; one visited "bad" women in order to enjoy sexual activity. This division of women into two distinct, non-overlapping groups gave implicit permission for men to seek sexual gratification from women outside their social circle and later outside their marriages, at the same time maintaining their image of women friends and wives as pure. There were also implications for women. Such a dichotomy meant that a woman had to suppress any sexual pleasure at the risk of being considered "bad" and at the expense of feeling guilty. The result, of course, was the double standard. Men were expected to have sexual relations apart from marriage, provided that they were discreet. Women were permitted to have and express no sexual craving or pleasure; their sexuality was repressed.

There is no doubt that a change in these attitudes has occurred, but the change has been less a matter of kind than of degree. One important reason for this change has been a shift from the traditional patriarchal family, with its stress on the family as a group, to the egalitarian family, which emphasizes satisfaction of the ego needs of the individual members.

There has been, then, a gradual reduction in the perceived difference between mens' and womens' sexual needs and pleasures. American women are slowly but surely becoming emancipated and therefore can more freely demand their sexual rights. Their educational and occupational opportunities have increased, and this has led to financial independence, first from fathers and then from husbands. Today it is not necessary for a woman to be sure that she has the financial protection of a husband before she can leave the protection of her father. Women today have greater freedom to select their own marriage partners—or to select none. Now a woman has more equality in courtship and dating decision-making than she had before, and this minimizes her parents' influence in her mate selection. Finally, many women now feel that they have an equal right to demand or withhold sexual privileges, and this also has been instrumental in bringing about changes in attitudes. Many women are no longer willing to accept the double standard; they are insisting that they are entitled to the same sexual pleasure as men.

Perhaps the most significant cause of the change in our attitudes toward sex has been the general switch from sacred to secular values. Religious teachings are losing their influence in our lives, and we are moving from asceticism to hedonism. Although there have been indications that we may be experiencing a religious revival, the evidence is not conclusive. Usually researchers cite increased church attendance to show that religion maintains and has increased its hold on American values. But increased church attendance does not mean that people are more affected by religious restrictions on sexual behavior. Indeed, most studies indicate that punishment is not strong for people who indulge in premarital sexual activity.[4]

Furthermore, even our churches are less stringent in their rules about sex because they themselves have been undergoing some internal changes. Several denominations, notably the Quakers, take the position that any sex act that occurs between consenting adults and that does no harm to anyone is to be considered moral. Many modern churches regard only entrapment, exploitation, and seduction as immoral.[5]

Education and science are supplementing religion as the dominant influence on our values. Studies indicate that a high percentage of college students trust information received from educational and scientific sources more than information provided by religious ones.[6] As more and more young people go to college, it is likely that the influence of religion on moral values will continue to decline in the general population, thus affecting our attitudes toward premarital sex.

In spite of these influences for a more lenient attitude toward premarital sex, it is still more restricted for girls than it is for boys. The norms continue to be that women should be both sexually attractive and sexually inactive. Although the American young woman has freedom to wear what she chooses, to select her own friends, to read whatever books she desires, to see explicit sex movies and plays, to seek as much education as she wishes, to find jobs in varied fields in any part of the world, she is still closely watched and supervised when it comes to sexual activity. If she behaves in any way that is suspect, she endangers her reputation and the possibility of finding a husband, although to a much lesser degree than in the past.

PREMARITAL SEX: BEHAVIOR

Although a few studies[7] of sexual behavior were made before the publication of the famous Kinsey reports in 1948 and 1953[8] and several were made after,[9] it was Kinsey and his associates who created the greatest amount of furor among social scientists and the American public, principally because Kinsey studied a very large sample—5,300 males and 5,940 females—and investigated a very wide range of sexual behavior.

Most professionals in the field of sex research agree that Kinsey made a lasting contribution to our understanding of human sexuality. But there has also been a great deal of criticism, especially concerning the sample. Kinsey did not have a probability sample. That is, his subjects were not selected so as to allow each individual in the population an equal chance of being included. Instead, Kinsey interviewed the total membership of various consenting groups and clubs. These groups were composed of people from urban areas in the northeastern part of the United States. The members were more highly educated than the average American, and their willingness to participate also set them apart from the general population. Thus, we can easily see that Kinsey's sample did not represent all the types of people in our society; therefore, his generalizations about human sexual behavior can, with justification, be questioned.

A second criticism was that Kinsey and his associates placed too strong an emphasis on the biological aspect of sexual life. These researchers used orgasm as a measure of gratification, thus minimizing the importance of emotion. The criticism is valid, but it is hard to suggest any other measure that could have been substituted, and it is even more difficult to ascertain the emotional components of sexual satisfaction.

A third criticism is that Kinsey required his subjects to recall events that may have occurred as much as a quarter of a century earlier. No one can really be sure of the accuracy of recall, so that in cases where Kinsey asked middle-aged people to relate sexual experiences during adolescence, we have cause to doubt the accuracy as well as the honesty of their reports.

Perhaps the most important result of Kinsey's work, which almost nullifies all criticism, is that it encouraged more research because it made sex research respectable. The best and best-known research to follow Kinsey was the work of Masters and Johnson, who interviewed, observed, and photographed 694 men and women during and after sexual relations and masturbation.[10] The Masters and Johnson book received remarkably favorable response from the general public, unlike that of Kinsey and his associates, which was often regarded by laymen with anger.* Apparently Kinsey laid the groundwork for the acceptance of such research.

What was learned about the premarital sexual behavior of Americans from the research conducted from the 1920s to the 1960s? For one thing, there are many ways in which people can respond to their sexual needs, and all are practiced by some members of our married and unmarried populations. However, the meanings we attach to these behaviors differ for the two groups. Married people are always permitted some expression of sexuality; unmarried people are permitted almost none. We appear to believe that sexuality among single people should be suppressed and that if it should rear its ugly head, proper individuals will ignore or repress it. Yet Kinsey was able to demonstrate that there were several practices widely used among the unmarried to gratify their sexual needs and that these met with varying degrees of acceptance by society.[11]

The most common practice was autoeroticism. Many years ago masturbation was condemned more severely than it is today, because it was thought to be the source of such problems as feeblemindedness, sterility, "moral degeneration," and "nervousness." Most of these superstitions have disappeared, and now most people recognize that no such dangers are attached to masturbation. Nevertheless, there is still some guilt that continues to be associated with masturbation.

In the Kinsey research 94 per cent of the men and 40 per cent of the women in his sample admitted that they had masturbated at

* The Masters and Johnson book was on the best-seller lists within four weeks after publication.

some time in their lives. Among his unmarried subjects, it was the most frequent form of sexual behavior, especially among the more highly educated females.[12] Kinsey explained this finding on the ground that better-educated women are less affected by superstition or feelings of sin, more likely to believe that women have equal sex rights with men, and likely to marry later than their less educated sisters.

A second major outlet for sexual expression among unmarried people, especially men, was nocturnal emissions. Eighty-two per cent of Kinsey's male subjects and 12 per cent of the females acknowledged that they had had orgasms during erotic dreams at least once before marriage. This type of sexual activity is not condemned by society, because no other person is involved and the act is involuntary.

Kinsey found that by the age of eighteen, 81 per cent of the girls and 84 per cent of the boys had "petted" to orgasm at least once.[13] Petting is used to stimulate one's partner sexually as a preliminary to sexual intercourse. Unmarried people, however, often use petting as an end in itself. Frequently, girls indulge in this sort of activity because it permits them to have orgasms while allowing them to retain their technical virginity.

Many things about the Kinsey reports were shocking to the general American public, but the most shocking was the finding that approximately 50 per cent of his female subjects were not virgins at the time of marriage. Kinsey also showed that there were differences between men and women as far as virginity was concerned. Males were more likely not to be virgins, and they were likely to have had more partners than females. Men, Kinsey noted, were more apt to be promiscuous; women were more likely to restrict themselves to one mate, usually a fiancé.[14]

Kinsey also found variations by education. The more education the female had, the greater the likelihood of her not being a virgin bride; the more education the male had, the greater the likelihood of his being a virgin bridegroom. Kinsey concluded that education makes a girl less rigid about virginity and that more educated boys have less opportunity for sex than less educated boys.[15]

An interesting aspect of this finding was that, despite societal pressures, 69 per cent of the women who had had premarital sexual intercourse did not express regret or guilt and, indeed, had found the experience pleasurable. Furthermore, the fear of pregnancy was not a common deterrent to sexual activity.

All this indicates that, despite the still operative double standard, the majority of unmarried women in our society who are engaging in coitus are doing so with satisfaction and without guilt or fear. We are not suggesting that promiscuity among unmarried women has become the order of the day. What is actually occurring is that virginity *per se* is no longer so important to our young women as it once was.

Ira L. Reiss has made an important contribution to our understanding of this phenomenon. He states that there is a continuum of sexual behavior. At one extreme is a *body-centered* orientation, stressing the physical aspect of sex. At the other extreme is a *person-centered* attitude, stressing emotional attachment to the person with whom one performs the sex act. Reiss identifies four types of premarital sexual behavior patterns:

1. Abstinence—under no circumstance is premarital sexual intercourse permissible for either men or women.
2. Permissiveness with affection—intercourse is permissible for both sexes when the relationship is stable, when there is strong love between the couple or when they are engaged.
3. Permissiveness without affection—if there is physical interest in each other, intercourse is permissible without stability.
4. Double standard—intercourse is not permitted to females but is acceptable for males.[16]

The double standard is the traditional pattern, and it continues, along with abstinence, to dominate the American scene. Sex without affection, Reiss claims, is probably the least acceptable standard, while sex with affection, which is seen as a means of communicating love rather than as an end in itself, is probably gaining approval in our society.

Let us now summarize the research findings up to the 1960s. In general, approximately half of the women appear to have been virgin at the time of marriage. Not being a virgin, however, did not signify promiscuity. Instead, it usually meant that the woman had had experience with one or two men—most frequently, only her intended husband. Finally, the research over five decades indicated little change in these patterns during the entire period of time.

Bell and Chaskes suggested that a change occurred in the 1960s in the direction of greater incidence of premarital coitus.[17] Bell and Chaskes compared rates of coitus for two samples of college girls, one in 1958 and one in 1968. The rates rose from 10 per cent in 1958 to 23 per cent in 1968 for girls who were dating. In general, these authors found that while engagement was the usual prerequisite for sexual intercourse in 1958, it was much less so in 1968. Bell and Chaskes attributed this change, first, to the development and acceptance of oral contraception. Although fear of pregnancy was never an important deterrent to premarital sexual activity, whatever fear did exist has been removed by the widespread distribution and easy availability of birth-control information and contraceptives.

Also, in recent years there has been a new openness about sex and sexual activity, so that many of the taboos surrounding it have been discarded or at least brought into question. When people feel freer to discuss a topic like sex, and information is readily available, it loses its mystery and its ability to produce guilt.

Two other researchers found no change in the rates for males but a decided increase for females in frequency of premarital intercourse during the 1960s. They concluded that there has been a sexual revolution among females and that males and females are now much closer in sexual attitudes and behaviors. "American females still are more sexually conservative than their [male] counterparts with respect to both attitude and practice, but the differences are less than formerly."[18]

PREMARITAL SEXUAL ATTITUDES AND BEHAVIOR IN THE FUTURE

I expect that the trend in premarital sexual attitudes and behavior will go in the direction of greater permissiveness. Before World War I chastity was a positive value, but since that time our society has become more accepting of what was once considered deviant behavior. I predict that there will be a gradual decrease in the percentage of virgin brides; it is likely that premarital sex relations will be the norm by the end of the century, especially between engaged couples.

This is not to say that society will lose its interest in the control of sexual behavior. No society can afford to do that. First, it is a function of any society to ensure that it maintains a population of a desired size. This is accomplished in part through emigration and immigration, but most effectively through the birth of new members. Therefore, during periods of high birth rates, societies must discourage reproduction by such means as legalizing abortion or dispensing free birth-control information and devices. Conversely, there are times when societies must encourage procreation, by rewarding large families and prohibiting abortion and birth control.

Secondly, all societies must provide for the care and socialization of newborn members by designating the adults who are accountable for this function, traditionally the parents. In other words, birth must be legitimate to ensure the care of the children. A large number of illegitimate births in a society is detrimental because socialization becomes haphazard. If too many new members fail to be properly socialized, there will be an insufficient number of people in the necessary statuses, or people will be performing their roles inadequately. The results would be a failure to accomplish the goals of the society and a decrease in the efficiency of other members in complementary roles.

Changes are occurring in our society, however, that make our older sex norms unnecessary for the ends of the society to be met. One change has been the development and distribution of effective, easily administered contraceptive devices, especially the Pill. This has the effect of separating the expression of sexuality from the consequences of biological reproduction. Society, then, need not worry that sexual activity will result in the birth of children who will not have legitimate parents to care for, socialize, and support them. In short, effective contraception means that society can lessen its interest in the sexual behavior of its members because such behavior no longer need result in the birth of children.

There is another group of factors that indicates a change in our attitudes toward premarital sex in the direction of more permissiveness. One of these is the trend toward "unisex"—the view that there is little or no significant difference between the sexes except in the most obvious biological respects, which need not be stressed. This notion of unisex can be seen in dress, in occupations, in domestic-task allocation, and even in sexual behavior. Our young men and women are coming to feel that distinctive marks identifying them as masculine or feminine are no longer important. We are coming to recognize that characteristics once considered to be exclusively in one domain or the other simply need not be so classified. Men can wash dishes, care for babies, be disinterested in sports, and cry without becoming emasculated. Women can hold important positions, open doors for themselves, and dislike cooking without appearing unfeminine.

Such a shift in attitude, when it filters down through the social-stratification system and across the United States, will have important peripheral effects. We will begin to evaluate our lovemates less for the older sexual traits—handsome, strong, money-making men and gentle, passive, beautiful women—and more for human traits. People will be valued because they are honest, open, productive, direct, not because they personify some unreal notion of a "real man" or a "real woman." We will love real people instead of the idealized images we have carried around.

The fact that we are already beginning to redefine sexual morality will have meaning for the future. Whereas in the past sexual morality meant abstinence, it increasingly means responsibility toward one's partner, with honest regard for the rights of others. Reiss calls this the "New Morality."[19] It means that all behavior is judged solely in terms of the amount and kind of love it generates between people. Those who subscribe to these "situational ethics" believe that any act that is likely to promote love in a given situation is a proper act, whether or not it has social approval.

The new morality justifies premarital intercourse if it occurs between two people who love each other and if no one is hurt in the relationship. It stresses tolerance of the life styles of others. Our young people are less likely than their parents to "disapprove" of beliefs that differ from their own. Whether or not one indulges in premarital sex is regarded as one's own business. Reiss argues that the new morality will eventually dominate American life:

> My feeling is that since the New Morality seems to predominate among the college-educated youth and since that group is increasing

in size and is destined to prominence in our society, therefore, I expect the New Morality approach to become even more emphasized in the last three decades of the twentieth century.[20]

Sexual relationships among our college population are characterized more and more by concern for each other's well-being. "The shift is from emphasis upon an act to emphasis upon the quality of interpersonal relationships."[21]

Reiss feels that the change in our sexual code is neither a revolution nor a sign of a general breakdown of morality. Instead, he says, "What *has* been happening recently is that our young people have been assuming more responsibility for their own sexual standards and behavior. . . . In short, today's more permissive sexual standards represent not revolution but evolution, not anomie but normality."[22]

Reiss goes on to point to other changes revealed by his study of 1,500 people over twenty-one from all over America and 1,200 high school and college students from three states. Guilt feelings apparently fail to inhibit sexual behavior. Reiss feels that, although many people feel guilty after their first premarital sexual experience, they tend to continue the behavior until the guilt disappears. The study also found that the subjects believe their sexual standards are very close to those of their parents and even closer to those of their peers, so that they do not feel they are engaging in deviant behavior. Reiss concludes from his data that one of the most important reasons for increased permissiveness is

. . . an intellectualized philosophy about the desirability of sex accompanying affection. "Respectable" college-educated people have integrated this new philosophy with their generally liberal attitudes about the family, politics, and religion. And this represents a new and more lasting support for sexual permissiveness, since it is based on a positive philosophy rather than on hedonism, despair, or desperation.[23]

An even stronger position is taken by John Cuber, who thinks that a sexual revolution is occurring:

There is a profound difference between someone who breaks the rules and someone who does not accept the rules. One is a transgressor; the other is a revolutionary. . . . The last generation—a sizable minority of it—broke the rules of sexual morality and in particular the rule of premarital chastity, but clandestinely and with great guilt. The members of this generation—a good many of them—simply do not accept the rules any longer. . . . They challenge the validity of the law—and *that* is revolution.[24]

The revolutionaries of whom Cuber speaks comprise only a very tiny segment of young men and women, but a very large group of other youth and older people support their revolutionary life styles. Cuber does not believe that this phenomenon will disappear. Unlike the rebellious youth of past decades, who eventually settled down into traditional patterns and accepted establishment norms, this generation, he feels, will not. The reason for this is lack of guilt. The present generation of young people does not feel that they are breaking the moral code; instead they question the code's validity. Because Cuber does not believe that the revolutionaries and their supporters will ever return to the old moral code, he suggests that Americans discard the notion of a single moral code and recognize that there are many codes operative in their society today.

In summary, I suggest that we are gradually but definitely moving toward greater permissiveness in our attitudes toward premarital sexual intercourse, with a concomitant increase in the amount of such activity.[25] This prediction is based on several factors: increased knowledge and availability of contraception; more frankness and openness in our media and in our personal lives about sex; a decrease in the perceived differences between males and females, which implies a diminution of the double standard; greater mobility for our young people, which means more opportunity for sexual encounters and less parental surveillance; and, finally, the new morality, the feeling, particularly among young men and women, that the emphasis in sexual relationships ought to be not on exploitation but on integrity and mutuality. The norm of permissiveness with affection, although not necessarily leading to marriage, can be expected to be dominant in the future.

MARITAL SEX: ATTITUDES

How does society think people *should* behave sexually after they are married? Good sexual adjustment should not be confused with good marital adjustment. A good sexual relationship in marriage does not necessarily mean that the marriage is a good one; nor is it always true the other way around.[26] Frequently the two do go together, but in this section I want to discuss only the sexual relationship in marriage.

What norms govern married sexual intercourse? Murdock found only one society in the World Ethnographic Sample of 250 societies that does not permit sexual relations between a husband and wife; most societies encourage it.[27] On the other hand, most societies proscribe such relations outside marriage, although a significant number do permit extra- or premarital sex. No society, however, allows conception outside a legal relationship. Marriage, then, universally licenses parenthood and legitimates children—that is its primary function. Secondarily, it regulates sexual conduct. Most societies have taboos against three forms of sexual conduct: incest, fornication, and adultery. Almost no society has expected or tried to ensure sexual monogamy for men, although many, including our own, demand premarital virginity and marital fidelity of women.

Upper-class preindustrial society stressed patrilineage; that is, descent was reckoned through the father. A male had an obligation to leave a legitimate heir to the family's name and position; the woman was the vessel carrying his seed. In such societies a man had to be absolutely sure that the child produced by his wife was indeed his child. It was of little consequence if someone other than his wife bore his offspring; it was of dire consequence if his wife bore a child by another man.

Thus the double standard derived from an upper-class patrilineal social structure in which paternity was socially more important than maternity. A virgin bride and a virtuous wife were essential; a non-virgin bride and an unfaithful wife endangered the patrilineal social system. These norms could be found in the upper classes in almost all ancient societies—Hebrew, Greek, and Roman. Among the early Semites, a non-virgin bride or an unchaste wife could be stoned to death along with her lover. High-born Greek men confined their wives to the house, permitting them to leave it only if veiled and accompanied by a slave. Romans could divorce their wives, kill them, or sell them into slavery if the wives committed adultery. All three societies had a class of prostitutes, so that they were able to distinguish between the women who bore their legitimate sons and those whom they could enjoy sexually.

With Christianity came the notion of premarital chastity for all, not only for women. Furthermore, the early Christians espoused celibacy even in marriage. Sexual intercourse was reserved for purposes of procreation only.

By the Middle Ages such attitudes toward sex had weakened, although virginity, chastity, and abstinence were still highly valued. The church retained its interest in preserving the family because of the continued concern about lineage. Toward the end of the Middle Ages and with the rise of a burgher class, the practice of arranged marriages became important. Marriages were arranged by parents along economic lines. These customs were, in part, carried over to the New World by the Puritans.

The Puritans combined the asceticism of the early Christians, their stress on chastity for both males and females, with the notion of thrift as practiced by the mercantile classes toward the end of the Middle Ages. This idea stressed conservation of time, energy, and money in matters of pleasure, and it extended into the sexual realm. The Puritans believed that sex should be strictly confined to marriage and practiced only for procreation, not for pleasure. Morality was enforced by civil government. Anyone indulging in premarital or extramarital sex could be executed. Any public display of affection, even between a man and his wife, was condemned. For example, Train reports the story of a Captain Kemble, "who, returning home after a long voyage, kissed his wife on the front steps and was promptly lodged in the stocks."[28]

By the end of the nineteenth century, women had come to be regarded as "delicate." Before that they had been blamed for the evil in the world, regarded as the source of sin and afflicted with moral weakness. The nineteenth century heralded the "new woman," who was morally so strong that she could prevent men from sinning by the example of purity, modesty, and fragility she presented. The nineteenth century offered almost no choice of life style for women other than marriage. Once married, a woman became totally dependent, socially and economically, on her husband. This delicate, sexually neuter, dependent wife had one function—to display her bourgeois husband's success to the world.

The double standard again gained control. Males were dominant; wives, dependent. Freedom prevailed for the males; women were once again divided into two classes: the "good" woman one married and the "bad" women with whom one consorted. The good women were dependent on their husbands and could do nothing to prevent their husbands from "straying."

Circumstances began to change during the early part of the twentieth century. By the end of World War I, new alternatives to marriage began to appear. There were now "good" marriageable women, "bad" play girls, and, finally, "career" girls. To some women a career began to seem a better choice than a bad marriage, although it was still not so desirable as a good marriage. However, women were no longer necessarily economically dependent, and this placed them in a better bargaining position. The double standard once more weakened. Paradoxically, an even more invidious dichotomy grew up in its place. Previously, "nice" women had not enjoyed sex; they had indulged in it to please their husbands and to have children. By the 1930s the notion of the virtuous asexual woman had become transposed by Freud into the "frigid" woman. Now "healthy" women were supposed to enjoy sex with their husbands. There was something wrong with them if they failed to do so.

This change in sexual attitudes was due in part to the fact that women were now able to get more education, which increased their economic independence from men. Upper- and middle-class women married more often out of choice. If they were going to indulge in sexual activity, they might as well enjoy it. Men and women began to demand more emotional and sexual satisfaction from marriage. People sought greater intimacy. Men, as well as women, wanted wives to be sexually gratified. The order of the day for the upper and middle classes became sexual responsiveness for women. People began to work to achieve this. Books on how to do it proliferated. Marital sex became self-conscious and pedantic.

The working classes of the 1920s and 1930s were not experiencing the same changes in sexual attitudes but were still practicing the marital sexual patterns of the late 1800s. Men still felt superior, and women subscribed to this view. Working-class people still believed that sex was intended for the pleasure of the man

SEX, MARRIAGE, AND SOCIAL CLASS[30]

	Highbrow	Upper Middlebrow	Lower Middlebrow	Lowbrow
How girl meets boy	He was an usher at her best friend's wedding	At college, in the psychology lab	In the office, by the water cooler	On the block
The proposal	In his room during the Harvard-Princeton game	In the back seat of a Volkswagen	After three drinks in an apartment he borrowed	In her home one night when Mom and Dad were at the movies
The wedding	In her living room, by a federal judge	College chapel (non-denominational)	City hall	Neighborhood church
The honeymoon	Mediterranean	Bahamas	Any Hilton hotel	Disneyland
Marriage manual	*Kama Sutra*	*Sexual Efficiency in Marriage*, Vols. I and II	Van der Velde	None
Sex novels she reads	Jane Austen	*Lady Chatterley's Lover*	*Myra Breckinridge* and any novel by Harold Robbins	*Valley of the Dolls*
Sleeping arrangements	Double bed	King-size bed or twin beds with one head board	Twin beds with matching night tables	Double bed
Sleeping attire	He: nothing She: nothing	He: red turtleneck nightshirt She: gown with matching peignoir	He: pajamas She: pajamas	He: underwear She: nightgown
Background music	Ravi Shankar or the Beatles	Wagner	Sound track of *Dr. Zhivago*	Jackie Gleason and the Silver Strings
Turn-ons	Pot	Champagne and oysters	Manhattans and whiskey sours	Beer
The schedule	Spontaneously, on an average of 2.5 weekly (that means 2 times one week and 3 times another)	Twice a week and when the kids go to a Sunday matinée	Twice a week and when the kids go to Sunday school	Twice on Saturday night

	Highbrow	Upper Middlebrow	Lower Middlebrow	Lowbrow
Number of children	1 each by a previous marriage, or as many as God provides	2.4	3	As many as God provides
Anniversary celebrations	A weekend in Dublin	He gives her a new dishwasher; she gives him a power lawnmower	Corsage and dinner out	Whitman Sampler and dinner at Howard Johnson's
Quarrels	"I don't care what your analyst says"	"I don't care if he is your brother"	"What do you think I'm made of?"	"Drop dead!"
If the marriage needs help	He consults her analyst She consults his	They go (a) to a marriage counselor (b) to the minister	He: to his successful brother She: to her best friend	He: to the bartender She: to her mother
The affair	"But I assumed you knew"	"It was basically a problem in communication."	"It was bigger than both of us."	"Some things no woman should have to put up with."
Sex education	"Ask Dr. Grauber, dear, when you see him tomorrow."	"Well, you see, Daddy has something called a . . . etc. And Daddy and Mommy love each other very much"	"Well, you see, Daddy puts the seed in Mommy's tummy," etc. etc.	"We got you at the hospital."
Vacations	Europe in May; she takes the children to the Cape; he commutes	Europe in July; family camping in Yosemite	He hunts or fishes She visits mother with the children	They visit brother Charles in Des Moines
Financial arrangements	Separate trust funds	Joint checking account	She budgets	He gets weekly allowance
Who raises the children	English nanny, boarding school, and Dr. Grauber	Mommy and Daddy, Cub Scouts, and Dr. Freud	Mom and Dad, the Little League, and Dr. Spock	Mom, the gang, Ann Landers, and good luck

or to produce children and the wife was to comply with her husband's demands. A study by Rainwater showed a correlation between social class and attitudes toward marital sex.[29] The higher the social class, the greater the probability that sexual relations with husbands will be regarded positively by wives. The chart on pages 58–59 illustrates the class differences in sex and marriage habits.

Part of the reason lower-class wives find marital sex distasteful lies in the negative attitudes instilled in them as children as a way of maintaining virginity. Working-class men continue to distinguish between the girls one marries and those who are "available." Lower-class parents try to protect their daughters and are concerned to see them marry "good" men. Marriage is still about the only alternative for working-class girls. What employment they can obtain is not likely to be interesting; often it is such drudgery that marriage is a means of escape. The working-class girl conceives of her proper role in life as wife and mother, and she is usually pleased to exchange a job for marriage.

How can we summarize American attitudes toward marital sex? Although various options are now open to young women in American society, marriage is still the preferred status. Although sexual gratification is no longer regarded solely as the right of the male, initiation of sexual activity generally remains the husband's prerogative. Although virginity is no longer essential for brides, it is still regarded as desirable. And, although variations are now recognized, Americans still subscribe to conventional sex techniques— that is, what has been called the missionary position. We still condemn infidelity in marriage. We still find many wives who are sexually inhibited. Our attitudes have changed, it is true, but obviously more change in behavior is needed to conform to our current attitudes.

MARITAL SEX: BEHAVIOR

Very little is known about actual sex practices in marriage. Research is limited by subjects' reluctance to discuss such intimate behavior and by the difficulty of ensuring their honesty. However, we can make certain inferences from the records of clinical psychologists and divorce lawyers.

First, it is probable that most American married couples practice conventional sex techniques within a very narrow range of innovation. It is also likely that a majority of married people are at least vaguely dissatisfied with their sexual lives. Masters and Johnson found that over 50 per cent of American marriages are sexually inadequate.[31] Sharon Price writes that only a minority of Americans are really sexually satisfied. She regards it as astonishing that more are not dissatisfied, given the taboos concerning sex in American culture. "We are still primitive in our sexual attitudes."[32]

Jetse Sprey agrees that marital sex is usually ungratifying, and he tries to explain why.[33] For one thing, Americans suffer from romantic notions that sex should be unfailingly wonderful. Novels, movies, and television give them the impression that, if bells don't ring wildly during sexual intercourse, they are not performing properly or are being deprived. In a performance-oriented society, Sprey writes, it is easy to regard oneself as a sexual underachiever.

Leonard Cammer, writing in the same issue of *Sexual Behavior* as Price and Sprey, says that most people have low expectations regarding sex, ignoring the experts who tell us how we should be behaving and what we may expect to experience:

> The stresses of today . . . leave little time or energy for the ideal romantic sensual pleasure scene. . . . Most people are so depleted just by struggling to cope successfully that they cannot afford the luxury of even trying to explore a higher level of sexual fulfillment. . . . Most persons, for the better part of their lives, seem to accommodate well to whatever sexual or other frivolities may be available to them.[34]

Part of the problem is that American society prefers brides to be virgins and bridegrooms to have just a little experience. Then, on the wedding night, they are expected to become perfect lovers. We fail to take account of the fact that sexual behavior is learned, not instinctive, and that time, knowledge, and adjustment are required in order to perform well.

Furthermore, males and females are socialized differently. They develop different attitudes toward sex. For example, boys learn to react more quickly and to more kinds of sexual stimuli than girls. This is not just because they are biologically different but largely because they are more frequently exposed to female sex symbols in the media than women are to the corresponding male symbols. Finally, for both biological and cultural reasons, males are more quickly and more frequently aroused sexually than females and more quickly and easily satisfied.

In sum, although almost no research data are available, it appears that, for a majority of American married couples, marital sex is disappointing. Males and females are socialized into sex roles differently, and so they develop unequal sexual needs and feelings of inadequacy. The pressures of ordinary living have become so great that we may not have the time or the energy to cultivate more varied and more gratifying sexual pleasures. Finally, the romantic notions endemic in Americans' culture are probably a major cause of our widespread feelings of incompetence and inferiority. We expect too much too quickly.

MARITAL SEXUAL ATTITUDES AND BEHAVIOR IN THE FUTURE

I predict that there will be an increase of sexual pleasure in marital coitus by the year 2000. One reason is the heightened awareness of potential satisfaction among women, which will lead to a diminution of inhibitions and a willingness to experiment. At first, this new freedom on the part of women will lead to more self-consciousness, resentment, and even impotence in men, but, ultimately, men will probably accept sexual equality and recognize the benefits it will produce for themselves as well as for women.

Kinsey's research in 1953 was already revealing a trend in this direction. Although the frequency of marital intercourse was slightly lower among his younger subjects than among the older subjects, the younger women had higher rates of orgasm. Kinsey inferred from this that the quality of marital sex was improving—women were becoming more interested in sex and more orgasmic.[35] It is likely that the frequency-of-intercourse rate will rise with the orgasmic and female-interest rates.

Another reason I predict increasing marital sex satisfaction is that there are signs of change in norms among youth. Many young adults recognize that an attitude of possessiveness, of owning one's sexual partner, is actually harmful to a relationship. Love, they tell us, must be free or else it is valueless. I expect that this new norm of freedom in love relationships will become stronger and will be passed down to the children of the present generation.

Accompanying this new norm of freedom in love relationships there is likely to be a change in the quality of sexual union. In the past sex was frequently a purely physical experience; now the stress is on the total relationship; in the future as well marital coitus will include not only sexual gratification but also a sharing of interests and of feelings.

Another reason for change will be the development of contraceptives that are wholly effective. This will remove any lingering fear of pregnancy that in the past may have resulted in what was called frigidity and will make sexual satisfaction easier to achieve.

As divorce becomes more acceptable, people will tend to stay married only so long as they are psychologically, emotionally, intellectually, and sexually satisfied. People will demand more of marriage because they know they can seek new relationships without incurring societal recriminations. We can expect that husbands and wives who stay married to each other then will be maximizing their sexual joys.

In sum, I predict that sex in marriage will become more pleasurable as a result of the expected increase in feminine awareness, response, and interest; the diminution of the stultifying effects of our norm of possessiveness; the change in emphasis in sexual union from physical sensation to a response that includes the total person; the development of wholly effective contraceptive methods; and, finally, the lessening stigma of divorce, which will make people less likely to remain in a marital relationship that is not sexually satisfying.

EXTRAMARITAL SEX: ATTITUDES

One very significant norm in our society holds that marriage is a permanent union with exclusive sex rights. This norm is more important and more severely enforced and sanctioned than the norm pertaining to premarital abstinence, because we consider that sex is available to married people and that extramarital sex is not only unnecessary for them but a threat to the institution of marriage.

Taboos against adultery are widespread. Although most societies recognize a need for such activity for men, it is rarely permitted to women. In a sample of 148 societies, Murdock found taboos against extramarital sex in 81 per cent. In only 19 societies was it conditionally allowed, and only 5 permitted total adulterous freedom.[36] Ford and Beach point out that 60 per cent of the societies they studied forbid adultery to women. Many societies forbid it to men as well, but the concern is always stronger for women.[37]

In early American society, husbands were permitted to indulge in adulterous relationships, but usually they exercised discretion, and, if their wives were aware of it, they were too dependent to do much about it. Partly, in fact, wives "understood" because as "good" women they could not be expected to satisfy man's "animal" needs. However, wives rarely had sexual relations themselves outside of marriage.

The taboo against adultery is still powerful in most societies, but it seems to be stronger in the United States than in other parts of the world. Hunt found that 80 per cent of a group of American wives declared that they would never have an affair; 36 per cent of a group of French and Belgian wives said that infidelity was not important in marriage; and 37 per cent felt that it was desirable.[38] Several factors account for this. One is the religious proscription against adultery. In the United States we retain many Puritan notions of right and wrong. Adultery is still a crime in this country, and it is also grounds for divorce in all fifty states. Further, there are moral implications that can be seen in American attitudes toward all sexual behavior. For women, love, sex, and marriage are inseparable. In most cases, if a girl is in love, she feels that she should marry and confine her sexual activities to her husband. Males also feel that wives should not share their sexual favors with other men. Men are frequently very possessive about their wives and feel that their masculinity would be threatened if their wives had sexual relations with other men.

In short, Americans in general firmly forbid adultery. Any incidence is likely to have widespread social repercussions. And yet the amount of adultery committed is not commensurate with this attitude.

EXTRAMARITAL SEX: BEHAVIOR

Kinsey's study of female sexuality revealed that, by the age of forty, some 26 per cent of the women and 50 per cent of the men had had extramarital affairs.[39] Cuber and Harroff reported on a study of five types of marriage among the upper class (see pages 101–3) and found incidences of adultery in all but one type, although the reasons given for adultery differed.[40] Psychotherapist Albert Ellis feels that the data presented by Kinsey and by Cuber and Harroff indicate that adultery is a much more common behavior pattern than was suspected.[41]

Robert Bell believes there are eight basic reasons why people commit adultery: (1) the adulterers are searching for variety; (2) they are retaliating against a real or imagined infidelity on the part of their mate; (3) they are rebelling against the norm of monogamy; (4) they are seeking emotional satisfaction; (5) they have had friendly relations with the outside partner that have developed into a sexual relationship; (6) the husband or wife encouraged the adultery; (7) they are proving that they are still young and sexually active; (8) they are engaging in extramarital relations for pure pleasure.[42]

Recently there has been a change in attitude toward adultery, with some experts taking the position that extramarital sex can be beneficial to marriage and to health. This new philosophy goes hand-in-hand with the notion that possessiveness is detrimental to good love relationships. The older idea that people are adulterous because their marriages are boring or inadequate is now being questioned, along with the idea that the results of adultery are always jealousy, guilt, and divorce. Myers and Leggitt studied adultery and found that the occasional, casual affair, the most common form of extramarital relations, need not threaten a good marriage.[43] Another type of affair is one in which the married person believes that he is in love with his extramarital partner; nevertheless, such a relationship neither necessarily destroys nor damages the marriage. Instead, it is peripheral to it; the adulterer derives a separate kind of pleasure from it that in no way affects his marriage. Some of the people interviewed said that their adultery supplemented marriage. While they loved their spouses, sex had become routine, and adultery added the spice that made the marriage tastier. Others regarded love affairs as growth experiences, giving them an opportunity to develop sensitivity to, and awareness of, the needs of others and themselves. Still others found in adultery a chance to experiment with forms of love-making that they regarded as improper in the context of marriage. There were also couples in which both partners agreed to condone adultery. Each member was aware of, and approved of, the other's having extramarital relations, claiming that such affairs strengthened their marriage.

Myers and Leggitt found that adultery can enhance marital relations by (1) lessening the feeling that marriage is preventing the partners from living a full life; (2) removing the need to participate in sexual relations within the marriage when desire is absent; (3) increasing the vitality and warmth of the adulterer; (4) motivating the spouse to become more attractive; (5) providing diversion; (6) allowing opportunity for discovering one's sexuality; (7) making mediocre marriages more bearable for the sake of the children, a place in the community, and so forth; and (8) providing excitement and joy.

Sexual Behavior asked several social scientists how an affair affects a marriage.[44] James L. Framo, chief of the Family Therapy and Training Unit at Jefferson Community Mental Health Center in Philadelphia, replied, "It is rare for the affair itself to break up the marriage. In some cases the affair turns out to have a therapeutic effect by revitalizing a depleted relationship. In others, the basic trust never gets re-established and the heightened suspicion gets incorporated into other problems that the couple have."

Herbert A. Otto, chairman of the National Center for the Exploration of Human Potential in La Jolla, California, said that an affair may have positive values, resulting in a "greater openness in communication," "one or the other member may make a greater effort to please," "new variety is sometimes introduced into the sex life," and a "greater appreciation and love for the spouse."

Carolyn Symonds, a marriage counselor in San Bernardino, California, stated, "It is probably safe to say that in a traditional marriage without close communication between the partners, if a man has an affair very little harm will come from it—even if he is discovered; if the woman has one and is found out it may dissolve the marriage."

Albert Ellis believes that the effects vary, depending on the reasons for which the mate had the affair and the attitudes he or she has about it. Ellis feels that the evidence is too scanty and that what there is draws on the replies of liberal, sophisticated individuals who report no particular effects on the marriage. However, Ellis claims, "That adultery *must* affect a marriage adversely is, of course, nonsense."

Lynn G. Smith, a graduate psychology student, and James R. Smith, a political scientist, both at Berkeley, felt that "One general effect of an affair is that it tends to make life more exciting; whether or not it satisfies, produces conflict, destroys, or uncovers a new dimension of life, it certainly intensifies." These writers stated further that "the ultimate effect on the marriage depends not only on the individual's motivation, whether positive or negative, but also on the spouse's interpretation of what the affair means."

Finally, Leon Salzman, deputy director of the Bronx State Hospital in New York, wrote, "Adultery is a widespread phenomenon which can be largely attributed to the failure of marriages to fulfill the needs of the partners, rather than to the more popular rationalizations regarding man's innate polygamous tendencies which cannot be satisfied with a monogamous social arrangement."

EXTRAMARITAL SEX IN THE FUTURE

According to Jetse Sprey, "each contact between a married person and anyone other than his or her spouse is by definition an extramarital one," although that is not necessarily the way most people, professional or otherwise, would define it.[45] Sprey then makes a distinction between sexual and nonsexual extramarital relations, asking which poses the greater threat to the marriage. With the shift in emphasis from the contractual to the interpersonal side of marriage, emotional involvement with an outsider may be a bigger threat than sexual involvement. To bolster his argument, Sprey points to the insistence of "swingers"—married couples who swap mates—that the sexual relations proceed on an impersonal level. Apparently they feel more threatened by emotional than sexual involvement.

Sprey makes several other distinctions between types of extramaritality. Are the affairs long or short? Do they occur only occasionally, when the adulterous spouse is away from home on vacation or on a business trip, or regularly? Is it the male, the female, or both partners who are married? Does either have children in his marriage? All these factors affect the adulterous relationship and the marital one.

Sprey believes that rates of extramarital relationships are increasing and will continue to do so for several societal reasons. One is our rising life expectancy. In the past, spouses could expect to live together no more than fifteen years; today they can anticipate forty years together. Secondly, we now demand much more of marriage, and when marriage is unavailable we seek fulfillment outside of it. Thirdly, women are participating more widely in our society and thus are finding more opportunity for engaging in extramarital relations.

Robert Bell estimates that one third of all married women and two thirds of all married men have had at least one extramarital experience.[46] Sprey wonders why the rest of the population refrains from such activity. The reason for some is lack of inclination; for others it is lack of opportunity. Some people find that extramarital sex requires too much time, energy, and money. Others abstain for ideological or religious reasons. Few, Sprey feels, plan to have extramarital affairs; most simply drift into these relationships.

In conclusion, Sprey posits that extramaritality has always been part of our culture and will continue to be so. He feels that it is found in stable as well as disorganized marriages. The main reason he finds for extramarital relationships is that Americans hold unrealistic expectations of marriage. It is probably not possible, as we like to believe, for two people to satisfy each other fully in all areas of life for four decades. Because it is unlikely that we will change our expectations about marriage in the foreseeable future, Sprey writes, extramaritality must continue to exist in secrecy, surrounded by guilt.

I agree with the many reasons Sprey offers to support his contention that extramarital sex is likely to remain part of our culture. I believe that more people will engage in this activity as the conditions Sprey describes become more institutionalized. Women will continue to enlarge their roles in society, increasing their desire and opportunity for wider sexual experience. Medical knowledge will continue to grow and will bring longer life spans. Finally, it is likely that we will increase our demands in the area of interpersonal relations, to the point where married couples will find it impossible to fulfill them, so that there will be greater acceptance of extramarital sex.

HOMOSEXUALITY

Homosexuality is a difficult term to define, but, in general, it refers to a sexual attraction between members of the same sex. In practice, many people use the term *lesbian* to refer to women with this proclivity, reserving *homosexual* for males. (The term *lesbian,* incidentally, comes from the Greek island of Lesbos, where Sappho, supposedly the first known homosexual woman, lived.)

The label *homosexual,* however, does not mean that all the people in question have no sexual interest in members of the opposite sex. Apparently there are many people who are physically attracted to members of both sexes. These people are usually referred to as bisexual. The point is that there are many kinds of sexuality—heterosexuality, homosexuality, and bisexuality, and, even within these categories, there is great variation.

According to Kinsey, 37 per cent of the males in his sample had reached orgasm within a homosexual context at least once in their lives by the time they were aged forty.[47] Kinsey was not, of course, saying that over one third of all males are exclusively homosexual. Most of his subjects were referring to a pattern of occasional homosexuality. Actually, Kinsey reports that between 3 and 16 per cent of his subjects were exclusively homosexual.

Homosexual men and women can fall anywhere on a continuum

from extremely feminine in dress, attitude, and behavior to the most masculine, athletic, muscular type. They can be found in all social classes, racial groups, ethnic groups, sections of the United States, religious groups, and occupations. They may be old or young, handsome or ugly, fat or thin, intelligent or stupid.

Many writers have made a point of classifying homosexuals as either "active" or "passive." This dichotomy implies that there is a distinct difference between the two groups, depending on the way they behave in bed—taking either the "masculine," active role or the "feminine," passive role. The truth is that most homosexuals cannot be clearly pigeonholed in this way, because they, like heterosexuals, vary their roles in the sex act.

In the classical world, homosexual love between older and younger men was considered the highest form of love and was practiced by the most exalted men. After the fall of Rome homosexuality came to be considered sinful, a violation of God's law. In this century, Freud and his followers have defined homosexuality as mental illness, arguing that a passive father and a domineering mother may produce a homosexual son:

> What he [Freud] had found in the case of inversion [homosexuality] was that the subjects had passed through a very early stage of fixation on their mothers and had then identified themselves with them. The objects from whom they later obtained gratification are narcissistic mirrors of themselves, loved as they had wished their mothers to love them.[48]

More recently investigators have been turning to biology for explanations. The newest thinking is that human animals, like nonhumans, are likely to inherit sex-role tendencies. Kallman, for example, examined 40 pairs of identical twins (developed from one fertilized egg) and 45 pairs of fraternal twins (developed from two separately fertilized eggs).[49] In all these pairs at least one of the twins was a known homosexual. Among the identical twins, Kallman found that in 100 per cent of the cases, the other twin was also homosexual; in the group of fraternal twins, there were no more homosexuals than one could expect to find in any male population. In 1962, another investigator studied 113 pairs of twins of which one member was a known homosexual. He found that, when they were identical, 95 per cent of the pairs were both homosexual; when fraternal, only 5 per cent of the pairs included two homosexuals.[50] These data suggest that sexual behavior and sex-role development are strongly influenced by genetic and hormonal factors, not, as Freud would have it, by disease.

In contrast to the theory that man's sexuality is at least partly biological, there is a theory that the infant is sexually undifferentiated, or neuter, at birth and that his sex role is determined by the social world, which impinges upon him as soon as his sex is determined at the time of delivery. This theory posits socialization as the most important factor in gender role (see Chapter 2). Money, Hampson, and Hampson[51] studied hermaphrodites, those rare individuals "in whom exists a contradiction between external genital appearance and sex chromatin patterns, gonads, hormones, or internal reproductive structures."[52] All but 7 of their 100 subjects displayed congruity between their sex socialization and gender role. These authors conclude that at birth a child's sex is determined on the basis of external sex organs. From that moment on, the child's femininity or masculinity is reinforced constantly.

> In place of a theory of instinctive masculinity or femininity which is innate, the evidence of hermaphroditism lends support to a conception that psychologically, sexuality is undifferentiated at birth, and that it becomes differentiated as masculine or feminine in the course of the various experiences of growing up.[53]

> Now it becomes necessary to allow that erotic outlook and orientation is an autonomous psychological phenomenon independent of genes and hormones, and moreover, a permanent and ineradicable one as well.[54]

The explanation, then, for human homosexuality is not clear. We cannot state unequivocally that any one factor accounts for it. "Man appears to be a creature of nature only if society enters into nature's conspiracy, and clearly, we can see that most of the time it does. Though man may be psychosexually malleable, he is not psychosexually neutral."[55]

In general much less is known about lesbianism than about male homosexuality. Lesbians are less visible and less active than males. They are less promiscuous, more selective and romantic, and more likely to form permanent attachments than are male homosexuals. Interestingly, homosexuality among males is most frequent among those who have no education beyond high school. For women, it is most frequent among college graduates. Finally, in the United States, it appears that there are far fewer lesbians than male homosexuals. We noted Kinsey's finding that 3 to 16 per cent of the males in his study were exclusively homosexual; he found only 1 to 3 per cent of the women to be exclusively homosexual.

Female homosexuality is more tolerated in the United States than male homosexuality, and women appear to be more tolerant of homosexuals, male and female, than men are.[56] No one is quite sure why this is so. We might postulate that male homosexuals are censured more than females because they violate the image of the ruling elite. Men are supposed to be rational, detached, and strong. They should not be weak and act out of impulse and intuition. The homosexual male violates the desired image when he acts like a female. In effect, he goes over to the enemy camp. As a feminized version of the powerful male, he becomes the deserter, and everyone hates a traitor. The standard argument is that male homosexuality is tolerated less than female homosexuality because it threatens men who suppress the tendency in themselves. This argument can of course be canceled out by saying that lesbianism threatens women who suppress that tendency in themselves.

HOMOSEXUALITY IN THE FUTURE

Homosexuality has been an aspect of human sexuality for as long as man has existed. And there is no doubt that it will continue to be a form of sexual activity in our society. However, there are grounds for believing that the stigma attached to it will disappear. One reason for this expectation is our increasing knowledge about homosexuality. We no longer condemn it as evil; we no longer "blame" parents. We now know that several factors—biological, chemical, and social—may play a role in this phenomenon and that we probably cannot consciously exercise any control over our sexual natures.

Furthermore, Americans are becoming more tolerant of their

pluralism. There is less demand for conformity, less stress on tradition. Slowly, we are beginning to acknowledge that we have room in our society for a variety of attitudes, behaviors, and values.

In addition, with our present concern for overpopulation, one reason for stigmatizing homosexuality—that such practices hinder our population growth—will no longer be valid. Finally, as bachelorhood becomes less maligned, we will stop thinking of the homosexual as depriving others of "normal" marital relationships.

Changes in the laws are beginning to give this prediction validity. In 1971 New York considered a bill prohibiting discrimination against homosexuals in employment and housing. In defense of the bill, Eleanor Holmes Norton, chairperson of the New York City Commission on Human Rights, said, "It is time we recognize the fact that there is yet another group in our society which suffers analogous [to race, creed, national origin, sex, age, and physical handicaps] prejudice and which faces unconstitutional deprivation of jobs, housing, and other rights due any citizen of this country."[57]

In the years ahead, homosexuality will probably become acceptable and recognized as no more and no less than one form of man's sexual expression. As Kinsey said, "The only kind of abnormal sex acts are those which are impossible to perform."[58]

The Incest Taboo

The incest taboo refers to the prohibition of sexual congress between blood relatives. The taboo is directed primarily at members of the nuclear family. In almost every known society, sex is prohibited between father and daughter, mother and son, and siblings. Some societies proscribe sexual intercourse between parents and adoptive children, between stepparents and stepchildren, of aunts and uncles with nephews and nieces, and even between cousins.

The most strongly tabooed relationship is between mother and son, with that between father and daughter a close second, followed by brother-sister relations. The only exceptions can be found among elite groups. Brothers and sisters intermarried in the ancient royal Egyptian family, in the Hawaiian royal family, and among the Inca Indians. Novelist John Updike has observed that incest seems to be the cardinal sexual sin among the elite, adultery among the middle classes, and rape in the lower classes.[59]

The origins of the taboo against incest are unknown, although the supply of theories has been ample. Today there is general consensus that there is nothing physiological or instinctive about it. There is also some agreement with Murdock's explanation, which begins by acknowledging that infants experience sexuality.[60] Children express this toward their parents and the parents reciprocate the feelings. But the adults reject the feelings because they are threatening and provoke guilt and anxiety. The society, in turn, concurs in this kind of discouragement on the part of the parents toward the children. There is good reason for this. The family is the basic economic, reproductive, and socializing unit, and its functions would be severely jeopardized if sexual competition should develop within its confines. There could be no stability or authority if fathers competed with sons for mothers and daughters. Such interchangeability in sexual relations could result only in chaos. If families consisted of daughters whose sons were also their brothers and if the sons were also parents to their sisters, "chaos" would be a mild term with which to describe the situation.

The incest taboo has other functions beyond maintaining the stability of the family and the regulation of the authority pattern. It also forces the younger members of the nuclear family to seek sexual partners outside the family, which strengthens the ties between families and enlarges the number of kindred.

One remarkable aspect of incest, beyond the strength and near universality of the taboo against it, is the emotional repugnance that accompanies it. This revulsion is strongest in reference to close blood ties and weakest toward the peripheral members.

Most societies enforce the incest taboo by inculcating this distaste during the socialization process in childhood. Apparently, this internalization of the norm prohibiting incest is very effective. One researcher reported only 1.1 offenders per million people in the United States.[61] However, if we take into account the records of psychotherapists and social workers, we might suspect that the rates are higher than that. At the present time, we cannot really be sure how high the incidence of incest is.

There is, of course, not the slightest evidence to support a prediction that incest, particularly within the nuclear family, will continue to be strongly tabooed. Yet, that is the prediction I make. One reason is historical. From all accounts, the incest taboo has been part of the culture of almost every known society in recorded history. Second, it is hard to imagine that the institution of the family, in any form, could continue unless sexual relations within it were regulated. The cooperation and authority patterns that are essential to its survival would surely be lost.

Notes

1. Milton Rokeach, "Definition of Attitude," in *Social Psychology,* ed. Edgar F. Borgatta (Chicago: Rand McNally, 1969), pp. 404–410.
2. R. T. LaPiere, "Attitudes vs. Action," *Social Forces* 13 (1934): 230–237; and R. D. Minard, "Race Relations in the Pocahontas Coal Field," *Journal of Social Issues* 8 (1952): 29–44.
3. M. L. DeFleur and F. R. Westie, "Changes in Interpersonal Perception as a Means of Reducing Cognitive Dissonance," *Journal of Abnormal and Social Psychology* 61 (1960): 402–410.
4. Thomas Poffenberger, "Individual Choice in Adolescent Premarital Sex Behavior," *Marriage and Family Living* 22 (November, 1960): 326.
5. Henry A. Grunwald, *Sex in America* (New York: Bantam Books, 1964), pp. 150–151.
6. *Newsweek,* 22 March 1965, p. 45.
7. K. B. Davis, *Factors in the Sex Life of 2,200 Women* (New York: Harper, 1929); L. M. Terman, *Psychological Factors in Marital Happiness* (New York: McGraw-Hill, 1938); and G. V. Hamilton, *A Research in Marriage* (New York: Albert and Charles Boni, 1929).
8. Alfred C. Kinsey, Wardell B. Pomeroy, and Clyde E. Martin, *Sexual Behavior in the Human Male* (Philadelphia: W. B. Saunders, 1948); and Alfred C. Kinsey, Wardell B. Pomeroy, Clyde E. Martin, and Paul H. Gebbard, *Sexual Behavior in the Human Female* (Philadelphia: W. B. Saunders, 1953).
9. Winston Ehrmann, *Premarital Dating Behavior* (New York: Henry Holt, 1959); and Ernest W. Burgess and Paul Wallin, *Engagement and Marriage* (Philadelphia: J. B. Lippincott, 1953).
10. William H. Masters and Virginia E. Johnson, *Human Sexual Response* (Boston: Little, Brown, 1966); and William H. Masters and Virginia E. Johnson, *Human Sexual Inadequacy* (Boston: Little, Brown, 1970).
11. Kinsey, Pomeroy, Martin, and Gebbard, *op. cit.,* 1953, p. 520.
12. *Ibid.,* p. 173.
13. *Ibid.,* p. 267.
14. *Ibid.,* p. 292.
15. *Ibid.,* p. 330.
16. Ira L. Reiss, *Premarital Sexual Standards in America* (Glencoe, Ill.: Free Press, 1960), pp. 83–84.

17. Robert R. Bell and Jay B. Chaskes, "Premarital Sexual Experience Among Coeds, 1958 and 1968," *Journal of Marriage and the Family* 32 (February, 1970), pp. 81–84.
18. Harold T. Christensen and Christina F. Gregg, "Changing Sex Norms in America and Scandinavia," *Journal of Marriage and the Family* 32 (November, 1970), p. 625.
19. Ira L. Reiss, *The Family System in America* (New York: Holt, Rinehart, and Winston, 1971), p. 394.
20. *Ibid.,* p. 396.
21. Lester A. Kirkendall and Roger W. Libby, "Interpersonal Relationships —Crux of the Sexual Renaissance," in *Intimate Life Styles,* eds. Joann S. Delora and Jack R. Delora (Pacific Palisades, Calif.: Goodyear, 1972), p. 93.
22. Ira L. Reiss, "How and Why Americans' Sex Standards Are Changing," in *Intimate Life Styles,* eds. Joann S. Delora and Jack R. Delora (Pacific Palisades, Calif.: Goodyear, 1972), pp. 104–112.
23. *Ibid.,* p. 108.
24. John F. Cuber, "How New Ideas About Sex Are Changing Our Lives," in *Intimate Life Styles,* eds. Joann S. Delora and Jack R. Delora (Pacific Palisades, Calif.: Goodyear, 1972), p. 116.
25. Jayne B. Burks, "The Delphi Study" (unpublished Ph.D. diss., Fontbonne College, 1973). A preliminary report of this study of sociologists' opinions of future trends confirms this point of view. Sixty-four per cent of the sociologists questioned felt that premarital sex will be an acceptable societal norm by 1985.
26. L. M. Terman, *op. cit.;* and Burgess and Wallin, *op. cit.*
27. George Murdock, *Social Structure* (New York: Macmillan, 1949).
28. Arthur Train, *Puritan's Progress* (New York: Charles Scribner's Sons, 1931), p. 347.
29. Lee Rainwater, "Marital Sexuality in Four Cultures of Poverty," *Journal of Marriage and the Family* 26 (November, 1964): 457–466.
30. William Simon and John Gagnon, "Sex, Marriage, and Social Class" in *Life Styles: Diversity in American Society,* eds. Saul D. Feldman and Gerald W. Thielbar (Boston: Little, Brown, 1972), pp. 86–87.
31. Masters and Johnson, 1970, *op. cit.*
32. Sharon Price, "Are Most People Dissatisfied with Their Sexual Life?" *Sexual Behavior,* December 1971, p. 52.
33. Jetse Sprey, *loc. cit.,* pp. 52–53.
34. Leonard Cammer, *Sexual Behavior,* December 1971, p. 55.
35. Kinsey *et al.,* 1953, *op. cit.*
36. Murdock, *op. cit.,* p. 265.
37. Clellan S. Ford and Frank A. Beach, *Patterns of Sexual Behavior* (New York: Harper, 1952), p. 115.
38. Morton M. Hunt, *Her Infinite Variety* (New York: Harper, 1962), p. 127.
39. Kinsey *et al.,* 1953, *op. cit.*
40. John F. Cuber and Peggy B. Harroff, *Sex and the Significant Americans* Baltimore: Penguin, 1968), p. 62.
41. Albert Ellis, "Healthy and Disturbed Reasons for Having Extramarital Relations," in *Extra-Marital Relations,* ed. Gerhard Neubeck (Englewood Cliffs, N.J.: Prentice-Hall, 1966).

42. Robert R. Bell, *Premarital Sex in a Changing Society* (Englewood Cliffs, N.J.: Prentice-Hall, 1966).

43. Lonny Myers and Hunter Leggitt, "A New View of Adultery," *Sexual Behavior,* February 1972, pp. 52–62.

44. *Sexual Behavior,* September 1972, pp. 46–51.

45. Jetse Sprey, "Extramarital Relations," *Sexual Behavior,* August 1972, p. 35.

46. Robert R. Bell, *Social Deviance* (Homewood, Ill.: Dorsey, 1971).

47. Kinsey, *et al.,* 1948, *op. cit.,* p. 488.

48. Ernest Jones, *The Life and Work of Sigmund Freud,* vol. II (New York: Basic Books, 1955). p. 287.

49. F. I. Kallman, "Comparative Twin Study of the Genetic Aspects of Male Homosexuality," *Journal of Nervous and Mental Diseases* 115 (1952): 283–298; and F. I. Kallman, "Twin and Sibship Study of Overt Male Homosexuality," *American Journal of Human Genetics* 4, (1952): 136–146.

50. W. S. Schlegel, "Die Konstitutionsbiologishchen Grundlagen der Homo-sexualität," *Zeitschrift für Menschliche Vereinbarung: Konstitutionslehre* 36 (1962):341–364.

51. J. Money, J. L. Hampson, and J. G. Hampson, "An Examination of Some Basic Sexual Concepts: The Evidence of Human Hermaphrodit-ism," *Bulletin of the Johns Hopkins Hospital* 97 (1955): 301–319.

52. B. G. Rosenberg and Brian Sutton-Smith, *Sex and Identity* (New York: Holt, Rinehart, and Winston, 1972), p. 32.

53. *Ibid.,* p. 316.

54. J. Money, "Sex Hormones and Other Variables in Human Eroticism," in *Sex and Internal Secretions,* vol. II, ed. W. C. Young (Baltimore: Williams and Wilkins, 1961), p. 1397.

55. Rosenberg and Sutton-Smith, *op. cit.,* p. 36.

56. Darrell Steffensmeir, "Male and Female Attitudes Toward Homo-sexuality" (Master's thesis, University of Iowa, 1966).

57. *New York Times,* 19 October 1971.

58. Quoted by Martin Duberman in the *New York Times, Book Review,* 10 December 1972, p. 7.

59. John Updike, "Van Loves Ada, Ada Loves Van," *New Yorker,* 2 August 1969, pp. 67–75.

60. Murdock, *op. cit.,* pp. 292–300.

61. S. Kirson Weinberg, *Incest Behavior* (New York: Citadel Press, 1955), p. 39.

4 Mate Selection

Most young people, when they are planning marriage and during the early stages of marriage, live in a romantic world of their own choosing and design. This conception of marriage, with its stress on personal satisfaction and romance, is uniquely American. No other culture at any time in history has considered love so necessary to the conjugal state. Nowhere else is there such strong stigma attached to being unloved. How did we arrive at this state of affairs? How did this notion of romantic love in marriage come about, and why is it the basis of marriage in the United States?

In the fifth century B.C. Plato wrote about love among the upper classes of Greece. According to his description, marriage was not associated with love, because marriage was related only to reproduction. Love was considered the highest form of human virtue. To be in love was to be honorable, kind, wise, and noble. The best possible love was that between a beautiful young man and a wise older man. Homosexual love was admired because it involved the spiritual, the intellectual, the soul, called *Agape,* in addition to or instead of sexual love, *Eros,* which was a less exalted form. Both were more valuable than the love between a man and a woman. Women were of inferior status—unworthy of being loved and incapable of returning love.

Six hundred years later, Ovid wrote about the Roman concept of love, which was quite different from the Greek concept. The Romans thought of love as sensual, not intellectual, spiritual, or romantic in a lasting sense. Love did not fulfill one; love was a game of mutual deceit and jealousy, similar in some ways to warfare.

The early Christians rejected sexual love in favor of total devotion to religion and to the church. Married sexuality was tolerated, but only in order to have children. The most splendid marriage was one in which abstinence was the rule. There were two reasons for this. First, the early Christians belonged to a radical and persecuted sect, and members of such a sect need to be encouraged to devote all their energies and passions to the movement itself. A man who is in love with a woman, it was thought, cannot be a good revolutionary. Second, women were regarded as the root of all evil. Men had to protect themselves against the inherent witchery of women, and to love, trust, or depend upon a female could end only in disaster.

No social order has ever successfully suppressed sexuality; the church put up a mighty struggle but it could not succeed. Gradually, out of this repression, the romantic ideal emerged at the end of the eleventh century among the noble class. Marriages were arranged along political and economic lines, so that love was extramarital. Ostensibly romantic love was asexual although there is disagreement among historians about this. The idea was for courtly men to fall in love with noble ladies, who were generally married, and to adore them from afar, writing odes and singing ballads to them, but not touching these fragile, divine creatures. Courtly love, of course, had little to do with mate selection or marriage.

From the twelfth century to the eighteenth there were many changes in the notion of romantic love. It filtered down from the upper classes to the middle and lower classes. As the idea spread, it created problems. The common man wanted romance, but he did not want adultery. Eventually the dilemma was resolved by shifting romantic love from the postmarital period to the premarital period and making it the basis for marriage. This, in turn, created another dilemma, because, if love was supposed to occur before marriage and lead to marriage, people wanted to have the right to choose whom they would marry.

During the nineteenth century and for centuries before that, parents chose their children's mates. Even though the early settlers in America believed in self-determination in marital selection as well as in religion and politics, love was not conceptualized in the same way we think of it today. Buckingham observed, "Love, among the American people, appears to be regarded rather as an affair of the judgment, than of the heart; its expression seems to spring from a sense of duty, rather than from a sentiment of feeling."[1] In other words, love developed after marriage; it was considered a function of the relationship and the roles, rather than of personal traits or interaction.

Gordon and Bernstein reviewed marriage manuals of the nineteenth century and noted that the most important criteria for mate selection were physical health, moral and character considerations, and religiosity.[2] Love, then, was dependent on these "good" characteristics.

By the second half of the nineteenth century marriage manuals began to show the influence of industrialization. The interaction between men and women began to gain prominence partly because middle-class women had more leisure time for personality development as technology released them from many household tasks. Thus, the personal nature of the marriage relationship came under consideration.

Today in America we have incorporated the elements of romantic love into marriage. For example, the notion persists that there exists in the world one ideal, perfect mate for each person. Each of us pursues this dream person, and when we fall in love we believe the miracle has occurred, that we have found the one man or woman on earth who was intended for us. Another concept Americans tend to accept is that of love at first sight. This means that, when the lovers who are meant for each other meet, they know each other instantly. We also put those we love on a pedestal. Selective perception allows us to screen out all negative qualities and exaggerate all positive ones. There are still other elements of romantic love in our courtship and early marriage. There is, for example, the belief that love conquers all; if two people love each other strongly enough, they can overcome all obstacles, all frustration, all opposition, and live happily ever after.

In a classic paper on the theoretical importance of love, Goode informs us that love is a universal psychological potential in every society, but it is always controlled by institutional patterns.[3] One pattern is child marriage, in which the child is betrothed or married before he is old enough to interact with potential mates. A second institutional pattern is one in which the pool of eligible mates is so narrowly defined that almost no choice is possible for the individual. Thirdly, a society can arrange to keep its young people separate by sex, so that little or no interaction can occur. This narrows the field to those considered acceptable as marriage partners. A fourth method for control of love is the chaperone system, which comes close to segregation. A fifth pattern is one in which choice is seemingly free, yet is controlled indirectly by encouraging young people to associate only with eligible peers. The only kind of society that could permit completely free choice of spouse would be one in which kinship lines were totally unimportant; Goode states that no such society exists. He modifies this, however, by pointing out that control of love is always more essential in the upper classes, gradually becoming less so as we go down the class hierarchy. Nevertheless, love is always under some control by social groups so as to preserve the existing social structures by directing young people into marriages that will maintain those structures.

It should be clear by now that there are many societal influences on love. Each culture exerts different pressures on people to fall in love for different reasons and in different ways. We are not born knowing how to love, or even knowing that we are supposed to love. Loving is something we learn to do during socialization. The child learns to love his parents and his siblings. Gradually, these feelings expand to include peripheral family members and peers. Most children are brought up to believe that love between the sexes is an adult thing, that they will "naturally" fall in love and marry (note the juxtaposition of love and marriage). Being in love implies being adult, and this is very significant for adolescents who try very hard to "prove" how grown up they are.

By the time we are in late adolescence we have internalized the value of being in love. Parents begin strenuous conditioning to prepare their children for marriage—not just any marriage, of course, but marriage to the "right" person. Peers add their own pressures to this, as they begin to fall in love and marry, by activating the always dormant fear that one will never find the right person and will be among the stigmatized unwanted minority.

During early adulthood, the differences between males and females become pronounced. Because marriage is a more important source of sex-role identification and status for girls than for boys, they are more concerned with love and marriage. Nevertheless, girls tend to be more realistic in terms of the future of these relationships; boys tend to be more romantic. Perhaps this is because love and marriage are of more practical concern to girls. For a female, we must bear in mind, marriage is generally her entire future; she must take care, then, in her selection. It must be romantic, no doubt of that, but she is also concerned about her total life style.

Kanin and his associates found that females score lower on romanticism scales, are less likely to recognize love than males are, and are more likely to be rational and cautious in their romantic behavior.[4] A woman, these investigators found, has a greater need to be certain of her feelings, but once she is sure, her feelings become more intense than a man's. Kanin explains that females are socialized earlier and more intensely into the notion of romantic love and marriage. Therefore, a woman invests more of herself in this kind of relationship once she commits herself to it.

THEORIES OF MATE SELECTION

As we have noted, in the United States we marry for love. The choice of a mate, however, is never so free as we would like to believe. Almost invariably, we select our mates from a pool of eligibles determined by social factors of which we may be hardly even aware. In reality, one cannot marry just anyone in the society. The probabilities are narrowed by socio-economic class, race, religion, age, and many other factors. The underlying reason for this is that marriage implies that the spouses are social equals, so that a marriage uniting people of differing social status can cause discomfort to the bride and groom and to their families. Therefore, society puts pressure on people to choose a "proper" mate. It is true that marriage can be a means of upward social mobility, but for most it serves to maintain the status quo by preserving the privileges and rights of the given social group.

The psychoanalytic school holds that people select their mates for unconscious reasons. As is typical of psychoanalytic theories, there has been little or no attempt at empirical verification. Indeed, Kubie claims that, because mate choice is unconscious, it cannot be subjected to empirical study.[5]

Most sociologists, on the other hand, believe that people have an image of an ideal spouse and consciously select marriage partners with that ideal in mind. The ideal image may be highly individualistic, but it is more usually determined by societal norms.

In a study of 372 college students who were either engaged or recently married, Strauss found that 80 per cent of the subjects had an ideal mate in mind; about half reported that they had actually compared this ideal with their real partners before making the choice.[6] Fifty-nine per cent said their partners matched their physical ideal; 74 per cent had partners who, they felt, matched their personality ideal.

Homogamy-Heterogamy

Whether the reasons for mate selection are conscious or unconscious is of less interest to sociologists than two other types of theories. Robert Winch tried to formulate a comprehensive theory of mate selection based on complementary personality needs.[7] Winch postulated that within the field of eligibles—that is, within the groups that are considered legitimate possibilities for marriage —the individual will try to select the person who is most likely to satisfy his personal psychological needs. Winch hypothesized that such a person will have needs that are complementary rather than similar to those of the prospective mate. Winch defined love as a positive feeling one individual has for another who meets his psychological needs. Each partner's needs complement the other's. Winch developed several areas of these complementary needs—for example, abasement-dominance, which means that one partner has a need to be blamed or criticized while the other has a need to control. Other examples: one partner may have a need for recognition, his mate, to admire and defer; one spouse may have a need to be nurturing, the other, to be cared for.

Winch set out to test his hypotheses. Unfortunately, his research methods left something to be desired, and later researchers either have refuted his rather weak findings or have been unable to substantiate them conclusively.[8]

Winch has since admitted that some of the criticisms are valid, and he has attempted to modify his theory.[9] A male-female relationship will probably be satisfactory, Winch now feels, if the complementary needs are compatible with the role norms. That is, if the paired needs are dominance and passivity for example, it is necessary that the male be the dominant partner and the female the passive partner, as these are considered the proper role norms in this society. Winch predicts that, if the male is the passive member and the female the dominant, the relationship will be less harmonious. It seems to me that Winch may have to re-examine his theory if our norms change in the direction considered desirable by the women's liberation movement. Such change would mean that we would no longer define such characteristics as "dominance" or "passivity" in gender terms.

The theory that competes with Winch's theory of complementary needs is called the theory of homogamy, which states that people marry those who possess similar personal and psychological characteristics. (The opposite term, heterogamy, refers to marriage to someone unlike oneself.) In short, in homogamy like marries like, as opposed to Winch's notion that opposites attract.

Several studies have shown that married couples tend to be similar in height, weight, and physical and mental health.[10] In addition, it has been found that attractive men usually marry attractive women.[11] Of course, what is considered attractive varies widely, depending largely on social class, which may account for Elder's finding that social mobility through marriage and female beauty are related.[12] He asserts that lower-class mobile women are considerably more attractive than their non-mobile sisters. Studies indicate that there is also a great deal of intelligence homogamy.[13]

Schellenberg finds that engaged and married couples are more likely to hold similar values than a group of people who are not interested in each other.[14] Kerckhoff and Davis find that, as couples tend to get more serious about each other, their values tend to become more similar.[15]

Endogamy-Exogamy

The term *endogamy* refers to the requirement that one marry within one's social group. When we say that a mate has been selected endogamously, we are referring to similar social characteristics. A good many of the norms of endogamy come from a feeling that is present in all groups—the sense of "we-ness." "We" usually consider ourselves to be superior to "them" in certain areas, so that a feeling of group-belonging is generally accompanied by antipathy to those outside the group. It follows, then, that "they" are not often considered proper mates for our sons and daughters.

Exogamy, the opposing term, refers to the requirement that we marry outside of certain groups in which we hold membership. Usually the group is the nuclear family; we are prohibited from marrying our parents, siblings, aunts and uncles, and, in some societies, cousins.

Endogamy seems to strengthen the in-group. People who are of the same class, race, or religion or who are neighbors or members of the same club are likely to feel closer to each other when they are united by marriage also. Endogamous social factors that are generally operative in our society are race, religion, age, education, and class.

Until approximately ten years ago, many states had laws that forbade miscegenation. At the present time it is difficult to obtain statistics on interracial marriage because few states today require such information on marriage-license applications. The *New York Times* reported that the Census Bureau has announced an over-all increase of 63 per cent in black-white marriages during the 1960s. The major increase was in marriages between black men and white women; a decrease was found in the number of white men and black women who married.[16] According to this report, the total of interracial marriages, including black-white, white–American Indian, and white-Japanese, as of 1970 represents only .7 per cent of the 44.5 million American marriages annually.

The most important factor that seems to operate to prevent white-black marriage is prejudice. However, it is also difficult to meet members of other racial groups, what contact takes place is frequently formal, and opportunity for the development of interpersonal relations is limited. Furthermore, most people are aware that if they intermarry they will face rejection from family and friends, and this seems to serve as an inhibitor.

We do not know very much about the kinds of people who marry outside their own race, because there has been little empirical research on the subject. Simpson and Yinger found that the interracial couples they studied were members either of the stable middle class, the sports world, the intellectual world, or radical groups.[17] Some were foreign-born people who were unaware of the implications of interracial marriage in this country. When interracial marriage does occur, it usually involves black men marrying white women, rather than the other way around.[18]

No one is quite sure why this is so. One explanation defines the racial groups in this country as castes. A caste is a closed social stratum that is based on heredity and that determines a person's prestige and status within the social system. The archetype of the caste system is the Hindu system in India. When caste exogamy does occur among Hindus, it is usually the higher-caste man who marries the lower-caste woman. If we consider the races in our society as castes, the reverse occurs: higher-caste (white) women are more likely to marry lower-caste (black) men than the other way around. This is especially remarkable because the white wife of a black man and her children are generally classified as socially "black"—and usually live in black areas of a city and associate primarily with black friends.[19] Why, then, do white women contract such marriages?

Pavela found that white women who married blacks were older than white women who married within their own caste.[20] He claims that this could mean that these women feared spinsterhood and therefore were less choosy than their younger peers. It could also mean that they felt less inhibited by the social mores because they were older, and that they could therefore make freer choices of mates. Blood adds to these conjectures by suggesting that, although low-caste people of both sexes may prefer to marry "up," low-caste males may exercise a sex-linked prerogative by suggesting such marriages while low-caste women do not feel free enough to do so.[21]

Beyond these meager and speculative explanations, we know very little more about the reasons for most marriages between black men and white women than we know about the reasons for those between white men and black women. Heer calculated that in thirteen generations, or 351 years, there could be a complete amalgamation of the races, provided that people cooperated toward that end.[22] If this should occur, the question as stated here will have become academic.

In general, Jews tend to be more endogamous than either Catholics or Protestants, and Protestants more than Catholics. The available data are very sparse because the matter of religion was removed from the Census questionnaire after 1950, so that the best information we have at present is from a 1957 study by the U.S. Bureau of the Census.[23] According to this study, only 7 per cent of all marriages that include at least one Jew are interfaith. Nine per cent of all marriages involving a Protestant are intermarriages, as are 22 per cent of those involving a Catholic.

The 1957 data suggest that religious intermarriage may well be a function of the population distribution. That is, when there are relatively few people in one's religious group, the chances of interreligious marriage are greater because the pool of eligibles is smaller. Jews have a high endogamy rate despite their relatively small numbers because they tend to cluster in cities and therefore are in a position to interact with many other Jews.

Reiss explains that the 1957 study is probably somewhat conservative. On the basis of data from Canada, he predicts that the trend is toward increased exogamy. He feels that the cultural similarities between the United States and Canada allow him to generalize in this fashion. In any event, the 1957 data underestimate the amount of intermarriage because the data do not take account of marriages in which one partner converted and because the sample contained a national cross-section. Reiss says that a true picture would require an emphasis on younger couples and on people married a year or less. Such a survey would probably yield a higher interfaith marriage rate.[24]

Religious intermarriage is much more common than racial intermarriage, probably because much less stigma is attached to it. Studies show that the rate of interfaith marriage is increasing, partly because "religious identity has lost most of its prejudicial and discriminatory salience."[25]

Heiss attempts to identify the people who intermarry.[26] Inter-marrying Catholics are likely to come from families where there was low family integration, where the parents were not religious, and where there had been intergenerational conflict. Protestants are likely to have had weak ties to both their families and their religion. Most Jews who intermarry were also not close to their families.

Age is another important factor restricting one's selection of a mate. The United States is an unusually age-conscious nation, and it is not surprising that this awareness can also be seen in its norms on mate choice. Apparently Americans find that they are more comfortable with their own age peers, and therefore they usually reject as mates those who are considerably older or younger.

Parke and Glick found that the median age difference between marrying couples was three years, with the woman the younger partner.[27] They also found that the older the man is at the time of marriage, the more likely he is to marry a woman younger than he.

The age difference between husbands and wives also seems to be decreasing. In 1890, for example, the average difference was 4.1 years; in 1930, 3.0 years; and in 1970, 2.4 years.[28] This is important because it may mean that a married couple will have a greater chance to survive together and have a longer marriage. In 1965, for example, Parke and Glick found that 64 per cent of women between fifty-five and sixty-four years of age were still living with their husbands.[29] They predicted that the rate would go up to 72 per cent by 1985. Such a situation would have many implications for divorce and remarriage rates.

There is an increased stress today on educational endogamy because education has more and more come to mean high status in occupation and prestige. When educational exogamy does occur, it is more acceptable if the woman marries "up." There is little difficulty if the man has more education than his wife, unless, of course, the difference is great enough to cause social embarrassment. However, when a woman marries a man with a great deal less education, she is often considered to have demeaned herself. Glick's data indicate that 45 per cent of the married couples in his sample were on the same educational level; in 27 per cent of the marriages the men were on a higher level; in 28 per cent the wives were on a higher level.[30]

When people are in the same social class, there is a tendency for them to share the same social values, goals, and attitudes. This means that they are likely to want the same kind of life style, to have similar ambitions, and to share views on child rearing. Although such sharing would tend to make the marital relationship easier, some studies have indicated that class-status endogamy is not so widespread as we might expect. Leslie and Richardson, who studied a group of married college students, conclude that, because a college contains students from diverse backgrounds, there is a tendency away from class endogamy among students.[31] Coombs's data also indicate that the norms on college campuses are less likely to produce endogamy than those in communities.[32] This means that when courting people are living at home with parents they are more likely to contract endogamous marriages than if they are living away at college.

To summarize these theories of mate selection—homogamy versus heterogamy and endogamy versus exogamy: It is probably true that most people are endogamous in relation to such social factors as race, religion, ethnicity, age, education, and class. From this pool of eligibles, probably most people select mates because some personality characteristics are similar and some are opposite. Continued research, using more sophisticated methods, may eventually resolve these questions.

MATE SELECTION IN THE FUTURE

Endogamy, the custom requiring people to marry within their own social groups, appears to be the norm in the United States today. Moreover, there also seems to be a tendency toward homogamy in terms of personal characteristics, such as personality, physical traits, and intelligence. We may speculate, then, whether these tendencies are likely to persist until the end of the century.

It is likely that we will continue the trend that has begun in our society toward equalization in all areas: race, religion, and social class.

In terms of race, more black students are in college than ever before, more black people are holding political office, and more are earning high salaries. This means that black people will become more visible to whites and less like strangers. They will mingle with white people at work, at play, and in the neighborhood. I predict that, as the black becomes the colleague, the golfing partner, and the man next door, his children will intermingle with white children, and, eventually, these children will intermarry.

In terms of religion, young people now are much less concerned with religion in their courtship patterns than people were in the past.[33] Nor do they tend to feel, as their parents did, that some religious groups have more prestige than others. Therefore, I predict that religion will not remain an important consideration for marriage.

Many sociologists believe that the gap between the lower classes and the middle classes is closing.[34] This is the theory of embourgeoisement, which argues that the working class is losing its identity as a separate group and is merging with the middle class. This theory is based on studies pointing to improved standards of living, rising income, increased occupational mobility, and new attitudes toward family life. I agree that, if indeed the working class and the middle class are converging, class distinctions in marriage selection will disappear, except among the very highest and lowest classes. In short, in these areas of differentiation—race, religion, and social class—major changes are occurring in the direction of similarity. Therefore, we may say that the pool of eligibles grows larger.

Furthermore, our cities are growing and it is in cities, where there is a pluralistic, anonymous, and mobile population, that exogamy is most possible. Also, because our population is so large, memberships in groups tend to overlap, with the result that in one sense or another every marriage breaks some rule of endogamy.

I predict, therefore, that endogamy will prove to be less and less of a criterion in mate selection. This will happen because blacks are moving into the mainstream of American society via education and occupation; because our young men and women are less concerned with religious and ethnic differences than their parents were; because our class boundaries are blurring; and, finally, because our cities are expanding at enormous rates, creating more anonymity and allowing less surveillance.

NOTES

1. J. S. Buckingham, *The Eastern and Western States of America,* 2 vols. (London: Fisher, Son and Co., 1867).
2. M. Gordon and M. C. Bernstein, "Mate Choice and Domestic Life in the Nineteenth Century Marriage Manual," unpublished manuscript (University of Connecticut, 1969).
3. William J. Goode, "The Theoretical Importance of Love," *American Sociological Review* 24 (February, 1959): 38–47; reprinted in *Sourcebook in Marriage and the Family,* 3d ed., ed. Marvin B. Sussman (New York: Houghton Mifflin, 1968).
4. Eugene J. Kanin, Karen R. Davidson, and Sonia R. Scheck, "A Research Note on Male-Female Differentials in the Experience of Heterosexual Love," *Journal of Sex Research* (February 1970): 64–72.
5. L. S. Kubie, "Psychoanalysis and Marriage: Practical and Theoretical Issues," in *Neurotic Interaction in Marriage,* ed. V. E. Eisenstein (New York: Basic Books, 1956), pp. 10–43.
6. A. Strauss, "The Ideal and the Chosen Mate," *American Journal of Sociology* 52 (1946): 204–208.
7. Robert F. Winch, *Mate Selection* (New York: Harper, 1958).
8. Charles E. Bowerman and Barbara R. Day, "A Test of the Theory of Complementary Needs as Applied to Couples During Courtship," *American Sociological Review* 21 (1956): 602–605; James A. Schellenberg and Lawrence S. Bee, "A Re-examination of the Theory of Complementary Needs in Mate Selection," *Marriage and Family Living* 22 (1960): 227–232; John A. Blazer, "Complementary Needs and Marital Happiness," *Marriage and Family Living* 25 (February, 1963): 89–95; Irving Rosow, "Issue in the Concept of Need-Complementarity," *Sociometry* 20 (1957): 216–233; and Jerold S. Heiss and Michael Gordon, "Need Patterns and the Mutual Satisfaction of Dating and Engaged Couples," *Journal of Marriage and the Family* 26 (August, 1964): 337–339.
9. Robert F. Winch, "Another Look at the Theory of Complementary Needs in Mate Selection," *Journal of Marriage and the Family* 29 (1967): 756–762.
10. Ernest W. Burgess and Paul Wallin, *Engagement and Marriage* (Philadelphia: J. B. Lippincott, 1953), pp. 80–81.
11. *Ibid.*
12. Glen H. Elder, Jr., "Appearance and Education in Marriage Mobility," *American Sociological Review* 34:4 (1969): 524.
13. Menford H. Kuhn, "How Mates Are Sorted," in *Family, Marriage, and Parenthood,* eds. Howard Becker and Reuben Hill (Boston: Heath, 1955), p. 263.
14. James A. Schellenberg, "Homogamy in Personal Values and the Field of Eligibles," *Social Forces* 39 (1960): 157–162.
15. Alan C. Kerckhoff and Keith E. Davis, "Value Consensus and Need Complementarity in Mate Selection," *American Sociological Review* 27 (1962): 295–303.
16. *New York Times,* 18 February 1973, sec. E, p. 4.

17. George E. Simpson and J. Milton Yinger, *Racial and Cultural Minorities* (New York: Harper, 1958).
18. Larry D. Barnett, "Research in Interreligious Dating and Marriage," *Marriage and Family Living* 24 (1962): 191–194.
19. Robert O. Blood, Jr., *The Family* (New York: Free Press, 1972), p. 302.
20. Todd H. Pavela, "An Exploratory Study of Negro-White Intermarriage in Indiana," *Journal of Marriage and the Family* 26 (May, 1964): 209–211.
21. Blood, *op. cit.*
22. David Heer, "Negro-White Marriage in the United States," *New Society* 6 (1965): 7–9.
23. U.S. Department of Commerce, Bureau of the Census, *Current Population Reports,* Series P-20, No. 79 (February 2). Washington, D.C.: Government Printing Office, 1958, p. 2.
24. Ira L. Reiss, *The Family System in America* (New York: Holt, Rinehart, and Winston, 1971), p. 326.
25. Robert F. Winch, *The Modern Family,* 2d ed. (New York: Holt, Rinehart, and Winston, 1963), p. 336.
26. Jerold S. Heiss, "Premarital Characteristics of the Religiously Intermarried in an Urban Area," *American Sociological Review* 25 (February, 1960): 53–54.
27. Robert Parke, Jr., and Paul C. Glick, "Prospective Changes in Marriage and the Family," *Journal of Marriage and the Family* 29 (May, 1967).
28. *Statistical Abstracts of the United States,* 1971 (Washington, D.C.: Government Printing Office, 1971), p. 60.
29. Parke and Glick, *op. cit.,* p. 250.
30. Paul C. Glick, "Bachelors and Spinsters," in *Marriage and the Family,* eds. Jeffrey K. Hadden and Marie L. Borgatta (Itasca, Ill.: Peacock, 1969), p. 117.
31. Gerald R. Leslie and Arthur H. Richardson, "Family Versus Campus Influences in Relation to Mate Selection," *Social Problems* 4 (1956), pp. 117–121.
32. Robert H. Coombs, "Reinforcement of Values in the Parental Home as a Factor in Mate Selection," *Marriage and Family Living* 24 (1962): 155–157.
33. Larry D. Barnett, *op. cit.*
34. Ira L. Reiss, *op. cit.,* p. 405.

5 Marriage

Most Americans marry at least once during their lifetime. Marriage has always been popular in this country, and apparently its popularity is increasing. In 1940, for example, 85 per cent of all American women were married by age 30; in 1960, 93 per cent in the same age group were married.[1]

Furthermore, Americans are marrying at younger ages. The modal age for males today is 21; for females, 18. The median age in 1960 was 22.8 for males, 20.3 for females.[2] Many young people marry while they are still in school. About 163,000 college women and about 77,000 high school girls in any given year are married. Older people marry also. In about 35,000 marriages per year in the United States, at least one of the pair is 65 years of age or older.[3]

LEGALITIES OF MARRIAGE*

Just as societies exercise control over most aspects of social life, so do they define the rights and obligations of marriage. In advanced societies such as ours, social control is formalized and extensive. We legislate the interaction between men and women, we

* I wish to thank my friend and attorney, Herman Taub, for his advice in this discussion and in the following sections dealing with legal matters. Any errors are entirely my own.

designate responsibilities for offspring, we regulate the transmission of status and property from one generation to another.

America's concept of marriage, from a legal point of view, is that of a contract. This means that a marriage cannot be discarded unilaterally. However, whereas most contracts can be terminated or modified if the parties involved privately agree to do so, marriage contracts can be broken only by the state. The state can be thought of as a third party to the contract primarily because of its interest in the preservation of the family unit. Thus, marriage can be seen as very much a matter of public concern. There are always legal restrictions placed on the marriage of two members of a society.

One restriction is on age. Many states permit marriage between adolescents (defined as people between 14 and 18 years old) provided that they have the consent of their parents. Generally marriage with consent is permitted to males of 18 and females of 16. Marriage without consent is usually permitted at 21 and 18, respectively. The law recognizes the social and physical differences between the sexes.

We also restrict marriage between certain members of the same family. One prohibition is based on consanguinity, or blood relationship. Thus, in the United States, marriage is not permitted between parent and child, between siblings, between grandparent and grandchild, or between aunt and nephew or uncle and niece. Some states forbid marriage between first cousins. A second prohibition is based on affinity, or legal relationship. This means that in some states marriage is not permitted between a stepparent and stepchild, or between siblings-in-law or parental in-laws.

Our laws also take mental and physical disabilities into account. When people who are deficient in these areas marry, they are frequently unable to discharge their social responsibilities. Society then takes a practical attitude, because the children of such a marriage may become an economic public burden. Many states legislate against the marriage of the insane, but such laws can, in some cases, be difficult to enforce, because unless the person has been legally declared insane, there are no standard definitions or guidelines.

States issue licenses to marry as a way of obtaining statistics on marriage and as an opportunity to refuse licenses to couples considered undesirable, for whatever legal reasons. Many states also require blood tests to ascertain if either of the couple has syphilis, because this dangerous communicable disease can be passed on to an unborn child.

Several states require a waiting period between the issuance of a marriage license and the time the marriage occurs. This delay is intended to prevent spur-of-the-moment marriages, and apparently it has some usefulness because it is estimated that 20 per cent of all couples who obtain a license to marry never do so.

When all requirements have been met—both are of legal age, have no mental illness or severe physical deformity, and are not closely related to each other; a license has been obtained; blood tests have indicated that no syphilis is present; and the waiting period has been observed—then the marriage is considered legal and valid. However, if a couple is married in a state that has fewer requirements, the marriage is considered legal in all fifty states. For example, only about fourteen states recognize common-law marriage; yet all states acknowledge such a relationship from one of those states.

Society remains interested in marriage after the wedding has taken place, and it continues to regulate the rights and obligations of the couple. For example, there are laws obligating a man to support his wife. Each partner is obligated to indulge in sexual activity with the other. There are legal responsibilities toward children born of the marriage.

Most domestic laws pertaining to the rights of husbands and wives discriminate against non-working wives. In the *Women's Role in Contemporary Society,* a report of the New York City Commission on Human Rights, Betty Barry testifies:

> I am speaking today as a member of the most economically vulnerable and largest group of women in America—the housewife. . . . Excluded from almost all protective or civil rights legislation, the housewife is sheltered and betrayed by a myth of economic security.
> . . . The occupation of housewife has no financial value in this society which is based on economic achievement. . . . The housewife should be compensated by receiving either a salary or a definite percentage of the income and property of the family. She should have her own pension plan, social security, medical insurance, etc., instead of receiving these benefits indirectly as a dependent of her husband.
> . . . The common law property rights of New York State dis-

criminate against the housewife because she has forfeited her financial independence. . . .

The housewife saves her husband thousands of dollars by signing
joint income tax returns, yet she is not legally entitled to one half of
this income or property. In New York, it is the husband's. The
housewife is not covered individually for social security, but only as
a dependent of her husband. Upon divorce she usually loses her
benefits and has no coverage or credit for the quarters spent as a
housewife.[4]

And another woman testifies:

I am a housewife, I am not a parasite, I work quite hard caring for
my husband, my child and my home. . . . I am a worker as sure as
any man on any payroll.

For my services I receive room and board and sometimes about
$5 a week. . . . I have absolutely no say whatsoever in determining
what is done with my husband's earnings, which are considerable.

I am a part-time graduate student. . . . My husband, however,
does not approve of my going to school. He has told me countless
times that in his opinion women have no need for higher education
and that he never wants me to work. His most heartfelt objection is
that on the one night a week that I happen to be in class, there is no
dinner for him on the table when he gets home. . . . He has told
me that it [money for tuition] will never come from him, although he
can well afford it.

. . . This term, however, the fees went up and the fees are much
more than I can afford. . . . I called the college financial aid office
and I told them I had no money and my education would have to be
subsidized. They told me not to worry, I could receive a waiver of
tuition if I was in need, just to come down with my husband's W-2
form. . . . I wrote them a long letter explaining my situation to
them. I also explained that I could not get a job to pay for my tuition since my daughter is a brain-damaged child and must be es-
corted to various therapy programs during the day.

Two weeks later I received a formal notice that my application
had been turned down. The reason given was that I did not meet the
qualifications for financial need. The fact that I have no legal access
to my husband's earnings was apparently considered to be my own
problem. . . . The [university] considers me an appendage of my
husband and not an individual in my own right.[5]

MARRIAGE RITUALS

A wedding is a rite of passage. Van Gennep tells us that all ceremonies are intended to symbolize separation, transition, or incorporation.[6] A marriage symbolizes the separation of the nuptial couple from its families of orientation, marks the transition from childhood to adulthood, and represents the incorporation of the newly married couple into a new family.

This ceremony, the wedding, is therefore important not only for the couple and its families and friends but also for the society itself. The couple assumes a new social status and takes on new social rights and obligations. So, although the United States is not a country that usually stresses ritual, it does seem to attach great significance to the marriages of its citizens.

The word *honeymoon* comes from a medieval custom in northern-European countries. For one month (moon) after the wedding ceremony the couple drank a special "mead," or wine made from honey; ergo, honeymoon. Of course the ancient origins of the custom have disappeared, but apparently about 85 per cent of all marrying couples still go on a honeymoon, if only for a few days.[7]

The Rapoports have devised a typology of honeymoons.[8] One type is apparently uniquely American. The Rapoports call it the lovers' nest type, and it means that the newly married couple goes to a resort or hotel that caters to newlyweds. A second type is called the *perpetuum mobile,* meaning that the couple sets out without plans and simply drives anywhere that seems appealing. A third type of honeymoon is called the vacation, because that is what it resembles.

The honeymoon is a commonly recognized activity throughout the world. Generally it is considered to involve a period when men and women can begin sexual intimacy away from the routines of everyday life. It also functions as a time to become reacquainted after the hectic activity of a wedding. It is a time to ignore "real" problems, to hide from the mundane affairs of the world, so as to get to know one another.

WHY PEOPLE MARRY

Although Americans always think they marry for love, there are several other reasons, some of which they are unaware of at the time they marry. Married people are, by definition, adult. As we saw in Chapter 4, one of the reasons for which many young people marry is to acquire unambiguous adult status. One who is not married, even as biological age increases, tends to be viewed as "not really grown up."

We also marry in order to fulfill our sex roles. This is especially true for women because, even though today women are discovering alternative life styles, marriage is still considered the best possible career a woman can have. Similarly, although occupation is the primary adult status for men, part of a man's success depends on his being a good provider for a wife and children. In a society like ours, it is more comfortable to conform to social norms and to be part of the accepted adult group.

Marriage is seen as the most intimate of all possible relationships. Husbands and wives belong together. Through the other, each strengthens his sense of his own value. This becomes especially important in technological societies, in which most relationships are in secondary groups. Together, the two members of the married dyad form a new societal unit—the couple. Even though the husband pursues his occupation as an individual and the wife has a separate status as a homemaker, they present themselves in all other activities as one unit.

"MARRIAGE WORK"

Benson has given us a useful list of six basic marital obligations that he claims obtain in almost all societies.[9] He calls these obligations "marriage work" because he believes, rightly, that effort is needed to perform them, although some are easier than others.

1. Husbands and wives have the right to expect that their spouses will be truthful and dependable. Because most of us are socialized early in life to be reliable and to tell the truth, one can-

not classify this obligation as "work." However, it is still worth noting that in a marriage relationship both partners should be free of suspicion of deceit.

2. Couples also should expect that each will help bear the work load of the relationship, that is, that there will be a sharing of the jobs and obligations that are undertaken in a marriage. Traditionally, labor has been divided into men's work (earning a living) and women's work (taking care of the house and children). This particular division of labor is changing now as we begin to question the traditional distribution of these obligations.

3. Spouses have a right to expect ego support and sympathy from each other. This is the sort of thing one expects of a friend, and if one is married to one's best friend the relationship is usually a happy one.

4. Married people also expect that each will communicate with the other, that confidences will be respected, and that they will be entertaining and interesting to each other. Benson feels that this is difficult work, that it involves more than just being sympathetic and giving ego support. He says that it takes a great deal of effort to listen to the things one's spouse is interested in and to take these things seriously.

5. Giving sexual satisfaction is, in Benson's opinion, a task. He feels that making love is learned behavior and that couples should work to avoid routine, monotonous sexual relations. This is not easy in today's world of variety and novelty, especially as time passes and the couple has been married for many years.

6. The last obligation is called volunteering. By this Benson means that married people should show a willingness to do things for each other that are beyond routine duty. Perhaps it is stretching things a bit to call this a basic obligation of marriage, but apparently most people believe that the mate they have selected should be willing to do more than is expected in order to please his spouse.

Types of Marital Roles

In previous chapters, several types of marriage were identified. Each type stresses different statuses and roles for the husband and wife. In each type there are different rights and obligations for each spouse. However, these are ideal types, and many features are overlapping.

Patriarchal Marriage

In the past, as we have noted, the dominant pattern in marriage was patriarchal. In this form of family organization the father was the undisputed head of the family, in whom all the authority and power were vested. In such marriages deference flowed from wife to husband and never in the other direction. Although it was probably true that the wife had some power in household matters and in child care, all other areas were under the jurisdiction of the male. Such a marriage was based on the assumption that there were sharp differences between men and women. Each had his status and role in the household, with no overlap. The husband commanded; the wife obeyed. This was the traditional marriage, and we can still see traces of it among the upper and lower classes, as well as in certain rural areas.

Matriarchal Marriage

This pattern of marriage grants the power and authority to the wife. However, the real power generally accrues to the mother's closest male relative. True matriarchy is rarely found in the United States, except perhaps among lower-class blacks and possibly in suburban homes. But these are matriarchies out of necessity rather than choice, and they occur because the husband is absent from home for long periods of time—the black because he is unable to support his family, the suburbanite because he is deeply involved in his work and time-consuming commuting. When these husbands are present, however, the power usually reverts to them or is shared.

Companionship Marriage

This type of marriage, described in Chapter 2, is based on the assumption that there is no difference between male and female sex roles and that either partner can fulfill the obligations and assume the rights of the other. This pattern of marriage is growing in popularity among modern, urban, middle-class couples that stress companionship, understanding, equality, affection, and democracy.

Colleague Marriage

The colleague marriage is very similar to the companionship form inasmuch as sharing, personal satisfaction, and comradeship are stressed. However, men and women in a colleague relationship recognize that there are role differences. They assume responsibility and authority for different areas of the marriage, each recognizing the abilities and interests of the other and according deference when it is applicable. The colleague couple, then, is aware of separateness. In their study of marriage, Blood and Wolfe found that most couples make joint decisions except in four areas: The husband has authority over his work and the car; the wife, over her job and the home.[10]

Both companionship- and colleague-type marriages can be found most frequently among upper-middle-class people. Such people tend to subscribe to the notion of "togetherness," stressing a sharing of interests and activities in recreation, church activities, sports, entertaining, and sometimes occupation.

MARITAL LIFE STYLES

Marriage types can also be discussed from the point of view of internal characteristics, the kinds of relationships within the marriage. Cuber and Harroff describe five life styles they found in a study of 211 upper-class husbands and wives.[11] By "life style" Cuber and Harroff mean the ways in which these couples organized patterns of living, brought up their children, expressed their sexuality, and conducted their lives in the outside world. These researchers noted that, although their study was based on upper-class marriages, the five relationship types can probably be found in all classes, with the possible exception of the lowest stratum. They expect, however, that the proportions would vary—that is, that there would be more of one type found at one class level and more of another type at another level. The most common types of marriage, regardless of class distinctions, are probably the passive-congenital and the devitalized, especially for couples in their middle age.

The *conflict-habituated marriage* is characterized by controlled tension. There is constant quarreling, nagging, and bickering, but it is usually kept private and quiet. The partners believe that no one else is aware of the nature of their relationship, although, generally, close friends and family members are fully cognizant of what is going on. Apparently people in this kind of relationship need conflict; in a sense, it is the conflict that cements the relationship. "The overt and manifest fact of habituated attention to handling tension, keeping it chained, and concealing it is clearly seen as a dominant life force. And it can, and does for some, last for a whole lifetime."[12]

The *devitalized marriage* is one in which the partners were deeply in love with each other before the wedding and during the early years of marriage. In the past they spent all possible time together, sex was an exciting part of their lives, and they were closely identified with each other. All this changed during the middle years of marriage. They avoid spending time together, sex is uninteresting and intermittent, and they no longer have shared interests. In short, the relationship has grown stale, dull, and boring. They have become habits to each other, and they take each other for granted.

Passive-congenital marriage is similar to devitalized marriage, except that the relationship was passive from the beginning. Couples with this relationship have never experienced the excitement and joy of being deeply in love. On the other hand, they are spared the disillusionment of the devitalized marriage, and there is little conflict because they do not share enough to fight about. This kind of marriage is often deliberately chosen by people who are afraid of deep attachments and commitment and by people who are involved in careers that allow little time or energy for personal relationships. Such couples stress other things in their marriage: successful careers, status in the community, children. According to Cuber and Harroff:

> The passive-congenital life style fits societal needs quite well also, and this is an important consideration. The man of practical affairs, in business, government service, or the professions, quite obviously needs "to have things peaceful at home" and to have a minimum of distraction as he pursues his important work. He may feel both love and gratitude toward the wife who fits this mode.[13]

The *vital marriage* is quite different from the three just described. Men and women in vital relationships are closely bound to each other in all the important areas of life. Everything is shared; indeed, the pleasure is in sharing, regardless of the activity, and nothing is pleasurable unless it is shared. Such couples will sacrifice anything in order to be together because their central life interest lies in each other. Conflict exists, as it must in every human relationship, but it is short-lived because arguing keeps these people apart and this is, for them, very uncomfortable.

The *total relationship* is similar to the vital, except that it is absolutely complete. Neither of the pair has any life at all without the other. Work and play are both shared. Frequently the husband and wife are in the same occupation, even in the same business concern, law firm, medical office, or college department. If they are not in business together, no business decision is made without mutual consultation. Such relationships are rare, but, when they do exist, it is as if neither partner has a private existence.

SUCCESS IN MARRIAGE

The concept of marital success poses several problems for sociologists. One problem has been how to define it. Do the terms *success, integration, adjustment, stability, satisfaction,* and *happiness* all mean the same thing? When we measure one of these features are we measuring the others? Somehow it seems that one can "adjust" to an unhappy marriage or be "integrated" into an unstable marriage. The interchangeability—or non-interchangeability—of these terms has led to confusion in family sociology.

Not only is there too much variability in the terms used to describe presumably the same state of the marital relationship, but there is also difficulty in obtaining honest information. For one thing, people may be happy for reasons quite apart from their marriage. For another, what is considered happiness in one marriage may mean unhappiness in another. Finally, we can expect subjects to give socially acceptable answers because the norm is to have a successful marriage. Thus, we cannot give full credence to self-reports; on the other hand, we have not developed objective criteria.

Another, and very serious, criticism of the studies on marital success is that too many investigators have based their conclusions on the responses of wives only, on the erroneous assumption that husbands and wives are likely to agree on their answers. Safilios-Rothschild points out that we have no basis in fact for this assumption and, indeed, that there is evidence that spouses differentially evaluate their relationship and their marriage.[14]

Robert Bell favors the term *adjustment* as a measure of marital success and satisfaction because he thinks the term is applicable in many areas of social life, which is, by definition, interactional.

> All functioning members of a society are adjusted to at least a set of basic social requirements and maladjusted to the degree that no individual can accept and conform to all of the requirements. Social adjustment is not an either/or proposition, but a matter of degree.[15]

Bell has suggested that there are some general criteria by which to measure the success of a marriage. He notes that these criteria are by no means universal but are "patterns that are frequently found in marriages defined by the couple as successful. In various successful marriages, not all the criteria will have the same significance or be related in the same way."[16]

Successfully married people enjoy being married. They find the roles they play pleasurable and the treatment they receive from their spouses satisfactory. Bell notes that no marriage can be perfectly satisfying all the time. However, when people like to live in a marriage situation, the dissatisfactions are manageable and do not really disturb the relationship.

Successfully married people feel that they are individuals in addition to being part of a dyad. That is, they find time and opportunity to do things separately from their spouses. In some marriages there is great stress on "doing things together" or "being one." Yet many people feel the need to express themselves independently at times. Bell believes that "pleasure for the individual through involvement with groups of his own sex is more common for men than for women"[17] because women are more dependent on men both socially and psychologically than vice versa.

A third characteristic of a successful marriage is the opposite of the previous one. The married person derives joy and pleasure from the things he and his spouse share. Marriage, then, seems to require that the couple recognize not only differences but also similarities and that it be accepting of both.

Finally, successfully married people are free in their affections and do not hesitate to verbalize and demonstrate their love for each other. All human beings from time to time require assurances that they are loved, and most of us expect to find such assurances in marriage. Thus, in a reciprocal, intimate relationship, it is necessary for each to be reminded that he is important and necessary in the life and for the welfare of the other.

STAGES OF MARRIAGE

Marriage can be divided into five stages: early marriage, before children are born*; the years when children are young; the years when children are teenagers; the postparental period, when children leave home; and marriage in old age. Parenting—the relationship of parents to children—is discussed in Chapter 6; here we shall talk about the relationship between the spouses during the other four stages of married life.

Early Marriage

Early marriage is characterized by romance and euphoria. This is the time of the excitement of a new sexual experience, of furnishing a home together, of learning about each other, of becoming a couple. But soon it becomes apparent that marriage cannot be lived in a dream world. Just as they had to learn the roles for each previous status, so the bride and groom must now learn how to play marriage roles.

We have already discussed the formal aspects of the marital role as spelled out by our legal code. However, there are informal aspects, and these are more meaningful to the young couple. The bride has known that she will be expected to cook, but she must

---

* Because 90 per cent of all married couples have children, I will talk about the stages of marriage from the point of view of this majority. Childlessness is discussed in Chapter 6.

learn what foods will be most satisfying to her husband. The husband has known that he will be expected to support his wife, but now he must decide, probably with her, on specific budgeting.

Many young couples today have already had sexual intercourse, at least with each other, by the time they marry. Nevertheless, they probably have only rarely, if ever, actually slept together for an entire night. Now they must learn to share a bed comfortably. It is this matter of sharing, the constant presence of another person, both in and out of bed, that makes early adjustment somewhat difficult. They must learn to be considerate of each other; they must re-allocate time and space.

Each member of the newly married pair will have to learn to accommodate himself to the needs and personality of the other and to adjust to being one of two instead of one alone. Each will have to make some sacrifices. The euphoria begins to dissipate, and eventually conflict enters the relationship. At first this may be shattering to a newly married couple, but conflict exists in all human relationships, especially marriage because it is so intimate.

Folsom developed a typology of conflict in marriage. It may, he says, be acute, progressive, or habituated.[18] Acute conflict is most prevalent during early marriage, when there are many undefined situations and when the newly married people are unaccustomed to their new statuses and therefore unfamiliar with their roles. This kind of conflict is characterized by intense hostility and emotional stress. Husband and wife lash out at each other and try to inflict as much pain as possible. Eventually, with effort and as time passes, a *modus operandi* is worked out and this type of conflict diminishes or even disappears. If the basic differences are resolved during early marriage, acute conflict will not do permanent damage. However, if the young couple are unable to work out compromises, then the second form of conflict will develop, namely, progressive conflict.

When acute conflict cannot be resolved, Folsom says, each argument leaves a residue, so that communication in that area breaks down. Issues develop that cannot be discussed calmly, and they become part of each new quarrel. This means that, over time, sensitive feelings on certain subjects remain in the background of each fight, but the couple cannot "talk it out," because too much antagonism has developed. These sensitive topics are silent participants in each subsequent disagreement and are potentially very dangerous to the relationship.

The last type of conflict Folsom discusses is not generally part of early marriage. So-called habituated conflict arises from situations in marriage that neither party can adjust to and that cannot be resolved. Such a conflict continues throughout the relationship, never very damaging and never resolved. It is not so explosive as acute conflict, nor does it worsen as progressive conflict does. It is just always there, and most couples learn to live with it.

Eventually the new husband and wife, it is hoped, will develop solidarity. They will emancipate themselves from their families; they will learn to give up some "self" in favor of the "other"; they will be able to manage conflict. The bride will come to think of herself as a wife; the groom, of himself as a husband. Gradually the young couple returns from a state of romantic euphoria to the real world and, over time, is able to work out a relationship that is comfortable and satisfying to both parties. Romantic love cannot survive in marriage; it requires mystery and distance. Empathy and acceptance must replace it. Perhaps this second kind of love is more real than romantic love because it acknowledges what is, not what should be. Any marriage that tries to maintain romance past the time when it should be undergoing transformation will be in trouble. Lovers are blind, and nothing is so likely to improve one's eyesight as a marriage ceremony.

The Childbearing Years

Married couples must decide at some time, usually within the first year or two, whether they want to have children and, if so, how many, when, and how far apart. These decisions are based on social norms to a much larger extent than the couple may realize. In the decade of the 1940s, a two-child family was considered ideal; by 1955, it had changed to four, and this figure held through the early 1960s.[19] If a couple feels itself out of step with current norms—if its family is too large or too small—this might affect the marital relationship.

Another change began to occur during the second half of the 1960s. In the past the first question was "When shall we start a family?" Now that is the second question, provided that the first has been answered in the affirmative: "Shall we have a family at all?" The third question is "How many?" Americans became conscious of the environment in the mid-1960s, noting the depletion and pollution of our natural resources. Part of this concern focused on the perils of overpopulation. Many Americans began to give serious consideration to limiting the size of their families. Thus the birth rate is a factor in personal decisions on family size.

Other variables, of course, also influence decisions on children. Career women, for example, are likely to want fewer children than women who are closely involved in the home.[20] Many young couples are pressured by their parents to have children. A wife may feel ostracized by her peers if she is the only one who has no children. Sometimes the sex of existing children influences the number of children. If a husband and wife had planned to have two children, for instance, but both are boys, they may decide to have a third in the hope that it will be a girl.

Because an important factor in marital satisfaction is the fit between the planned number and spacing of children and reality, it is desirable that the husband and wife be in accord. The crucial point is not how many children of which sex the couple has but whether or not the couple gets what they both want. If they prefer to have seven children and they have them, that is the key issue, not the number in and of itself.[21] Therefore, family planning is important. To this end, a great deal of information is available. At the present time the two most popular methods of controlling whether and when conception is to occur are the intrauterine device, called the IUD, and the oral contraceptive pill for women.

The IUD is a small, irregularly shaped plastic or metal device that is inserted directly into the uterus by a physician. It can be left in place indefinitely, although most gynecologists prefer that the woman have it removed and checked yearly. The IUD is almost 100 per cent effective, although no one knows exactly how it prevents the fertilized ovum from lodging in the uterus. Greek women inserted small stones into their uteri with the same effect and the same lack of understanding. The only problem with the IUD is that it occasionally causes excessive bleeding and pain. In such cases, a physician will often try a device of a different shape, which may not produce these side effects.

The Pill, if properly used, is also 100 per cent effective. Starting on the fifth day of her menstrual cycle, a woman takes one pill every day until the twentieth day. The Pill induces a hormonal reaction that puts a woman into a state of pseudo-pregnancy, thus preventing ovulation. Because a woman taking the Pill is, in effect, in an early stage of pregnancy, it is not unusual for her to experience some of the symptoms of that stage, such as nausea, breast sensitivity, changes in skin and hair, and weight gain. However, most of these side effects disappear after a time, and not everyone experiences them. There has been continuous research to reduce these side effects, and the newest oral contraceptive pills are less likely to induce them.

These two methods of contraception are considered the most effective because they entail the lowest probability of technological or human failure. When a method is used that requires self-control or interruption of the sexual act, we can guess that it will be less efficient, not because such methods are technically less effective, but because of human fallibility. In the lower classes especially, there are usually greater indifference and less knowledge than in the middle and upper classes.

Research has indicated that contraception is approved of by nearly 90 per cent of all married couples in the United States.[22] Not only do married people approve of birth control, they also practice it. Campbell found that 81 per cent of his subjects were using some kind of birth control.[23]

Rainwater found a relationship between social class, religion, and choice of contraceptive method.[24] Lower-class Catholics and Protestants select douching, withdrawal, or the condom. Middle-class Protestants prefer the Pill and the IUD. Lower-middle-class Catholics use the rhythm method. In general, Rainwater found that belief in the efficacy of contraception was also class- and religion-influenced. Middle-class Protestants have the greatest amount of confidence in contraception. Members of the lowest class in both religions have the least, because many of them feel that God decides if and when people should have children; therefore, they are likely to use contraceptive methods carelessly, if at all.

Women in the lower classes, Rainwater concludes, are likely to be less interested in, or perhaps downright hostile to, sexual intercourse. For this reason, they tend to favor such contraceptive methods as douching, withdrawal, or the condom because these methods either prevent them from coming into direct contact with semen or remove the semen. Furthermore, the notion that sex is for the satisfaction of the male still prevails to some extent in the lower classes; therefore, contraception is his responsibility. Lower-class people also use these less effective methods because they are more readily obtainable.

Rainwater found a relationship between effective contraception and sexual satisfaction.[25] Seventy-five per cent of those reporting satisfactory sexual relations were successfully using birth-control methods, compared to only 40 per cent of those who were negative about their sex lives.

Middle-Age Marriage

There comes a time in every marriage when the children leave home, to attend an out-of-town college, to get a job, to get married, or for some other reason. This results in a new adjustment for the couple. For approximately twenty years they have been involved in several relationships beyond the marital one, and now they must revert to the earliest period of the marriage—the time when they were alone together. The primary statuses are once again those of husband and wife, not father and mother.

This time of life, the postparental period, is often referred to as the "empty-nest" stage. Because Americans are marrying earlier than ever before and because their life span is increasing, this stage of life is getting longer. At the beginning of the century a newly married man of twenty-five and a newly married woman of twenty-two had only a 50 per cent chance that they would both be living forty years later. Today a pair who marry at the same ages stand a 65 per cent chance of both being alive when the wife reaches sixty. In the last decade of the nineteenth century, the average wife could expect to be a widow before her last child left home; by 1950, she could anticipate fourteen years alone with her husband in the empty nest. Just eighteen years later, by 1968, 40 per cent of all couples who had not been divorced could expect eighteen years alone together; 25 per cent of these couples could expect twenty-three years. If we average out these data, most postparental couples will have about one third of their entire marriage after the children are grown and gone.

How well do couples readjust to this renewed concentration on each other? Early studies found a correlation between postparental marital satisfaction and the ability to fill the gap left by departed children.[26] Thus Sussman in 1955 reported that there was frequently an increase in the activities couples did together, such as taking a trip, decorating a home, or starting a hobby. He found they were likely to be supportive of each other and to look to each other for recreation. Two dominant patterns were identified: Some couples anticipated their new freedom with pleasure and concentrated on doing the things they had long waited to do; others maintained close ties to married children and filled their time by babysitting and otherwise helping their families. In general, early research indicated that newly emancipated middle-aged parents turned to each other and were pleased with the easing of their financial problems and the increase in their free time to pursue personal interests, alone or together.

More recent research indicates that the picture is less rosy. This period is now seen as a time of great loneliness for the couple and increasing isolation from each other. Perhaps there is more time to pursue interests, but there is little in which they are interested. Pineo reports that in the postparental years, as compared to the period of childrearing, couples are less close to each other and there is less sexual activity, less social activity, fewer things shared or discussed, and less confiding in each other.[27] Blood and Wolfe found that these husbands and wives are less likely to turn to each other with problems, less likely to share tasks, and more likely to pursue separate lives.[28]

According to both of these reports, part of the difficulty of the postparental period is that several changes occur at the same time in addition to the loss of the children, and all require adjustment. One is the advent of the menopause in women and the climacteric in men, both of which frequently have psychological as well as physical and hormonal consequences. Another is the need for the husband, because of his age, to acknowledge the failure or success of his efforts to achieve his occupational goals. Still another is that women feel that their reason for living is past because they no longer have children who need their attention and care. Relatively few women are trained or educated to work, and they are therefore left with many hours in which they have little to occupy their attention, time, or energy. At this time also both men and women experience a sense that they are becoming sexually unattractive. Men, in addition, frequently cannot perform sexually as often or as competently as they could in the past. All these factors combine to make this new marital adjustment difficult and often unsuccessful.

Deutscher's study of middle-class postparental couples is less depressing and probably more realistic.[29] He had a small sample, but his insightful, in-depth interviewing compensates for the sample size. Deutscher concludes that, if two people had a good relationship during the child-rearing years, they are likely to continue to share activities and to enjoy each other during the empty-nest phase. If the marriage has been one of conflict or boredom, it is unlikely to improve after the children leave home. What Deutscher tells us, then, is that a good relationship will continue to be good and a poor one will remain poor. Little will change just because the children are gone.

Deutscher noted the satisfactions many couples find during this time. There is a general increase in the pleasure of being together and a decrease in irritability, nervousness, financial worry, and the sense of being tied down. Other couples mentioned the dissatisfactions: the necessity of acknowledging failure to achieve occupational goals, the physical and psychological discomforts of aging, and the sense of emptiness without the presence of children.

Old Age and Marriage

Today about 9 per cent of our population, approximately twenty million people, is over sixty-five years of age. This represents an increase in the number of old people as the result of technological developments. But our social norms have failed to parallel our technology. Americans unfortunately do not treat the aged very well. We have learned how to extend life but not how to cope with the financial, social, and psychological problems that accompany it. We cannot as yet handle the problems of housing, health care, loss of status and loss of functions.

It is important that we address ourselves to these problems and soon. Townsend noted that more than 40 per cent of his sample of Americans over sixty-five years of age were great-grandparents, and that the increase in the number of four-generation families is marked.[30] One reason, of course, is longer life expectancy. Further, people marry younger now and have children earlier.

All this means that new relationships are developing in families. Townsend contends that, in the four-generation family, the two older generations are likely to interact more frequently and with more intensity than we might expect. Grandmothers find themselves busier than in the three-generation family because they divide their time and energies between their own very old parents and their grandchildren. The extended family, then, is beginning to include four generations, and this will result in a wider and more complex range of relationships.

If we follow Deutscher's argument—that the quality of the empty-nest stage is determined by the quality of the marital relationship during the childbearing and child-rearing years—we can say that the relationship of the couple in old age is also dependent on the relationship during earlier stages. If the pair related well to each other in the past, there is little reason to think they will not continue to do so into old age.

The crucial factor appears to be ego support, just as it was during other stages.[31] Nevertheless, old age means a gradual change in one's self-evaluation, and ego support probably becomes more significant because more proof of personal worth is needed.

Little is known about the sex lives of old people. According to Masters and Johnson there is a sharp drop in sexual capability and interest among men over fifty.[32] One reason is monotony; the other is fear of failure, which in itself is reinforcing.

Although fear of failure is virtually absent among women, they also experience declining interest in sex during old age. And yet, according to Masters and Johnson, many women find their sexual interest increasing. One reason is that they no longer need to worry about pregnancy; another is emancipation from household and child-rearing chores, which gives them more time, less worry, and less fatigue. This increased interest can remain unsatisfied, however, because either elderly women are widowed or, if their husbands are alive, the husbands lack interest in sexual intercourse.

Deutscher's theory that the past will continue into the present also holds in terms of old-age sex. If men and women have enjoyed frequent and stimulating sex lives during preceding stages of their marriage, the probability is high that, unless there are physiological barriers, sex will continue to be pleasurable into old age.

One theory about old age that has occupied the attention of sociologists is the theory of disengagement, first developed by Elaine Cumming and her associates.[33] The theory suggests that as people age they withdraw from the community and from younger people; at the same time young people withdraw from them, so that the process is a mutual one. Furthermore, it occurs regardless of the health or financial status of the elderly person, which indicates to these researchers that the process is normal. Streib claims, furthermore, that his data from other societies, both literate and preliterate, show that the phenomenon may be universal.[34]

The process supposedly begins in middle age. Disengagement is slow until a stable level is reached that is appropriate for the elderly. Old people spend less time with others, there is greater social distance, and roles are simplified. Behavior and interaction are scaled down until the aged person retains only those activities and those people who are of basic significance to him.

Cumming feels that we can evaluate the importance of social involvement by noting how much disruption would occur if a man were to die suddenly. Very involved people often leave confusion behind them, but, as people age and limit their involvement, death means little change for those left behind. The disengagement process, then, is preparation for death. The process is seen in four stages of increasing withdrawal. The first stage occurs between the ages of forty-five and fifty-four; the preretirement stage is from fifty-five to sixty-four; retirement is from sixty-five to seventy-four; and old age is from seventy-five to the end of life.[35]

The theory of disengagement has met with severe criticism. Basically, it is a pessimistic theory, relegating old people to the shelf regardless of their health and financial status. While most of us can believe that youth withdraws from age, it is difficult to accept the notion that age is willing to withdraw from youth. Arnold Rose has been the most outspoken critic.[36] Like Deutscher, he feels that the evidence indicates that people who have been engaged and active during earlier periods of life will continue to be so into old age. Rose also points out that when older people are active they are likely to report greater satisfaction in life than inactive old people. Rose takes issue with the notion that disengagement is universal, pointing out that it occurs only in certain types of societies, such as the United States, where old age brings a low status. Finally, Rose notes that several recent trends contradict the theory of disengagement. In fact, he thinks re-engagement, not disengagement, is more likely for several reasons. Retirement from primary statuses (occupational for men, parental for women) is occurring earlier; social security and pension plans provide economic security; educational opportunities for older people and job opportunities for women are increasing, as are leisure-time activities. All these factors combine to invite the elderly to participate rather than withdraw. Rose feels, in short, that Americans are beginning to cope with the problems of the aged and to invite them in, not push them out.

"Un-marriage"

Bachelorhood and spinsterhood are viewed with suspicion in the United States. Social pressure to conform by marrying is applied to single people. Unmarried people are treated, and tend to think of themselves, as "different." Ours is a two-by-two world, and there is little room in it for the unaccompanied individual. Furthermore, unattached people, especially women, are considered a threat to married people. To justify their own state, married people think of marriage as "natural," and anyone who does not conform to this point of view is challenging the social values.

In 1960 there were approximately 3 million men over thirty-five and 3 million women over thirty who had never been married. About 10 per cent of these men and 5 per cent of the women were in some kind of custodial institution, primarily mental hospitals. Another 5 per cent were members of religious sects in which marriage is forbidden. Of the remainder, probably most would like to marry, but only about 20 per cent of each group will.[37]

To date there has been very little empirical research on the state of singleness, and virtually none on single men. Sociologists are as human and as culture-bound as anyone else and thus tend to ignore those segments of society that do not conform to our cultural norms. This obvious omission tells us something about our society and our discipline. Surely the oversight is not because sociologists are unaware that a sizable proportion of our population is unmarried. Rather, the neglect reflects our adherence to the ideal that everyone should marry and that, if he really wants to, anyone can.

Margaret Adams describes the situation of the single woman, explaining that she is writing out of her own experience and that of women friends, including not only spinsters but also widows and divorced women, who have similar life styles.[38] She shows how many of the problems of the unattached woman stem from the fact that she is a deviant member of society. "Women who eschew this *modus vivendi* [family life] are subject to a subtle array of social sanctions that erode their self-esteem, distort their relationships and disturb their sense of homeostasis in the shifting world scene."[39] For one thing, like any other minority group, these women are stereotyped. Their spinsterhood is often attributed to lack of sexual appeal, psychosexual conflicts, inability or unwillingness to commit themselves to one person, or, of course, lesbianism.

Another problem is insecurity. An independent unmarried woman is open to exploitation in the male-dominated world of work. Of course all females suffer from discrimination in hiring practices, lower salaries, fewer promotions, and less power, but the single woman, according to Adams, is a special target.

Friendships, too, cause difficulty. Each time an unmarried woman starts a relationship with a man, she must re-examine her commitment to spinsterhood. Relations with other single women are hampered because there is always the suspicion that each would prefer to spend the time with a male and that the other is being used to fill in time and ward off loneliness. Friendships with married couples are not easy either, although it is in this context that the unmarried woman has the best opportunity to be herself. She may be able to play a special role in the lives of her friends' children. She may be able to help the wife consider alternatives to the homemaking role. She may be able to provide the husband with Platonic feminine companionship. The danger, of course, lies in becoming a surrogate spouse, either in reality or in fantasy, and eventually arousing the distrust of the entire family.

Adams notes that, with rare exceptions, the single life is a lonely one for a woman. "A significant lack in the single woman's life is a congenial, trustworthy, and accessible person to serve as a soundingboard and provide the requisite feedback."[40] It seems logical to assume that the same loneliness would be present in a bachelor's life.

Adams suggests two factors that can make singleness a pleasure rather than a burden for women. The first and indispensable factor is the ability to be economically independent. The single woman, in other words, must be capable of supporting herself entirely. Secondly, the modern single woman must be socially and psychologically autonomous. This means that she is not involved in a relationship with a male in the sense of a long-term commitment and that she has no obligations to dependents, such as children.

Such a woman is free to take advantage of all the experiences available in the world today. She can take a job in a new city or even a new country. She can take a chance by giving up one type of employment for a new type that may be more attractive. She can travel, go to school, or join reform movements. Adams feels that by age thirty "most women who are not married are beginning to build up economic independence, an investment in work, and a viable value system that allows them to identify and exploit major sources of personal and social satisfaction in other areas than marriage and family."[41] In short, there is little to prevent the single woman from experiencing whatever appeals to her within the range of her financial situation.

Adams notes that the women's liberation movement has three primary goals: (1) to free women from the narrow roles they have been forced to take in a male-dominated society, (2) to show that women are no different from other powerless minority groups, and (3) to release and channel the energies and talents of women. To date the movement has directed the major part of its attention to married women. Little consideration has been given to single women, who have also suffered from feelings of deprivation, deficiency, and alienation, because of the stress on marriage and motherhood as the only "normal" roles for women. But, if the goals of the women's liberation movement are realized, single women also will gain a sense of their own worth. Indeed, unmarried women may serve as role models for their married sisters.

For one thing, because single women are in the labor market, they have learned how to cope and how to be independent in that "man's world." They understand the weaknesses and strengths of their male colleagues. The results of their experiences can be extremely important as women seek their roles in the world.

Just as she can help the movement because of her understanding of men and work, so the movement can help the spinster. If marriage comes to be seen as an antiquated, socially dysfunctional institution, the single woman may find herself no longer in a deviant minority; instead she may become a model of the good female life. Spinsters will no longer need to feel apologetic for their singleness. They will feel free to reject close interpersonal relations in favor of careers, independence, and freedom. Adams believes: "This trend has already been set in motion. When it attains its full momentum the more obvious differences between the officially single and the officially married woman will be absorbed in a new common life pattern."[42]

MARRIAGE IN THE FUTURE

Marriage as it is practiced in the United States today is considered by most scientific observers to be very much in need of study and change. Many openly deplore the institution, declaring that it is in a state of decay. Even those who do not advocate radical change recognize that modifications are in order. John Edwards writes that a large proportion of marriages, not only those that end in divorce, are characterized by severe unhappiness.[43] Vance Packard speculates that a marriage occurring in the latter part of the 1960s had no more than a 50 per cent chance of remaining intact.[44] Clifford Adams[45] reports that, although divorce now ends two out of every five American marriages, the true divorce rate is closer to 70 per cent.* Lederer and Jackson found that at least 80 per cent of all married people seriously consider divorce at some time during their marriage.[46] Rustum and Della Roy state without

---

* A true divorce rate would include informal separation, annulment, and desertion, as well as those marriages in which couples continue to live together without any positive interaction.

qualification that "the total institution* of marriage in American society is gravely ill," largely because "marriage as an institution is partly governed by warring churches, a society without a soul, a legal system designed for lawyers, and a helping system [designed] for psychiatrists who almost by their very mode of operation in the marriage field guarantee its failure."[47] Orleans and Wolfson tell us that American marriage "as we have known it is slowly disintegrating. Evidence of its collapse is visible in the multitude of unhappy, broken families and miserable people."[48]

And so it goes, with many sociologists decrying the state of matrimony today. Let us now see what several of them have claimed is wrong with marriage and what alternatives they foresee for the future.

Olson writes that although marriage continues to be our most popular voluntary institution (only 3 per cent never marry), the divorce rate also is constantly rising; one out of every four marriages since 1967 has ended in divorce.[49] Olson places part of the blame on our myths about marriage, which are responsible for the unrealistic expectations we bring to it. Among the myths: "Marital relations will improve spontaneously over time"; "A child will improve a poor marriage"; "If one child doesn't work, two will"; "People marry for love and married people are in love"; etc.

The most hazardous expectation is that one's spouse will satisfy all one's needs—spiritual, sexual, emotional, social, psychological, and intellectual. Marriage is seen as a context in which the mates are to find complete satisfaction from each other only. The truth, as Olson sees it, is that most couples cannot attain such utopian relationships but are unprepared by society to accept anything more realistic. Change is definitely indicated, and Olson suggests the following:

1. Society must discourage early marriage and encourage peo-

---

* The adjective "total" is no accident. "A total institution may be defined as a place of residence and work where a large number of like-situation individuals, cut off from the wider society for an appreciable period of time, together lead an enclosed, formally administered round of life." (Erving Goffman, *Asylums* [Garden City, N.Y.: Anchor Books, 1961], p. xiii.) If we eliminate the words "and work" and "large," the Roys' implication should not be difficult to understand.

ple to wait until they are emotionally mature and professionally established.

2. People should not be pressured into marriage but instead
   should be allowed to experiment with many life styles until
   they find the one in which they are most comfortable.

3. Several laws require revision. It should be made more difficult to marry; tax laws should not favor married over single
   people; laws on sex should permit sexual freedom to consenting adults.

In short, Olson does not propose radical alternatives to monogamous marriage. Instead he offers possible solutions to existing
problems in order to make monogamy more satisfying and enduring.

Osofsky and Osofsky, in an article entitled "Androgyny as a
Life Style," define "androgyny" as "a society in which there are no
stereotyped behavioral differences between the roles of males and
females on the basis of their sex alone."[50] They envision a society
in which androgyny will be the dominant value. Changes in this direction, they believe, are already apparent. Women are being encouraged to participate in a meaningful way in the labor force.[51]
Husbands are sharing in the tasks that have traditionally been defined as female. Options are opening for men to be dependent, passive, and nurturant; for women to be aggressive, independent, and
competitive. However, we need changes in socialization and educational patterns to encourage these embryonic beginnings.

From birth we must treat all infants alike, avoiding even differences in the colors in which we dress them, which evoke differential
treatment for boys and girls. We must also have more adult males
visible for children. Fathers must take a more active role in both
the home and the school. Men must be encouraged to become
teachers at the elementary and high school levels. Textbooks that
picture women and girls always in "feminine" statuses, such as
mothers, wives, nurses, airline stewardesses, and secretaries, and
men in "masculine" statuses, such as business executives, doctors,
lawyers, firemen, and athletes, must be replaced. Most important,
perhaps, is a need to change the sort of counseling young people
get in high school. Boys are told that they have no choice; they

must select an occupation. Girls are given a choice: career or marriage. But they are not told that the two can be combined, nor are they advised that a career may be preferable for them.

The Osofskys, then, like Olson, believe that monogamous marriage will continue to be the dominant life style in the future. Olson believes that we can improve monogamy principally by demythifying it; the Osofskys think we can improve it by changing socialization and education so that marriage will involve two people whose roles are undifferentiated by sex.*

Several researchers believe that serial monogamy will be the pattern. This theory, of course, includes the assumption that divorce rates will increase. Somerville thinks that serial monogamy will be especially prevalent during the middle and older years because today's youth have experienced some innovation, and they are likely to carry this flexibility into maturity.[52] Furthermore, Somerville thinks that the middle and older years are ideal for serial monogamy because they are free from the cares of childbearing and child rearing.

Alpenfels also envisions what she calls "progressive monogamy."[53] She writes that there is nothing new in this behavior pattern, despite the proscription that it is incompatible with the American ideal. What is new is that remarriage is now cross-cutting all social categories because of our unrealistic cultural values which expect marriage to result in complete self-fulfillment. Since total fulfillment by one person is highly unlikely, Alpenfels believes we will continue to divorce and remarry in a constant search for personal satisfaction.

Orleans and Wolfson also take the position that serial monogamy will be the dominant marriage pattern of the future.[54] They feel that long-term sexual monopoly is not only impossible but harmful. People will realize before they marry that there is little likelihood of permanence, and they will probably divorce for no more reason than a need for novelty. Thus we will have several mates during a lifetime, with exclusive sexual rights during the course of each marriage.

* It is interesting that although their focus is on equality of the sexes, the Osofskys still select a male-biased word to describe this state of affairs. Why androgyny? Would not gynandry have served as well?

Orleans and Wolfson do not see serial monogamy as the only form marriage will take, acknowledging that in a pluralistic society no one form can be suitable to all people. They expect that, along with serial monogamy, we will see polygamy, most commonly among two females and one male, because there is a paucity of eligible males, especially in the older age groups. These authors believe that as triadic marriages proliferate, we will give up our current notions of jealousy and possessiveness until eventually totally free sexual interaction will become the norm.

Larry and Joan Constantine apparently endorse the triadic form, but they prefer to call it multilateral marriage, which is "an essentially egalitarian marriage relationship in which three or more individuals (in any distribution of sex) function as a family unit, sharing in a community of sexual and interpersonal intimacy."[55] Like Alpenfels and Olson, the Constantines believe that personal satisfaction is the primary goal for people today and that multilateral marriage is the best possible vehicle for achieving it. These authors suggest that in the expanded family, which in some ways resembles the older extended family of three generations in one household, there will be a greater chance for community, as well as variety in sexual relationships, and greater security and stability than are now available in dyadic marriage.

However, the Constantines do not see multilateral marriage as a viable possibility for the majority of Americans, although it is likely to become prevalent among older people. Instead they believe that the most widespread new structure will be what they label the "intimate network," "a cluster or chain of families, maintaining separate domiciles and family identity, but coupled by intimate relationships between families," with intermarital sexuality an intrinsic part of these relationships.[56] These writers believe that the intimate network will be more acceptable than multilateral marriage because it will incorporate all the most desirable aspects—sexual and intellectual variety, security, stability, and extended emotional support —without the dangers of constant group interaction, as when several people actually live in one household.

In summary, then, Somerville, Alpenfels, and Orleans and Wolfson all believe that serial monogamy—the marriage of one person to several partners, one at a time—will be an important new form of marriage in the future, although Somerville believes that it is most likely to occur among older people. Furthermore, Orleans and Wolfson and the Constantines advocate multilateral marriage, or group marriage—a form in which three or more people live together in a marital state—although, again, they suggest that it is most appropriate for older people. The Constantines further believe that the intimate network—a form of group marriage in which several families share everything except residence—will become more common.

Rustum and Della Roy take a humanistic stance.[57] They feel that traditional monogamy, which stresses permanent marriage to one person, the nuclear family, and restricted sexual relations, is in grave danger. They believe that we can no longer expect people to confine all sexual expression to one partner for life. The permissiveness resulting from the sexual revolution, the vast amount of eroticism in our mass media, and the increased interaction between men and women because of women's greater involvement in the labor market, all vitiate our social norm of monogamy.

The Roys propose several modifications based on their notion that community is one of the primary goals of man. One change they advocate is acceptance of several patterns of marriage because traditional monogamy is not feasible for all people in this society. They believe that monogamy can survive if we thus allow it more flexibility. Marriage should be made more difficult; however, we must recognize human sexuality by permitting engaged couples to live together, although not to have children. Such a norm would provide training for marriage, which the Roys believe should improve the quality of marriage when the time comes. They also suggest that we recognize people's need for variety in sex by permitting extramarital relationships. They note that there is no evidence that extramarital sex is harmful to a marriage, and, indeed, there is some evidence that it may be beneficial (see pp. 65–67).

The Roys recommend that those who prefer to be single should have our respect and should be included in our two-by-two society. Single people should be allowed to become family members with the same rights to belong, to have obligations, responsibilities, and community. On the other hand, they should also retain the right to remain apart.

Finally, the Roys advocate polygyny. They believe that the ratio of women to men will go as high as seven to five, especially among people over sixty-five, and that we must therefore legalize polygyny so that women who otherwise would have to live alone for many years after their husbands die could enjoy the companionship, stability, security, and sexuality of married life.

Psychotherapist Harold Greenwald argues that marriage should be a non-legal voluntary association, without state supervision or sanction.[58] He feels that legal marriage is considered valuable in our culture as protection for children and women, as a stabilizing influence for the society, and as a regulator of taxes and property rights. However, he thinks that these are not valid reasons for perpetuating it. Marriage does not ensure that a father will care for and protect his children, nor will it prevent him from leaving or deserting his wife should he wish to do so. Greenwald does not think it guarantees societal stability; nor is marriage necessary to protect property when agreements can be made between people in a voluntary association.

If, then, we remove all state authority from marriage, we would have people staying together because they want to, which is the only viable reason for marriage in the first place. Furthermore, non-legal marriage would eliminate the need for divorce, which is always humiliating, embarrassing, guilt-provoking, or farcical. Finally, Greenwald says, "Changing marriage to a free voluntary association would also permit experimentation in varieties of family life which would possibly be more in keeping with the needs of many individuals for whom life-long monogamous marriage is unsuitable."[59]

Margaret Mead suggests that marriage should be arranged in two stages.[60] In the first stage, which she calls "individual marriage," the couple would legally live together but would not be permitted to have children. This marriage could be terminated easily without obligation for either party. The second marriage, called "parent marriage," is undertaken after the first one has proved successful. This would be a permanent marriage, difficult to dissolve, and the couple would be permitted to have children. Others have suggested a third stage which would occur after the children are grown and out of the house. At this time the parent marriage could be terminated without penalty and another, middle-age marriage, could be contracted.

Let us now evaluate what these writers have said. Olson, Orleans and Wolfson, the Roys, and Greenwald stress the pluralism in our society, arguing that it is not rational to expect that one form of marriage will be appropriate for everyone. Cultural pluralism is a model of society in which racial, ethnic, and religious differences are valued because the diversity they yield strengthens the society culturally. America is a huge country in geographical area, number of people, and types of subgroups. This means that several different value systems, attitudes, and behaviors exist simultaneously. We must provide a system of male-female relationships that will reflect these differences and be acceptable to as many subgroups as possible. Thus, I must agree with these authors' stress on pluralism and suggest that there should be several acceptable and accepted alternatives to monogamous marriage in the United States. If certain segments of society are comfortable with premarital sexual freedom, with extramarital sexual freedom, and with group or multilateral marriage, they should be permitted to live in the style they find suitable. However, I am not suggesting that society abdicate its control over marriage. Rather, I am saying that such forms of marriage should be legalized and regularized by the state in exactly the same way it now regularizes monogamous marriage. There must be rules governing who is allowed to have premarital or extramarital sex relations, who may live in multilateral marriages. Laws must continue to define the obligations and rights of these members toward their children, the authority patterns, and the distribution of property. For this reason I reject the suggestion of Greenwald, who believes that the marriage of the future should be a non-legal, voluntary association.

It is not possible to accept Greenwald's point of view because no society can exist unless it has at least some control over large segments of human behavior. Since marriage is a behavior that almost all members of our society engage in, it is reasonable that the state, representing society, should provide rules, sanctions, and controls over it. As I have said before, government has established controls over the interaction between men and women, over the rights of children, over the transmission of property, and over the authority patterns within the family. It is difficult to believe that any society would voluntarily surrender this responsibility, or that its members would wish it to do so.

Olson, the Roys, and Margaret Mead all feel that we should have new laws making marriage more difficult to enter. This is an acceptable suggestion. In the United States, it is easier to marry than to obtain a driver's license, form a business partnership, enter college, or purchase a house. Getting married is one of the major decisions of life, and the easy access to it seems in a sense to trivialize the decision. I would agree, then, that there should be more prerequisites for marriage, such as longer waiting periods, required training with formal structures, and more stringent qualifications, such as proof of the ability to retain financial independence.

The suggestion by the Osofskys that we institutionalize the norm of androgyny in marriage is heartily acceptable. It seems obvious that if there were greater equality in marriage in terms of the division of labor and the amount of respect accorded the partners, both the husband and the wife would be happier within themselves, a condition that should extend into the marital relationship. Men have been deprived for a long time of the right to show their feelings, to be nurturing and tender, to be dependent and passive. Women have been equally deprived of the opportunity to participate in the work world, to be competitive and aggressive. If both males and females were encouraged to be human, to express the entire range of human feelings, it seems that they would be more content with marriage, with their statuses within society, and, most important, with themselves.

In other words, I am suggesting that many of our values be changed in order to enhance the marriage relationship. Among these, in addition to the value of androgyny, I would urge that Americans discontinue the pressures to marry that they have heretofore exerted. In a pluralistic society, we must recognize that there are those who prefer to live alone, and we must accord them the same respect and sense of community that we accord to married people. Discrimination against single people in taxation, exclusion, and sexual restraints should be removed so that those who select this life style are welcomed into the society with the same privileges as those who select any other life style.

Moreover, it is essential that the myths surrounding marriage be dissipated. Young people must be made to see that marriage is not an endless romance. We must socialize them to understand that hearts will not continue to beat faster after ten years; that all problems cannot be resolved simply because two people love each other. Most of all, we must teach our young men and women that they cannot expect total fulfillment from each other in all areas of life. Rarely can one person wholly satisfy another sexually, intellectually, and psychologically for a lifetime. People must allow each other freedom to seek some of these satisfactions from others. They must loosen the ties that are so strangling both to the one who is tied and to the one who ties. It is disappointing to seek and fail to find, but it is equally frustrating to try to satisfy all the time and be unable to do so. Married people must be socialized to be less possessive, to be freer to form relationships with others without threatening the spouse. The grass is greener on the other side of the fence only because there *is* a fence. In short, if we could socialize our children to have realistic expectations about marriage, then, when the spouse falls short in some area, as he inevitably must do because he is human, the disappointment will not be so overwhelming and the tendency to run away and seek perfection elsewhere will diminish.

In summary, I agree with some of the writers we have reviewed in believing that marriage in the future will be based on a recognition of pluralism. Therefore, we will have laws that uphold the individual's right to adopt reasonable alternatives to monogamous marriage, including bachelorhood. At the same time, we will strengthen marriage as it currently exists by encouraging changes in socialization procedures so that males and females are treated as equals and we face what marriage really is instead of disguising it in romantic ways.

I have said that we must seek and encourage the growth and legitimation of alternative forms of marriage. For example, we can anticipate a society that will acknowledge two needs of youth heretofore largely unrecognized. One is for sexual expression and the other is for marriage training. In modern industrial society young people require a longer and longer time to acquire the education that will enable them to enter the labor force. This, in turn, delays marriage, especially for youth in the upper strata. Additional education, however, does not suppress sexual impulses. Indeed, many would argue that the years of the twenties, especially for males, should be the most sexually active period. We suggest, therefore, that we institutionalize a form similar to what Margaret Mead calls individual marriage, in which young men and women can live together in a sexual relationship and learn what it is to be married, without the notion of permanence. Of course, there should be no obstacle to making such unions permanent at some later date.

Mead is not the only social scientist to suggest legalized premarriage as a vehicle for sexual expression and as a means of education for marriage. Olson incorporates this notion when he anticipates that society will begin to discourage early marriage. For very young people, much of the impetus to marry is the desire to engage in sexual activities. Freedom of sex without marriage will eliminate this motive. Rustum and Della Roy make the same proposal when they recommend living together for engaged couples. In sum, it is probable that one form marriage will take in the future is institutionalized premarriage with sexual relations permitted, without financial obligation, and without children. This form, best suited to youth, will serve as an outlet for sexual expression and as a training program for the monogamy of the child-rearing years.

After their education is completed and young women and men can demonstrate financial responsibility and emotional maturity, they could enter what Mead calls parental marriage. This period, from approximately age twenty-five to forty-five, would be the years of bearing and rearing children in permanent monogamy. Divorce would be extremely difficult during this stage of life, and the society would do everything possible—for example, provide free counseling services, free child-care centers, free contraceptive advice and materials—to facilitate this middle marriage.

There is no reason to believe that these couples would not stay together after the child-rearing years. However, if they preferred to separate, no stigma would be attached to the decision even if the reason were as shallow as a need for variety. Then, for the next ten- to twenty-year period, approximately to the age of sixty-five, I envision a time of what Somerville and Orleans and Wolfson call "serial monogamy" and what Alpenfels calls "progressive monogamy." Since these years are relatively free of financial and child-rearing responsibilities, people might wish to experience several relationships and several life styles. Quite probably, a large number of people will remain with the partner from the parental marriage; another large segment will contract a third relationship and stay in it. However, others may seek and find several spouses, and they should all have societal approval and sanction. This type of serial monogamy I believe is preferable to the extramarital relations advocated by Olson, the Constantines, and the Roys.

It does not seem likely that extramarital relations will be institutionalized in the United States. The rates of adultery may increase, as Reiss believes, "for those who are in process of getting a divorce and for those who are unsatisfied with their marriages and those with narrow self-involvement in their marriages."[61] But if our society should adopt the custom of serial monogamy during the middle part of the life cycle, then there should be little need for adultery.

When old age approaches, some time after sixty-five, group marriage as advocated by the Roys, the Constantines, and Orleans and Wolfson is the preferable marital structure. Group marriage during old age can be a great financial help. Old people, especially women, are usually poor.[62] If three or four elderly people were to live together and pool incomes, the standard of living would rise for all of them. Health would also improve, particularly for men. Widowers are generally less able to take care of themselves than widows. Men are not usually skilled in domestic tasks, and they tend to neglect their homes and their diets. In multilateral marriage, the women would be able to help each other with the housework. This is important because people over 65 often do not have the energy and strength of youth.

Group marriage offers special advantages for men, who adjust less well than women to widowhood. Because most men derive status from their occupations, retirement means a loss of standing and also of a great deal of male bonding. Their common interest in work holds men together in a group, and many find themselves friendless when they are no longer part of the work force. If, as often happens, they are widowed during this same period of life, they suffer a great deal of loneliness. On the other hand, women retain old friendships and make new friends more easily than men because they have practiced integrative skills all their lives.

Lowenthal and Haven[63] studied elderly people and found that nearly twice as many women as men, whether married or widowed, had an intimate same-sex friend. These researchers claim that women are more personally responsive and more versatile in choosing companions. Furthermore, most men report that their wives are their confidantes, while women generally report that this place is occupied by a child or a female friend.

In sum, I suggest that the most desirable marital structure in old age is group marriage, although unquestionably it would be difficult to resocialize people of this age to accept what to them would be very radical and perhaps immoral. Both sexes stand to gain from the arrangement, not only for practical reasons but, most important, because man is happiest when he is living in community with others who love, respect, and accept him. Too many of our elderly widowed and retired men and women live alone and isolated. Group marriage could bring them back into a community of their peers.

I predict, then, that the institution of marriage will expand rather than change in order to accommodate the many different life styles in our society. Premarriage for youth, parent marriage during the childbearing and child-rearing years, and serial monogamy for middle age will probably all be accepted forms by the end of this century. Indeed, they are all well along the way to acceptance now. Multilateral marriage for old age may be somewhat more prevalent, but, for reasons I have explained, will probably not soon be institutionalized.

I further predict that the content of marriage, in any of these forms, will also change. Indeed, the trends are already quite obvious. As our world becomes more bureaucratized, we will develop even greater need for personal warmth, companionship, and intimacy. Marriage will prevail. But we will redefine sex roles, both occupational and domestic, in the direction of less differentiation along sex lines. Marriage will take on more of the attributes of friendship—greater trust, equality, and freedom. People will stay together only as long as they are content with each other, and when they separate it will be without the pain and stigma that apply today.

NOTES

1. U.S. Department of Commerce, "Marriage and the American Woman," *Population Profile* (Washington, D.C.: Population Reference Bureau, June,1963).
2. U.S. Department of Commerce, Bureau of the Census, *Current Population Reports,* Series P-25 (Washington, D.C.: Government Printing Office, 1960).
3. Isadore Rubin, *Sexual Life After Sixty* (New York: New Amsterdam Library, 1965).
4. Eleanor Holmes Norton, *Women's Role in Contemporary Society: The Report of the New York City Commission on Human Rights, September 21–25, 1970* (New York: Avon, 1972), pp. 776–778.
5. *Ibid.,* pp. 792–793.
6. Arnold Van Gennep, *The Rites of Passage,* trans. Monika B. Vizedom and Gabrielle L. Caffee (Chicago: University of Chicago Press, 1960).
7. Theodore B. Johannis, Jr., "Married College Students and Their Honeymoons," *Family Life Coordinator* 7 (1959): 39–40.
8. Rhona Rapoport and Robert N. Rapoport, "New Light on the Honeymoon," *Human Relations* 17 (1964): 33–56.
9. Leonard Benson, *The Family Bond* (New York: Random House, 1971), pp. 9–11.
10. Robert O. Blood and Donald M. Wolfe, *Husbands and Wives* (Glencoe, Ill.: Free Press, 1960), p. 20.
11. John F. Cuber and Peggy B. Harroff, *Sex and the Significant Americans* (Baltimore: Penguin Books, 1966), ch. 3.
12. *Ibid.,* p. 46.
13. *Ibid.,* p. 53.
14. Constantina Safilios-Rothschild, "Family Sociology or Wives' Sociology? A Cross-Cultural Examination of Decision-Making," *Journal of Marriage and the Family* 31:2 (1969): 290–301.
15. Robert R. Bell, *Marriage and Family Interaction,* 3d ed. (Homewood, Ill.: Dorsey, 1971), p. 295.
16. *Ibid.,* p. 291.
17. *Ibid.,* p. 293.
18. Joseph K. Folsom, *The Family and Democratic Society* (New York: John Wiley, 1943), pp. 445–447.
19. Pascal K. Whelpton, Arthur A. Campbell, and John E. Patterson, *Fertility and Family Planning in the United States* (Princeton: Princeton University Press, 1966).
20. Lee Rainwater, *Family Design: Marital Sexuality, Family Size, and Contraception* (Chicago: Aldine, 1969), p. 191.
21. Harold T. Christensen, "Children in the Family: Relationship of Number and Spacing to Marital Success," *Journal of Marriage and the Family* 30 (May, 1968): 283–289.
22. Catherine S. Chilman, "Child-Rearing and Family Relationship Patterns of the Very Poor," in *Sourcebook in Marriage and the Family,* 3d ed., ed. Marvin B. Sussman (Boston: Houghton Mifflin, 1968), pp. 201-210.
23. Arthur A. Campbell, "Population Dynamics and Family Planning," *Journal of Marriage and the Family* 30 (May, 1968): 202–206.

24. Rainwater, *op. cit.*
25. *Ibid.,* p. 240.
26. Arnold M. Rose, "Factors Associated with the Life Satisfactions of Middle-Class, Middle-Aged Persons," *Marriage and Family Living* 17 (1955): 15–19; and Marvin B. Sussman, "Activity Patterns of Post Parental Couples and Their Relationship to Family Continuity," *Marriage and Family Living* 17 (1955): 338–341.
27. Peter C. Pineo, "Disenchantment in the Later Years of Marriage," *Marriage and Family Living* 23 (1961): 3–11.
28. Blood and Wolfe, *op. cit.*
29. Irwin Deutscher, "The Quality of Postparental Life: Definitions of the Situation," *Journal of Marriage and the Family* 26 (1964): 52–59.
30. Peter Townsend, "The Emergence of the Four-Generation Family in Industrial Society," in *Middle Age and Aging,* ed. Bernice L. Neugarten (Chicago: University of Chicago Press, 1968), pp. 255–257.
31. Benson, *op. cit.,* p. 249.
32. William H. Masters and Virginia E. Johnson, *Human Sexual Response* (Boston: Little, Brown, 1966).
33. Elaine Cumming, Lois R. Dean, David S. Newell, and Isabel McCaffrey, "Disengagement: A Tentative Theory of Aging," *Sociometry* 23 (1960), 23–25; Elaine Cumming and William E. Henry, *Growing Old: The Process of Disengagement* (New York: Basic Books, 1961); and Elaine Cumming, "Further Thoughts on the Theory of Disengagement," UNESCO, *International Social Science Bulletin* 15 (1963): 377–393.
34. Gordon Streib, "Disengagement: Scientific Theory or Sociological Interpretation?" (Paper read at Southern Sociological Association meetings, New Orleans, April 12, 1969).
35. Wayne E. Thompson and Gordon F. Streib, "Meaningful Activity in a Family Context," in *Aging and Leisure,* ed. Robert W. Kleemeier (New York: Oxford University Press, 1961), pp. 177–211.
36. Arnold M. Rose, "A Current Theoretical Issue in Social Gerontology," *The Gerontologist* 4 (1964): 46–50.
37. Paul C. Glick, "Bachelors and Spinsters," in *Marriage and the Family,* eds. Jeffrey K. Hadden and Marie L. Borgatta (Itasca, Ill.: Peacock, 1969).
38. Margaret Adams, "The Single Woman in Today's Society: A Reappraisal," in *The Women's Movement,* eds. Helen Wortis and Clara Rabinowitz (New York: John Wiley, 1972), pp. 89–101.
39. *Ibid.,* p. 92.
40. *Ibid.,* p. 96.
41. *Ibid.,* p. 91.
42. *Ibid.,* p. 101.
43. John N. Edwards, "The Future of the Family Revisited," *Journal of Marriage and the Family* 29:3 (1967): 505–511.
44. Vance Packard, *The Sexual Wilderness* (New York: David McKay, 1968).
45. Clifford R. Adams, "Evaluating Marriage Prediction Tests," *Marriage and Family Living,* 12 (1950): 55–56.
46. William J. Lederer and Don D. Jackson, *The Mirages of Marriage* (New York: W. W. Norton, 1968).

47. Rustum Roy and Della Roy: "Is Monogamy Outdated?" *The Humanist* (1970): 19–26.
48. Myron Orleans and Florence Wolfson, "Future of the Family," *The Futurist* 4:2 (1970): 48–49.
49. David H. Olson, "Marriage of the Future: Revolutionary or Evolutionary Change?" *Family Coordinator* 21:4 (1972): 383–393.
50. Joy D. Osofsky and Howard J. Osofsky, "Androgyny as a Life Style," *Family Coordinator* 21:4 (1972): 411–418.
51. Jayne B. Burks, "The Delphi Study" (unpublished Ph.D. diss. Fontbonne College, 1973). In this study 51 per cent of the family sociologists polled believed that by 1990 the labor force would contain about an equal number of men and women.
52. Rose M. Somerville, "The Future of Family Relationships in the Middle and Older Years: Clues in Fiction," *Family Coordinator* 21:4 (1972): 487–498.
53. Ethel J. Alpenfels, "Progressive Monogamy: An Alternate Pattern?" in *The Family in Search of a Future,* ed. Herbert A. Otto (New York: Appleton-Century-Crofts, 1970), pp. 67–73.
54. Orleans and Wolfson, *op. cit.*
55. Larry Constantine and Joan Constantine, "Where Is Marriage Going?" *The Futurist* 4:2 (1970): 44–46.
56. *Ibid.,* p. 46.
57. Roy and Roy, *op. cit.*
58. Harold Greenwald, "Marriage as a Non-Legal Voluntary Association," in *The Family in Search of a Future,* ed. Herbert A. Otto (New York: Appleton-Century-Crofts, 1970), pp. 51–56.
59. *Ibid.,* p. 56.
60. Margaret Mead, "Marriage in Two Steps," *Redbook Magazine,* July 1966, pp. 48–49, 84–85.
61. Ira L. Reiss, *The Family System in America* (New York: Holt, Rinehart, and Winston, 1971), p. 409.
62. Irving Rosow, "And Then We Were Old," *Trans-Action,* 2, Jan.–Feb., 1965, 21–26.
63. Marjorie Fisk Lowenthal and Clayton Haven, "Interaction and Adoption: Intimacy as a Critical Variable," *American Sociological Review* 33 (1968): 20–30.

6 Parenting

Parenthood is usually expected to follow marriage. Only about 10 per cent of all married couples remain childless, and childlessness is voluntary for only about 2 per cent.[1] The other 8 per cent, then, have a sterility problem. Most societies in the past have "blamed" childlessness on the wife, but we now recognize that there is an equal probability of some impairment on the part of the husband. It has been estimated that between one third and one half of all cases of involuntary childlessness are due to problems of the male.[2] Farris found in his study of male fertility that 40 per cent were highly fertile, about 35 per cent relatively fertile, about 15 per cent subfertile, and the remaining 10 per cent sterile.[3]

Because the female reproductive system is highly complex, male sterility can be diagnosed more readily than female sterility, but this does not mean that it is more readily cured. The problem in male sterility focuses on a deficiency in the structure, number, and/ or strength of the sperm. The cure, if one is possible, is usually chemical. Female sterility may be due to a lack of ovulation; the sperm may be blocked from reaching the cervix; the egg may be blocked from reaching the uterus; the egg may not survive fertilization; there may be secretions that destroy the sperm; and there may be other factors as well, including psychological ones, that prevent impregnation. Treatment for female sterility can be very long and difficult and is by no means invariably successful.

There is also variation in fertility potential among females. The period of highest fertility is between the ages of twenty-one and twenty-five. After that fertility decreases until by age forty the average woman is only about 60 per cent as fertile as during her twenties.[4]

Women are socialized to place great value on having children. Therefore, when it becomes apparent that there is a fertility problem in a marriage, it is the wife who is more likely to investigate the reasons. Men are apparently threatened by the possibility that they are sterile and are therefore more likely to resist diagnosis, not to mention medical attention.

Women are also more receptive to adoption than are men, probably for similar reasons—they need children more in order to fulfill their primary role. In 1963 there were 127,000 legal adoptions, mostly through the offices of adoption agencies.[5] The demand for adoptive children exceeds the supply, and the gap will probably increase now that the Supreme Court has passed a ruling permitting abortion. Beigel estimated that in 1961 there were ten times as many pairs of prospective parents as children.[6] In the same year, Vincent estimated that about 100,000 people annually applied to adoption agencies, and that 70 per cent of all illegitimate white infants were given up for adoption, comprising 40 per cent of all the children in the adoption market.[7] Most adopted children go to upper-middle-class couples, because the agencies that control adoption believe that they make the best parents.

Another solution to childlessness is artificial insemination, of which there are two types. One is AIH (Artificial Insemination by Husband), which utilizes the husband's sperm. Insemination in these cases must be artificial because for some physical reason the sperm cannot meet the egg by natural means. The second type is AID (Artificial Insemination by Donor), artificial insemination with an anonymous donor's sperm. This occurs when the problem rests with the husband. In 1953 Baber estimated that there were about 20,000 people in the United States who were conceived through AID, and that success was achieved in 50 to 80 per cent of the cases.[8]

Actually, AID could help many more childless couples than it does. One reason is that there is little attempt to publicize this solution to childlessness. Another reason is opposition by the Catholic

Church. Finally, many couples resist the procedure even when it is available to them. One study showed that 22 per cent of the males but only 14 per cent of the females approved of the procedure.[9] The subjects gave the following reasons for their rejection: preference for adoption, moral reasons, religious reasons, and nonagreement between spouses.

Freedman and his associates found that there were correlations between childlessness and some social variables.[10] For instance, women who had been married more than once were more likely to be childless than once-married women. Of course, this may simply mean that childless women were more likely to divorce than those with families. Working women were more likely to have fecundity problems than non-working women. Again, this may simply reflect the fact that mothers are less likely to be employed than childless women. Kunz and Brinkerhoff found that, contrary to the stereotype, black couples were more likely to be childless than white couples.[11]

ABORTION

Childlessness is generally regarded as involuntary, and there is a tendency to be compassionate toward those who are unable to produce offspring. However, the other extreme, which can be equally distressing, is to have unwanted children.

Abortion is defined as the interruption of a pregnancy and the destruction of the embryo before birth can occur. Almost every society has been known to practice abortion, and attitudes toward the phenomenon vary over time and from one society to another.

Until recently, three types of abortion could be identified: spontaneous, therapeutic, and illegal. A spontaneous abortion, often called miscarriage, occurs involuntarily. Neither the mother nor any other person performs a deliberate act designed to destroy the fetus. It is estimated that 10 per cent of all pregnancies end in spontaneous abortion.[12] A therapeutic abortion is performed if a medical reason is established proving that a continued pregnancy would be harmful to the mother. This occurs in approximately 1 out of every 200 pregnancies (.5 per cent).[13] Illegal abortion means that the embryo is removed from the mother without lawful authority. No one can know, of course, how many illegal abortions have been performed, but estimates range between 4 and 22 per cent of all pregnancies.[14]

Although at this writing most states continue to carry laws on their books prohibiting abortion except to preserve the life of the mother, the Supreme Court of the United States on January 22, 1973, ruled that states could prohibit abortion only during the last ten weeks of pregnancy, and then only if a full-term delivery was necessary to preserve the mother's life. The states have begun to conform to the Court's decision. However, these laws have not made it easier for poor women to obtain an abortion.

The question of abortion reform turns on the question of the woman's right to control her own body and determine her own life. Many people believe that the rights of the unborn child are greater than those of the mother and that she has no right to destroy life in her own interest.

THE FUTURE OF CHILDLESSNESS AND ABORTION

There is little doubt that the rate of childlessness will rise. Indeed, the trend is already apparent. The *New York Times* reported on December 5, 1972, that, according to the latest federal statistics, the birth rate in the United States was below the level of replacement.[15] Each family needs to produce 2.1 children in order to maintain the population with zero growth. In the first nine months of 1971, the rate dropped to 2.08, in spite of the fact that there was an increase in the number of women of childbearing age. This means that by the year 2000, if the trend continues, there will be 17 million fewer Americans than there are today.

Demographers offer several explanations for the decline of the birth rate. There are more young people who are choosing to remain unmarried; many married couples are opting to have children later; and many couples are limiting the size of their families. Furthermore, there are more women than ever in the labor force; there is wider dispersement of contraceptive devices; and abortion laws are being liberalized.

The sum and substance of all these reasons is that many women are seriously questioning the necessity of becoming mothers. "The Motherhood Myth—the idea that having babies is something that all normal women instinctively want and will enjoy doing"—is coming under attack.[16] Almost all social scientists agree that the motherhood myth is nonsense. Goode says, "There are reflexes, like eye-blinking, and drives, like sex. There is no innate drive for children. Otherwise the enormous cultural pressures that there are to reproduce wouldn't exist. There are no cultural pressures to sell you on getting your hand out of the fire."[17]

There is, then, reason to believe that the myth is losing power. If it continues to do so, there will no longer be any cultural compulsion for women to bear children. There will be no stigma attached to childlessness. The result will be less motherhood. Less motherhood means that those who do choose to become mothers will do so freely, not because of feelings of anxiety. Mothers, children, fathers—people—will be better off and happier. I predict, then, that childlessness will increase, as will the number of small families.

As far as the future of abortion is concerned, preliminary results of the Burks study indicate that 74 per cent of the sociologists questioned believe that there will be no legal restraints on abortion in America by 1980.[18] Legislation reflects this trend.

The women's liberation movement is largely responsible for the liberalization of the abortion laws. The fight has been a difficult one because through most of human history, societies have tried to prevent autonomy in the area of human reproduction. There have always been laws outlawing contraception and abortion. Justifications have ranged from religious dogma stressing the sacredness of human life, to the need of the military for soldiers, to economic needs to enlarge the labor force. In short, historically, women have been denied the right to determine whether or not to have children.

Today, it is true, abortion cannot legally be denied to a woman in any state, and birth-control information and devices are more readily available than they have ever been. However, the old mores continue to prevail; in spite of the law, informal customs still restrict abortion. Often physicians and health agencies refuse to prescribe contraception to unmarried people, especially minors. Long waiting periods and high costs still make abortions unobtainable for many. Bureaucratic procedures are still punitive; that is, the informal structures in hospitals and health clinics, the nurses, aides, and doctors, still try to extract penalties from women for what they consider immoral behavior.

We in the United States have the resources to make abortion available to every woman who wishes it. Without this step, the equality of women cannot become a reality. I predict that in the very near future our attitudes and mores will change to conform with the new ruling of the U.S. Supreme Court.

PLANNING FAMILIES

In the past people had less control over the number and spacing of their children than they have now. Today, however, with highly effective and widely distributed contraceptive devices, having a child has become a matter of choice, not chance. Most people have from two to four children.[19] Evidence indicates that families with more than four children are less likely to consider themselves happy; the children appear more likely to be dependent and to have lower intelligence test scores, and to achieve less in their occupations.[20]

Why do people want to have children at all? The reason can no longer be economic. Whereas children were economic assets during the period of America's growth, they are economic liabilities today. Blood and Wolfe report that only 2 per cent of their subjects gave "economic security" as a reason to have children.[21] The notion of maintaining the family name is also no longer relevant, especially in the middle class, which lays so much stress on individualism, not kinship. Blood and Wolfe found that 15 per cent of their couples had children for this reason.[22]

It seems, then, that people have children primarily to satisfy ego needs of their own. This does not imply selfishness but, rather, a desire to both give and receive love from their children. In the Blood and Wolfe sample 48 per cent said having children was good because it brought them "pleasure and emotional satisfaction."[23]

Parenting and the Marital Relationship

Obviously the relationship between the parents affects the child and his personality, but the child also affects the parents' relationship and their self-evaluations. Now let us examine how becoming parents affects the marital relationship.

Before the first child is born the parents develop patterns of interaction. The advent of a baby is disruptive, and they must readjust their dyadic interaction to include a third person. A baby is more than just an intrusion into a relationship because a baby is a special kind of person. He is totally unsocialized and therefore totally selfish and inconsiderate of his parents. He does not care that he disturbs their sleep, interrupts their sexual activity, and interferes in every possible way with their social relationships and with their private relationship with each other.

More than likely, the first child's insensitivity to his parents' needs and demolition of their routine have probably not been anticipated by the young parents. Our social norms, amplified by mass media propaganda, have conditioned the young couple to expect parenthood to be glamorous and exciting. They picture a perfect little angel sleeping peacefully in a crib, not a little demon who constantly demands their attention. Just as young people must accept the reality of marriage in spite of society's unfair representation of it as a romantic dream, so they must come to grips with the realities of parenthood, for which our society has not adequately prepared them.

It should be no surprise, then, that studies of parents at the time of the birth of their first baby show that the event often produces a state of crisis.[24] In general these studies report that after an initial period of four to six weeks during which parents are ecstatic over the baby, the necessary readjustments produce "severe" to "extensive" feelings of crisis. The new mother experiences post-partum depression and chronic fatigue because of loss of sleep, increased household tasks, worry over how well she is performing as a mother, restricted social contacts, and a lowering of household efficiency. The new father is concerned over his inactive social and sexual life, financial pressures, and fear of another pregnancy. However, the picture is not all black. It does not usually take the couple long to alter its expectations so as to include comfortably the third person and to readjust its personal relationship to allow its new statuses—father and mother—room within the older husband and wife statuses.

The arrival of subsequent children into the family rarely has the same impact on the marital relationship. After all, once a third person is introduced into a dyad, the entrance of two or three more cannot cause the same upheaval and cannot require the same degree of interactional readjustment. I am not saying that adjustment is not needed as each successive child is born; of course, it is. But the feeling of crisis that often appears when the first child is born is not re-experienced, at least not to the same degree, when others arrive.

Each new child certainly does change the family structure. A four-person group is subtly different from a three-, five-, or seven-person group. The result is continually shifting coalitions within the family. Caplow points out that these shifts help to maintain vitality in the family and may even contribute to its cohesiveness because one pattern does not have an opportunity to become rigid. If a coalition should become frozen—for example, if one parent and one child should permanently unite against the other parent—serious difficulties could arise in the socialization process and personality development.[25]

In summary, then, the husband-wife relationship is inevitably altered when children arrive in a family. The relationship may be strengthened or weakened, depending on how each parent adapts to his role and depending on the relationship before the child was born. Conflict may develop that will be everlastingly harmful to their relationship. Much depends on their ability to transform preparenthood fantasy into reality, just as much depended on the transition from premarital euphoria to marital reality. The most difficult part of parenthood is not bearing and rearing children *per se,* but adapting to the status of parent and helping one's partner make the transition.

"PARENT WORK"

Although all known societies hold positive attitudes toward the bearing of children because birth is the best method of increasing or maintaining population, over time, parents have not always had the same obligations toward their children. One function that has almost always been delegated to the family is the care of the newborn infant through the first several years of life. Parents have historically been entrusted with the task of socializing the child (see Chapter 2).

Benson has described what he calls "parent work," which is a modern conception of parental obligations.[26] The first obligation is maintenance; that is, parents must supply their offspring with food, shelter, and clothing. Secondly, parents are expected to provide guidance, to influence their children in socially and morally acceptable attitudes and behaviors. Parents are also required to discipline children and to help them in matters beyond basic survival; i.e., homework, finances. A very new obligation is to love the children. Parents are expected to have wanted their children in the first place and to love and respect them as they mature. Finally, parents should release children when they are ready to leave home; that is, they must train their children for independence.

Fashions in child-rearing practices have also changed over time. In Colonial America, children were considered naturally evil; they had to be trained in order to fit into society. Relations between parents and children were very formal. Parents gave orders and children unquestioningly obeyed. So one theory—that children were ruled by the devil—influenced the child-rearing practices of the Puritans. Another theory—that children were small adults—was also important because it meant that no allowances were made for immature judgment or behavior.

After the Civil War, when America began to industrialize, children became an economic asset. They were expected to internalize the ideals of the Protestant Ethic, which were essential to our development as an industrialized society, so that boys as young as ten were expected to be self-controlled, thrifty, self-denying, and self-sufficient.

After 1900 and until World War II, the concept of scientific childrearing gained prominence, especially among middle-class parents. Adjustment, not achievement, was stressed. Equality between parent and child became the norm. "Understanding" was the keynote. Kendel sees this as a response to the need to prepare children for life in a bureaucratized society, which emphasizes conformity and compromise.[27]

Since World War II, the lower class and the middle class have become more similar in their attitudes toward rearing children. Whereas in the past only the middle class sought advice from experts, after 1945 the lower class turned away from the advice of kin and friends and also sought the opinions of experts. One trend that the majority of Americans are now following in their child-rearing practices is toward greater permissiveness. Another stresses friendship between parent and child; a third is toward more affection and less authoritarianism.

PARENTAL ROLES

Mothering

Parenthood is one of the most significant and demanding statuses we acquire in our lifetime. However, it is different for men and women. Moreover, the role of each parent in the United States is quite different from their roles in other societies.[28] In general, other cultures are likely to define parental roles more sharply; in America, the sex distinction is blurring.

From a societal point of view, the role of "mother" is clear. It is, to begin with, a primary status, far less ambiguous than "father." It follows, then, that there are strong social pressures on the woman who is a mother to remain out of the job market and stay home to take care of her children. Even when she claims that it is financially important for her to work, society is skeptical.

All other statuses are subordinate to a woman's role as mother. Only after she has satisfactorily discharged all her obligations to this status is she socially permitted to engage in others. Let me make this point very clear: in our society, all non-maternal responsibilities are considered secondary to the maternal responsibilities. Thus, socially speaking, the status of mother is primary and unambiguous.

The personal role of mother, however, is ambivalent. On the one hand, mother occupies a nearly sacred status; on the other, she is damned as an emasculator. On the one hand, women are claiming that being a mother is a satisfying, full-time occupation; on the other, they are claiming that motherhood is a prison from which they want to escape.

In spite of the ambiguities, certain things appear to be true. The primary aspiration of the young woman is to become a wife and a mother. This status is still seen by the majority of American females as the most desirable in a woman's life. Second, becoming a mother calls for major role adjustments. Gurin and his associates found that mothers often equated having children with loss of freedom and with feelings of anxiety.[29]

Although we socialize our daughters to desire motherhood, we do not adequately prepare them for the status. The result is often disappointment, apprehension, role insecurity, and conflict, especially with the first baby. One Gallup poll revealed that 20 per cent of the new mothers sampled were disappointed, and 40 per cent said they often thought they would not want to have more children.[30]

Women, then, must learn to find satisfaction in the mothering role. If mother love were instinctive and universal, all children would be loved, none would be placed in foster homes, and none would be abused. Yet we know of rejecting mothers; it has been estimated that sixty thousand children a year are neglected or severely mistreated by their mothers, and our hospitals report a constant increase in the number of battered children diagnosed and treated.[31]

The interaction between the mother and the child is more frequent and more complex than that between father and child. Winch believes that the mother is usually the preferred parent, and that the son is the mother's preferred child.[32] Furthermore, of the four possible relationships—mother-son, mother-daughter, father-son, and father-daughter—mother-son is the strongest of all.

Although children derive their sex-role identities from the same-sex parent—that is, girls identify with their mothers and boys with their fathers—there is some evidence that children of both sexes identify more strongly with the mother. However, the son's identification is usually not in those characteristics that are clearly sex-typed.[33]

Working Mothers

An old and persistent question asked by family sociologists is: Does working have a negative effect on a woman's performance of the mothering role? In one major study in this area, Yarrow and her associates found, in general, that working had little impact on mothering.[34] They reported no difference between two matched groups of subjects, one working and one non-working, in terms of acceptance of the feminine role in marriage. There was also no difference in the quality of the care the two sets of children received. Yarrow also found that when women were satisfied with their roles, there was no difference between the employed and unemployed, in their ability to be mothers. However, when they were dissatisfied, the non-working mother was less effective as a parent than the working mother.

There have been innumerable studies of the effects of working mothers on children, too many to detail here. Nye and Hoffman reviewed this research and concluded that "none of the studies done thus far has found meaningful differences between the children of working mothers and the children of nonworking mothers."[35]

Apparently, contrary to old myth, a mother's employment has no necessarily negative effects on the children. This is fortunate because between 1900 and 1970 the proportion of women in the labor force rose from 18 to 37 per cent. The increase is due to an increase in the number of married women at work, especially in the number of working women who are older and financially comfortable. Mead and Kaplan point out that over a third of all mothers in the United States are working. The age of the child seems to be the major determinant of the amount of time worked; the older the child, the more likely it is that the mother is working full time.[36]

Fathering

The transition from husband to father is less difficult than the transition from wife to mother. The latter requires a complete transformation in daily routine and highly innovative adaptation; the former is less demanding and immediate. The reason for this is the same as the reason the transition from singleness to marriage is more difficult for females than for males. The male's primary role is in the occupational sector, and it is not altered very much by either marriage or fatherhood; nor is the focus of his daily life, except in the sense that he has a heightened awareness of financial responsibility. This concern about money may be his chief source of frustration and anxiety, especially because the presence of children may decrease, or appear to decrease, his mobility.

Throughout his childhood, one is likely to interact less with his father than with his mother. Modern middle-class, upwardly mobile fathers tend to come home from the office in time to kiss their children goodnight and spend weekend hours in pursuit of personal relaxation. When fathers do direct attention to their children, especially their sons, they tend to relate in terms of competition and athletics. Fathers try, sometimes in odd ways, to prepare their sons for the aggressive world of business, and if they worry about the children at all, it is in terms of occupational expectations. Daughters are apt to be treated more casually and more affectionately by fathers, who leave the training of girls to their wives.

Absent Fathers

There has been a long-standing assumption that when a child lives in a home with two parents, his socialization will be more successful than the socialization of a child whose father is absent. Undoubtedly, it is advantageous for a youngster to have both parents in his home. However, we have leaped from this assumption to the next obvious one—that when a parent (usually the father) is absent, the consequences for the child will be very negative. Research shows the assumption to be incorrect.

Nye compared the adjustment of children in unhappy intact homes with the adjustment of children in broken, or one-parent, homes and in remarriage.[37] He found no difference in adjustment among the three kinds of homes. Two other researchers compared children who lived in one-parent and remarried homes in terms of school achievement, psychosomatic problems, and juvenile delinquency and found no difference.[38] Crain and Stamn found that prolonged father absence did not alter the child's perception of either parent in terms of love and authority.[39]

These data contradict our assumptions that the absence of a

father causes delinquency, sexual problems, role confusion, neurosis, and school difficulties. It is probable, instead, that the father's absence has little bearing on these conditions.

PARENTING THROUGH THE LIFE CYCLE

Let us now look at the relationships between parents and their children through the various stages of the child's life cycle.

During his infancy and childhood, the parents dominate in the child's life, but as he passes into adolescence, early adulthood, and the early years of his own parenthood, other forces come into play and the parental influence diminishes.

Early Adolescence

Puberty can be defined in biological terms: it is that period in life when the child's body gradually changes to an adult's. But adolescence is an American social invention. We use it as a transition stage between childhood and adulthood. Primitive societies have no such stage; a child is a child until he goes through the puberty rites at a prescribed age, and then he is an adult. Part of the reason we have adolescence is to delay the time of entrance into the job market. Thus, these years, which correspond approximately to the teen years, are ambiguous. The young man or woman is physically adult but socially has neither the privileges of childhood nor the responsibilities of adulthood. It is no wonder, then, that the 18 million Americans between the ages of thirteen and seventeen are frequently frustrated, confused, and alienated, which leads very often to difficulty with parents.

Compounding this difficulty is the parents' own stage in the life cycle. Parents are trying to adjust to middle age at the same time that their children are trying to adjust to growing up. Parents are jealous of the youth and strength of their children, and children are jealous of the privileges of their parents. Perhaps the current norm that adolescents and parents should be pals, implying that they are nearly age peers, is an attempt on both sides to make the one group seem older and the other younger.

One frequently cited source of difficulty between the generations is independence: how much and under what circumstances? This is complicated by the fact that not all parents have the same standards, so that a young person can easily find himself outside the peer group if his parents happen to be more stringent than his friends' parents. Conflict can develop over dating, money, dress, hair, the use of a car, smoking, drinking—almost anything. But out of all this conflict, the adolescent is probably learning to become independent.

He is learning to question arbitrary authority and to search out his own goals and the means of achieving them. His parents may try to hold him back because his maturity implies their aging, but ultimately, most young people become self-sufficient. In any event, it is possible that the generation gap is not so wide as we are led to believe. One study showed that only 13 per cent of the teenagers felt that they disagreed with their parents often; another 31 per cent said occasionally; and the remaining 56 per cent claimed that they rarely or never disagreed with their parents.[40] Unfortunately, this problem has not been studied recently, so we do not really know how teenagers feel about their parents today.

Young Adulthood

It is during this period, when children are beginning to leave home to work, to marry, or to go away to college, that the adolescent becomes an adult by breaking the dependency ties to his parents. Neither parents nor children may find this easy to do. Expectations may be diametrically opposed, with children seeking independence and parents wanting to continue to be needed. Furthermore, in spite of themselves, young adults may not really want to be freed from parental authority.

The conflict with their children may also have negative effects on the marital relationship. One study reported that many couples who rated the early child-rearing years of their marriage high rated their marriage low during the period of their children's young adulthood.[41] The researchers feel that this may indicate that the respondents enjoy parenting more than marriage itself. This strain between the parents ultimately worsens the relationships between the child and the parents.

Just as the role of parent is different for mothers and fathers during infancy and childhood, it is also different during young adulthood. The mother experiences greater emotional stress because, for most women, this is the end of her most important adult role. Even for the mother who is employed, the loss of her major role leads to frustration and new adjustment. The father, on the other hand, is less affected when his children grow up because his ego is primarily invested in his occupation. His way of life is much less threatened.

There comes a time, however, when all the children have finally left the parental home. We discussed the effect on the marriage in Chapter 5. What happens between married children and their parents has been the subject of a long-standing debate among family sociologists.

One theory, defended chiefly by Talcott Parsons, holds that the married son or daughter drifts away from the family of orientation and forms a nuclear family which is quite isolated from the kin group.[42] Parsons argues that the nuclear family does not share its residence with parents and frequently lives far away from the rest of the kin group. Census data support these arguments. In 1959, 97.2 per cent of all married couples lived in their own homes, and only one in ten lived with relatives other than children.[43] Reiss found that parents and married children often would prefer to live close together, but not too close.[44]

Parsons also stressed the economic independence of young married couples, but this viewpoint has received scant support. Almost all research indicates that parents help their children in many ways: babysitting, advice, information, and chiefly, financial aid.[45]

A second theory argues that the kin group maintains close ties with the young married couple and performs many of the old functions from childhood, plus several new ones. The sociologists most frequently associated with this second viewpoint are Sussman, who described a "helping pattern,"[46] and Litwak, who spoke of the modified extended family system."[47]

The mother in particular may establish modified ties with her adult children which are very meaningful to her as well as to the children. Sussman found that middle-class parents continue to give service, advice, and financial assistance to their married children, especially to their daugthers.[48] Adams noted the same pattern in the working class.[49] He found that this help was greatest during the first ten years of the children's marriages, and that the geographical

distance between the parents and the children did not greatly influence the amount or kind of help supplied.

The generation gap between parents and children seems to narrow after the children marry. Parents and children continue to be
emotionally attached to one another. This is not to say that there is
no tension between them. There is almost inevitably some ambiva-
lence between the child's desire to be totally emancipated and his
desire to be cared for.[50]

In general, as I examine the evidence for the two theories, I
must conclude that the relationships between parents and their
married offspring will depend a great deal on the relations between
them before the children's marriages. If the parents were possessive
and domineering, the break caused by the marriage will probably
be difficult and unpleasant. If the relations had been friendly, they
should continue to be. Ideally, parents' help should gradually
lessen over the years. Parental aid is probably greatest during the
early years of the children's marriages, decreasing until the
"young" people are middle-aged. Then the roles may well be re-
versed, and the "children" tend to manage their elderly parents'
lives.

Young Parenthood

One of the activities that helps to fill the gap when children leave
home is grandparenting. As grandchildren are born, older couples
acquire new interests and discover that there are things they can
contribute to the world in terms of helping to launch yet another
generation. The role of grandparent, however, has been changing
over time. One reason is the earlier age at which we become grandparents because we are marrying younger and having children
younger. (I myself was a grandmother at age thirty-seven.)
Younger grandparents are likely to accept and perform the role differently from older grandparents.

Neugarten and Weinstein studied these variations in grandparenting.[51] Nearly 59 per cent of their subjects enjoyed being grandparents, and about one third found the role uncomfortable and disappointing. Neugarten and Weinstein were able to discern five
styles of grandparenting: formal, fun-seeking, distant-figure, surro-
gate-parent, and reservoir-of-family-wisdom.

The most common type was the formal grandparent, either male or female. This is more characteristic of older than younger grandparents. Formal grandparents do the things they believe are correct in this status. They are careful not to interfere between their children and their grandchildren, and they provide the "goodies" to make life more pleasant for the young family—special gifts and outings, treats, surprises, and occasional babysitting.

The second most common form, particularly among younger grandmothers, is the fun-seeker. Such grandparents think of their grandchildren as sources of pleasure and objects of indulgence. The relationship is characterized by play and informality. These are the grandmothers who spoil their grandchildren. They are probably responsible for the belief that grandparents and grandchildren are such good friends because they have a common enemy—the parent.

Grandfathers are more likely to fall into the category of distant-figure than are grandmothers. These are the grandparents who are seen at Christmas and at birthday parties, but not much in between. Such grandparents are likely to be younger, and their social distance is based on such factors as difficulty in accepting the status of grandparent, occupational interests, or poor relations with in-law children.

The surrogate parent refers only to grandmothers in the study by these investigators. These grandmothers do the work of the mother, usually at the parent's request, because the mother is fully employed, chronically ill, or for some other reason unable to fulfill the mother's role.

The least prevalent style is the reservoir-of-family-wisdom. When it does occur, it is the grandfather's, not the grandmother's, role. This is an authoritarian position which may be taken because the grandparent is very wealthy or for some reason is seen as a source of special skill or knowledge. When such a grandparent is on the scene, it is likely that both the children and the grandchildren will defer to him and will accord him special respect.

In-Laws

Marriage, of course, means a new relationship between a man and a woman, and eventually between them and their children.

However, it also means new relationships with each other's family. The woman becomes not only a wife but a daughter-in-law and perhaps a sister-in-law. Her husband becomes a son-in-law and perhaps a brother-in-law. These statuses are answerable to the expectations of all concerned, and they may not always be identical expectations. Thus, problems with in-laws are frequent in marriage, especially at the beginning. Family patterns and social roles must be reconsidered and modified, and this requires time, effort, intelligence, understanding, and cooperation. All the status occupants must make adjustments.

Mothers seem to have more difficulty than fathers in making adjustments to their child's new spouse. Mothers, as we have seen, play a larger part in raising children and consequently are usually more emotionally involved with them. In this situation, too, the mother is again reminded of the loss of her primary role and must recognize that she has to take a secondary position in her child's life. Her new role as mother-in-law is not socially comfortable. Much of her status is defined by such societal attitudes as are implied by mother-in-law jokes, which show her, albeit in humorous terms, as domineering and interfering. Her relationship with her in-law child, especially her daughter-in-law, is often one of mutual jealousy, with each competing for the attention and affection of the husband-son. Of course, this stereotype of a mother-in-law, like all stereotypes, is exaggerated and frequently does not apply in individual situations.

A father, because the marriage of a child does not threaten his primary status as provider, is subject to less trauma and needs less readjustment. Moreover, daughters-in-law often are very attentive to their male in-law parent, which fathers-in-law are very likely to reciprocate and to enjoy.

One study showed that the most troublesome of these relationships is between the mother-in-law and the daughter-in-law. Fifty per cent of the young wives reported that this relationship was a problem to them.[52] Another study, however, found that although the mother-in-law has an adjustment problem when her son marries, she is often seen by her daughter-in-law as helpful to the young couple, and that daughters-in-law are more likely than sons-in-law to say they love their mothers-in-law.[53]

The second most difficult in-law relationship is between the wife and her sister-in-law. Thus it appears that the distaff members of a family encounter more problems with each other than the male members do among themselves and with females. Christensen and Johnsen offer the following explanations:

1. Role adjustments are more extensive for women.
2. Family roles are more central in the lives of women.
3. The wife's role is subject to more criticism because it is more visible than the husband's.
4. The mother-in-law, because she is more emotionally attached to her son than his father is, is more apt to compete with the young wife.
5. A daughter is more likely than a son to be dependent on her mother, and this dependency may threaten the relationship between the girl and her husband.
6. As transmitters of the culture, females bring certain attitudes to their marriages about foods, child rearing, special occasions, religious rituals, and so on. If the notions of the wife differ from those of her mother-in-law, she may be criticized.[54]

Leslie suggests another reason: Because males have more power in our society, a man's mother-in-law is less likely to challenge him because he could make contact between the mother and her daughter uncomfortable or difficult.[55]

The problems between a mother-in-law and a son-in-law are minimal. Their roles are very different and, therefore, there is less opportunity for comparison and competition than there is between mothers-in-law and daughters-in-law. There are really only two possible areas of difficulty: the mother-in-law may not approve of her son-in-law's treatment of her daughter or her grandchildren, and the son-in-law may view his wife's mother as trying to interfere too much in his marriage.

The least conflicted relationship is between the father-in-law and his daughter-in-law. In the Landis study only 11 per cent of the wives complained about this relationship.[56] The reasons for this compatibility seem obvious. The father-in-law is only peripherally involved in the personal life of his married son. Moreover, these two people may develop a flirting relationship that enhances both egos—he because a young girl is attracted to him, she because he may be similar to her father and/or her husband in many ways.

The relations between fathers-in-law and sons-in-law are also relatively trouble-free. Landis and Landis report that only 15 per cent of the young men felt they had problems with their fathers-in-law.[57] The reason is probably that although for both the primary status is occupational, in this case too there is little opportunity for direct comparison or competition. Furthermore, unlike the mother-in-law, the father-in-law rarely attempts to tell his son-in-law how to play his marital role.

To summarize, then, all in-law relationships demand some adjustment and compromise from the status occupants. However, the greatest difficulties are experienced by the women in the family with each other: the mother-in-law, the sister-in-law, and the daughter-in-law. As the necessary adjustments are gradually made, the tensions are usually reduced. If not, the two families may, by unspoken agreement, interact as infrequently as possible.

There are no trends in the in-law relationship *per se* that we can use as cues to the future. However, there are trends that I have described in other contexts that may have an indirect influence on these relations. One is the increasing pluralism in our marriage institution; the other is the women's liberation movement.

If my predictions concerning marriage become reality—that is, if young couples enter premarriage, then parental marriage, and, in middle age, serial monogamy—then the tensions surrounding in-law relationships, which are especially characteristic of the early and parental phases of marriage, should relax. The two couples involved will be mindful that in all probability their relationships are not permanent and can therefore be taken less seriously.

The women's liberation movement is related to this. With less stress on the feminine role of housekeeper, with women dividing their time, energy, and attention between their homes and their occupations, they will have less interest in competing for the husband-son. The most troublesome of all in-law relationships, that between mother-in-law and daughter-in-law, should improve. Mothers-in-law aged forty-five or fifty will be at the most productive time of their careers instead of at the end of the only career they have had before—homemaker and mother. They will, furthermore, be entering new marriages and will be more attentive to their own happiness in these new relationships than to their sons' lives.

Women in general will no longer be investing all their lives in men
—son or husband—and therefore competition with other women will
be less threatening than in the past.

I predict, then, that as women find greater activity and interest outside the home, as they find new excitement in new sexual
relationships, and as they acknowledge that their children's marriages may not last forever, they will be more likely to form friendships rather than rivalrous relationships with their daughters-in-law.
The younger women too will be caught up in outside experiences
and will not need to feel judged on their homemaking talents alone.
I have noted that one reason male in-laws get along better than
females is that they are not in directly competing roles. When
women also are involved in the work world, they will not be competing directly either.

Sibling Relationships

Unfortunately, the relationship among young siblings has been
largely neglected by sociologists.[58] Those authors who have considered this relationship generally do so from a psychological perspective, concentrating on sibling rivalry, birth order, sibling displace-
ment, and the like.

The variable most frequently discussed is sibling rivalry because
it is often very obvious in families and can be very destructive to
the sibling relationship. Sibling rivalry may be defined as a feeling
on the part of one child in a family that he is in some way inferior,
or is treated as if he were inferior, to another child in the family.
Such feelings may occur in a first-born child when subsequent children arrive, or in second- or third-born children who may feel that
the oldest child is privileged. In either case, there is jealousy and
frustration. Sibling rivalry may take the form of overt hostility. It
may result in regression on the part of the older child, who may return to wetting his pants, sucking his thumb, etc.

Many researchers believe that sibling rivalry is unavoidable in
American families because all children would like to feel that they
are loved by their parents most of all. One study showed that there
was no treatment the mother could offer to the oldest child that
would assuage his sense of having been displaced.[59]

We have already mentioned (Chapter 2) that there are both ad-

vantages and disadvantages to having a sibling. There is no need
to reiterate these here. We can only note that relationships between
brothers and sisters are usually a mixture of happiness and unhappiness. And although there has been almost no research interest
directed to interaction between child siblings, there is some evidence that relations improve considerably when the children grow
up.[60]

Adams's findings are very interesting:

> Regarding frequency of sibling interaction, the major determinant—
> as between young adults and their parents—is the distance which
> separates them. Blue-collar siblings tend to live closer to each other
> and therefore to see each other more often. However, when resi-
> dentially separated, it is only sisters who are likely to overcome the
> distance with extremely frequent utilization of the means of com-
> munication. For brothers and cross-sex siblings, a substantial separa-
> tion comes close to producing isolation.
>
> Occupationally disparate siblings, even brothers, do not manifest
> a lesser frequency of interaction or contact than two white- or blue-
> collar siblings.[61]
>
> The relationship between age-near siblings is predicated upon a basic
> family interest, upon the desire to know how and what one's brother
> or sister is doing. The role of social companion is seldom played by
> age-near siblings . . . even when they live close enough to be good
> friends. Nor are these siblings a recurrent source of mutual aid . . .
> adult relations between siblings are to a great extent a continuation—
> mitigated by changing interests and distance considerations—of a
> relationship which has been developing during childhood and
> youth.[62]
>
> In summary, on the one hand enjoyment of the sibling is quite simi-
> lar to that expressed toward parents. Obligation, on the other hand,
> is usually not felt to be as great, and specific obligation, or obliga-
> tion to help, is virtually non-existent. . . . General obligations to
> keep in touch, while not dominant, are still an important aspect of
> sibling relations.[63]

There is, perhaps, one other word to be said about child-child
relations. They can affect all other relations within the family—
those between a parent and a child and those between the parents
themselves. Negative sibling interaction can be a divisive force in

a family. For a family to be well integrated, there must be good relations between the dyads within it.

THE PARENT ROLE IN THE FUTURE

At other times in our history, mothers were less important in the role of rearing children than they are now. The frontier mother was too involved with her husband in the struggle for survival to pay full-time attention to her family. In our small towns, women worked with their husbands in the family store or on the farm, and grandmothers and older children helped with younger children. Wealthy families had nursemaids, black mammies in the South and immigrant girls in the North.

In most American families, then, surrogate mothers—grandmothers, older siblings, servants—performed the everyday functions of bringing up children. But during the 1920s, when restrictions led to less immigration, and during the 1930s, when the Depression forced middle-class families to limit their expenditures, the mother's role as chief parent gained ascendancy. At the same time, as industrialization increased, men moved farther and farther away from their families and assumed less and less responsibility, other than financial, for their children. "The two significant changes in the socialization of American children in the last hundred years are the increasing role of the mother and the declining role of the father."[64]

Until recently, Americans have taken this division of roles for granted. The "natural" way, we tend to believe, is for the woman to bring up the child and for the man to play a peripheral, mainly financial, role. This is the present situation in our society. It is now becoming obvious, however, that this family structure is being replaced by an urban family whose members are increasingly involved in and gain satisfaction from relationships outside the family. The question, then, is: Where does the status of parent go from here?

Many social scientists today are urging that we license parenting, just as we license marriage, making a sharp distinction between the right to have sexual intercourse and the right to have children. This means that people who request a license for "parental marriage" would be asked to furnish assurances that they are qualified to be parents, biologically, financially, and emotionally. I believe that the new norms will permit freedom in choice of living arrangements, but the society will retain an interest in who becomes a parent.

I also predict that planned parenthood will become the norm, even among the lower classes. This will be made possible by the development of even more effective and convenient birth-control methods, which will need to be disseminated more widely. Along with acceptance of planned parenthood will go acceptance of abortion. As a result, we will have fewer unwanted children and fewer children in adoptive and foster homes.

When family planning becomes universal, and when people will be permitted to have children only after they have demonstrated a true readiness and ability, we can look forward to happier and healthier parent-child relationships. Nationally institutionalized family planning, then, is one strong possibility for the future. There are, however, more radical possibilities.

Virginia Satir offers several suggestions for changing our social norms so as to increase the satisfactions of all family members.[65] First, she would like to alter the image of parenthood. Instead of assuming, as we do, that anyone capable of having a child is capable of rearing it, we should recognize that not everyone is able or willing to do this job. To implement this notion, Satir proposes that each neighborhood establish a "Family Growth Center" where people could learn how to be human. Furthermore, birth should be the concern of all three people involved: mother, father, and child. We should change child-rearing practices so as to stress the child as a person, not as a dependent; and we should allow children completely free sexual expression and experimentation. Most important, the goal of becoming human—loving, close, productive, and responsible people—should be primary in society.

In *Walden II*, B. F. Skinner designed an entire society. Frazier, the major character, discusses the parent-child relationship in this way:

Many parents are glad to be relieved of the awful responsibility of being a child's only source of affection and help. Here [in Walden II] it's impossible to be an inadequate or unskilled parent, and the vigorous, happy growth of our children is enough to remove any last suspicion that we have been deprived of anything.[66]

In *Walden II*, the parent-child relationship has been de-emphasized. Children are reared together by male and female nurses. They are regarded as the children of everyone in the community so that they cannot become overly dependent on their mothers, so that those members of the community who are childless are still involved in family life, and, finally, so that children are not damaged if their parents are divorced.

Skinner responds to the question of identification in children:

We know very little about what happens in identification. . . . No one has ever made a careful scientific analysis. . . . All we really know is that children tend to imitate adults, in gestures and mannerisms, and in personal attitudes and relations. They do that here, too, but since the family structure is changed, the effect is very different.

Our children are cared for by many different people. It isn't institutional care, but genuine affection. . . . Remember that the adults who care for our children are of both sexes. We have broken down prejudices regarding the occupations of the sexes, and we have worked particularly hard to keep a balance in the nursery and school system. . . . By balancing the sexes we eliminate all the Freudian problems which arise from the asymmetrical relation to the female parent.[67]

Carl Levett offers another suggestion.[68] He proposes that if the two biological parents have highly demanding and time-consuming occupations, third and fourth parents should join the family unit to fill the gap left by the parents' absence and inattention. The point Levett wishes to emphasize is that we must change our conceptualization of the family model wherein only the biological parents can successfully rear the children. In the age of specialization, we should have parents who are skilled in rearing children. Levett believes that this notion of parents could be especially useful when the biological parents are divorced. He concludes: "Ultimately, a uniquely educated, trained, professional corps of alter-parents could help to overcome many parental difficulties in future family models."[69]

The most radical suggestion on future parent-child relations comes from Alvin Toffler, who believes that because the new birth technology will cause such enormous changes future parenting will have a meaning different from that it has today.[70] Toffler says this new technology will allow us to predetermine the sex of the child, his intelligence, his appearance, and even his personality. But, Toffler asks, what happens to our notions of parenthood when babies can be grown in laboratory jars or purchased from a corporation? Who will be a parent?

Toffler thinks many things are possible. People may remain childless or postpone having children until after retirement so that they can pursue careers without the interference of other obligations. "The post-retirement family could become a recognized social institution."[71] Or, he predicts, we might have professional parents who would rear children for other people. These pro-parents would be trained for their occupation just as any professional is trained. Children would be assigned to family units of pro-parents, which might even be three-generational so that the children could have several role models. The real parents, "bio-parents," would be more like godparents, interested and friendly strangers. In this way, Toffler suggests, we could continue to breed a genetically wide variety of babies, and the children could be reared by groups of families who are trained professionally to care for children.

One thing sociologists seem to agree on is that the relationship between parent and child will change dramatically as a result of two major trends: the change from sex-role differentiation to equality between men and women, and the enlarged role that government agencies will play in child rearing. The two trends are evidently related to each other. Both reflect, at least partially, the aims of the women's liberation movement.

The thrust of this movement is equality for women in the occupational sector and at home. Women are demanding that they be allowed to reject the traditional role of wife and mother and seek their identity, as men do, in the labor market. At the same time, women believe that as workers and as contributors to the household budget, they should no longer be solely responsible for housekeeping and parenting. They want to share these tasks with men.

All the various women's groups, from conservative (National Organization of Women) to radical (Female Liberation Front), see the present family structure as destructive of women's identity. They see housework as demeaning subservience and motherhood as unnaturally binding if they are forced on a woman. The movement continues to grow. Whereas it began among educated, middle-class, white women, it has moved through the social classes and cut across racial lines. Many colleges now offer at least one course on women or sex roles. It seems clear that the women's liberation movement has already had a strong impact on the family, on marriage, and on parenting. It will undoubtedly continue to do so.

The first change will be a de-emphasis on the role of mother. This will come about as contraception allows more women to choose when and if they will have children, so that women can no longer be "trapped" into having huge families. It will also be made possible by a new stress on the female occupational role and the concomitant lessening of the stigma of working when one has children. Indeed, for a tiny minority of upper-class, professional, educated women, there is already a stigma attached to *not* working, to *just* staying home and caring for children.

As women reject the maternal role as the only possible full-time occupation for them, we will need to find replacements to serve this function. There are three possible ones: the father, a privately employed trained professional surrogate parent, and government facilities, such as day-care centers. The father would not be expected to change places completely with his wife and take over the entire child-rearing task, unless that is what the couple agreed to do. Instead, he will come to share this occupation. No one person will be solely responsible for raising children. Fathers and mothers will play equal roles, and all will benefit. Mothers will be released from the full-time routine of parenting and will be able to fulfill other ambitions in the work sector. Fathers will be released from having to suppress all nurturant, gentle qualities in their personalities and will be permitted to fulfill such needs of expression with their children. Children will benefit most of all because they will have deeper and more meaningful relationships with two parents, who are both more complete in themselves.

A second substitute for the mothering role now occupied by women will be professional parents, of the kind advocated by Toffler and Levett. Such a parent will be a specially trained individual —male or female—with a certified degree in parenting. His job will be to train, socialize, love, and give attention to children. This does not mean that biological parents must abdicate, but they will not have responsibility for their children on a day-to-day routine basis. Instead, their position will be similar to that of grandparent, aunt or uncle, or godparent. As Toffler suggests, pro-parents may be older people, retired, healthy, interested in children.

The third possible mother-surrogate is the government agency, of the type envisioned by Skinner in *Walden II,* or like the children's house in the Israeli kibbutz, or like the day-care centers in this country. This suggestion has been severely criticized by many social scientists, notably psychiatrist Abram Kardiner, who claims that the surrogate parent is a poor substitute for the real thing.[72] Having children unites parents and strengthens marriage. With only one professional parent for several children, children will have to compete for his affection and attention and will not get enough of either.

The evidence is against Kardiner. Studies of kibbutz children show them to have more positive attitudes toward their parents than traditionally raised children. They showed less conformity, greater maturity, higher intellectual interests, and stronger egos. The most beneficial aspect of collective child rearing is that parents need not be disciplinarians and can be more symbolic of love and affection.[73]

Nimkoff is apparently very much in favor of collective child rearing. "The kibbutzim may very well prove to be harbingers of the future with respect to patterns of child care. With the continuing growth of culture and the increasing professionalization of child-care services, it seems realistic to anticipate more community responsibility for child care."[74]

In summary, I believe that families in the future will be more carefully planned than they are today. Couples will need to show proof of stability, both financial and emotional, in order to obtain a license for parental marriage, permitting them to have a child. I also believe that the female role in parenting will diminish. Because we are a pluralistic society, there will be several possible alternatives. Some people will prefer to have the two parents share the responsibility equally. Some will prefer to have professional parents raise their children. Some will want them reared in government children's houses with themselves as involved and interested outsiders.[75] Some will want their children cared for by day in government-sponsored day-care centers but will want to take them home after work and spend evenings and nights with them. Any of these alternatives will be possible without stigma. The results should be greater happiness and fulfillment for the parents, for the children, and for the professionals who will be involved in caring for the children.

NOTES

1. Ronald Freedman, Pascal K. Whelpton, and Arthur A. Campbell, *Family Planning, Sterility, and Population Growth* (New York: McGraw-Hill, 1959), p. 26.
2. Robert R. Bell, *Marriage and Family Interaction*, 3d ed. (Homewood, Ill.: Dorsey, 1971), p. 419.
3. Edmond J. Farris, "Male Fertility," in *Sourcebook in Marriage and the Family*, ed. Marvin B. Sussman (Boston: Houghton Mifflin, 1955), p. 135.
4. Paul H. Gebbard, Wardell B. Pomeroy, Clyde E. Martin, and Cornelia V. Christenson, *Pregnancy, Birth and Abortion* (New York: Harper, 1958), p. 81.
5. U.S. Department of Commerce, Bureau of the Census, *Statistical Abstracts of the United States: 1964* (Washington, D.C.: Government Printing Office, 1964), p. 312.
6. Hugo G. Beigel, "Illegitimacy," in *The Encyclopedia of Sexual Behavior*, eds. Albert Ellis and Albert Abarbanel (New York: Hawthorn, 1961), p. 513.
7. Clark Vincent, *Unmarried Mothers* (Glencoe, Ill.: Free Press, 1961), pp. 13, 195.
8. Ray E. Baber, *Marriage and the Family* (New York: McGraw-Hill, 1953), pp. 534–535.
9. Glenn A. Vernon and Jack A. Boadway, "Attitudes Toward Artificial Insemination and Some Variables Associated Therewith," *Journal of Marriage and the Family* 21 (1959): 46.
10. Freedman, Whelpton, and Campbell, *op. cit.*, pp. 43–53.

11. Philip R. Kunz and Merlin B. Brinkerhoff, "Differential Childlessness by Color: The Destruction of a Cultural Belief," *Journal of Marriage and the Family* 31 (November, 1969): 719.
12. Alan F. Guttmacher, "Abortions," in *Modern Marriage and Family Living,* eds. Morris Fishbein and Ruby Jo R. Kennedy (New York: Oxford University Press, 1957), p. 402.
13. *Ibid.,* p. 410.
14. *Ibid.*
15. National Center for Health Statistics, *Monthly Vital Statistics Report* 1:9 (1972).
16. Betty Rollins, "Motherhood: Who Needs It?" in *Family in Transition,* eds. Arlene S. Skolnick and Jerome H. Skolnick (Boston: Little, Brown, 1971), p. 346.
17. Quoted by Rollins, *ibid.,* pp. 346–347.
18. Jayne B. Burks, "The Delphi Study" (unpublished Ph.D. diss., Fontbonne College, 1973).
19. Robert O. Blood and Donald P. Wolfe, *Husbands and Wives* (New York: Free Press, 1960), p. 118.
20. Catherine S. Chilman, "Fertility and Poverty in the United States: Some Implications for Family-Planning Programs, Evaluations, and Research," *Journal of Marriage and the Family* 30 (May, 1968): 213.
21. Blood and Wolfe, *op. cit.,* p. 138.
22. *Ibid.*
23. *Ibid.*
24. E. E. LeMasters, "Parenthood as Crisis," *Marriage and Family Living* 19 (1957): 352–355; Everett D. Dyer, "Parenthood as Crisis: A Restudy," *Marriage and Family Living* 25 (May, 1963): 196–201; Daniel F. Hobbs, Jr., "Parenthood as Crisis: A Third Study," *Marriage and Family Living* 27 (August, 1965): 367–372; and Harold Feldman, "Development of the Husband-Wife Relationship: A Research Report," in *The Family in Social Context,* ed. Gerald R. Leslie (New York: Oxford University Press, 1967), p. 530.
25. Theodore Caplow, *Two Against One—Coalitions in Triads* (Englewood Cliffs, N.J.: Prentice-Hall, 1968).
26. Leonard Benson, *The Family Bond* (New York: Random House, 1971), pp. 11–13.
27. William F. Kendel, *The Family in Perspective* (New York: Appleton-Century-Crofts, 1966), p. 250.
28. Edward Z. Dager, "Socialization and Personality Development in the Child," in *Handbook of Marriage and the Family,* ed. Harold T. Christensen (Chicago: Rand McNally, 1964), p. 770.
29. Harold Gurin, Joseph Veroff, and Sheila Feld, *Americans View Their Mental Health* (New York: Basic Books, 1960), p. 30.
30. George Gallup, "The Woman's Mind: America's Young Mothers," *Ladies' Home Journal,* March 1962, p. 72.
31. Bell, *op. cit.,* p. 435.
32. Robert F. Winch, *The Modern Family* (New York: Henry Holt, 1952), p. 299.
33. David R. Lynn, "The Process of Learning Parental and Sex-Role Identification," *Journal of Marriage and the Family* 28 (November, 1966): 468.

34. Marion Yarrow et al., "Childrearing in Families of Working and Non-working Mothers," Sociometry 25 (1962): 122–140.
35. F. Ivan Nye and Lois W. Hoffman, eds., The Employed Mother in America (Skokie, Ill.: Rand McNally, 1963), p. 191.
36. Margaret Mead and Frances B. Kaplan, eds., American Women: The Report of the President's Commission on the Status of Women (New York: Charles Scribner's Sons, 1965).
37. F. Ivan Nye, "Child Adjustment in Broken and in Unhappy Unbroken Homes," Marriage and Family Living 19 (1957): 356–361.
38. Joseph B. Parry and Erdwin H. Pfuhl, "Adjustment of Children in 'Sole' and 'Remarriage' Homes," Marriage and Family Living 25 (1963): 221–223.
39. Alan J. Crain and Caroline S. Stamn, "Intermittent Absence of Fathers and Children's Perceptions of Parents," Journal of Marriage and the Family 27 (August, 1965): 344–347.
40. Thomas L. Langner and Stanley T. Michael, Life Stress and Mental Illness (New York: Free Press, 1963), p. 255.
41. Boyd C. Rollins and Harold Feldman, "Marital Satisfaction over the Family Life Cycle," Journal of Marriage and the Family 32 (February, 1970): 26.
42. Talcott Parsons, Robert F. Bales et al., Family, Socialization, and Interaction Process (New York: Free Press, 1955).
43. U.S. Department of Commerce, Bureau of the Census, United States Census of Population: 1960, Final Report PC (2)-4A (Washington, D.C.: Government Printing Office, 1963).
44. Paul J. Reiss, "The Extended Kinship System: Correlates of and Attitudes on Frequency of Interaction," Marriage and Family Living 24 (February, 1962): 333–339.
45. Marvin B. Sussman, "The Help Patterns in the Middle Class Family," American Sociological Review 17 (1953): 22–28; J. Joan Moss and Marian Myers MacNab, "Young Families," Journal of Home Economics 53 (1961): 829–834; Marvin B. Sussman and Lee Burchinal, "Kin Family Network: Unheralded Structure in Current Conceptualizations of Family Functioning," Marriage and Family Living 24 (1962): 231–240.
46. Sussman, 1953, op. cit.
47. Eugene Litwak, "Occupational Mobility and Extended Family Cohesion," American Sociological Review 25 (1960): 9–21.
48. Sussman, 1953, op. cit.
49. Bert N. Adams, "Structural Factors Affecting Parental Aid to Married Children," Journal of Marriage and the Family 26 (1964): 330.
50. Paul H. Glasser and Lois N. Glasser, "Role Reversal and Conflict Between Aged Parents and Their Children," Marriage and Family Living 24 (1962): 46–51.
51. Bernice L. Neugarten and Karol K. Weinstein, "The Changing American Grandparent," Journal of Marriage and the Family 26 (May, 1964): 199–205.
52. Judson T. Landis and Mary G. Landis, Building a Successful Marriage (Englewood Cliffs, N.J.: Prentice-Hall, 1953), p. 289.
53. Alan L. Switzer, "Some Factors Related to In-Law Difficulty and Conflict" (M.S. thesis, Purdue University, 1966).

54. Harold T. Christensen and Kathryn P. Johnsen, *Marriage and the Family,* 3d ed. (New York: Ronald Press, 1971), pp. 359–360.
55. Gerald R. Leslie, *The Family in Social Context* (New York: Oxford University Press, 1967), p. 321.
56. Landis and Landis, *op. cit.*
57. Landis and Landis, *op. cit.*
58. Donald P. Irish, "Sibling Interaction: A Neglected Aspect in Family Life Research," *Social Forces* 42 (1964): 279–288.
59. Allison Davis and Robert J. Havighurst, *Father of the Man* (Boston: Houghton Mifflin, 1947), p. 120.
60. Philip Garigue, "French Canadian Kinship and Urban Life," *American Anthropologist* 63 (1961): 498–507; Bernard Farber, *Family: Organization and Interaction* (San Francisco: Chandler, 1964); Michael Young and Peter Willmott, *Family and Kinship in East London* (Baltimore: Penguin, 1964); and Bert N. Adams, *Kinship in an Urban Setting* (Chicago: Markham, 1968).
61. Adams, *op. cit.,* p. 103.
62. *Ibid.,* p. 108.
63. *Ibid.,* p. 114.
64. Gail Putney Fullerton, *Survival in Marriage* (New York: Holt, Rinehart, and Winston, 1972), p. 158.
65. Virginia Satir, "Marriage as a Human-Actualizing Contract," in *The Family in Search of a Future,* ed. Herbert A. Otto (New York: Appleton-Century-Crofts, 1970), pp. 57–66.
66. B. F. Skinner, *Walden II* (New York: Macmillan, 1948), p. 118.
67. *Ibid.,* pp. 119–120.
68. Carl Levett, "A Parental Presence in Future Family Models," in Otto, *op. cit.,* pp. 161–169.
69. *Ibid.,* p. 169.
70. Alvin Toffler, *Future Shock* (New York: Random House, 1970), ch. 2.
71. *Ibid.,* p. 215.
72. Abram Kardiner, "Bringing Up Children in Russia," *Saturday Review,* 26 August 1961.
73. A. I. Rabin, "Attitudes of Kibbutz Children to Parents and Families," *American Journal of Orthopsychiatry* 29 (1959): 172–179; A. I. Rabin, "Personality Maturity of Kibbutz and Non-Kibbutz Children as Reflected in Rorschach Findings," *American Journal of Orthopsychiatry* 27 (1957): 48–53; and A. I. Rabin, "Infants and Children Under Conditions of Intermittent Mothering in the Kibbutz," *American Journal of Orthopsychiatry* 28 (1958): 577–584.
74. M. F. Nimkoff, ed., *Comparative Family Systems* (Boston: Houghton Mifflin, 1965), p. 360.
75. Burks, *op. cit.*

7 Marital Breakup

There are couples who go through many decades of marriage without ever considering terminating the relationship. For others, there is less and less pleasure and joy in the relationship over the years. As we saw in Chapter 5, Pineo believes that diminishing satisfaction in marriage is the more common pattern.[1] Three processes are involved. They are *alienation,* the opposite of early idealization, which includes feelings of anger and resentment toward one's mate; *disenchantment* or disappointment in the marriage, probably the result of early over-romanticism; and *disengagement,* which marks the end of intimacy, confidence, sexual play, shared interests, and so on. According to Pineo, the process of deterioration in a marriage is generalized into every area of the relationship; all aspects deteriorate simultaneously. Blood, who studied marriage in Detroit and in Tokyo, came to the same conclusion, even though these two cities are very different in their courtship patterns and marital relationships.[2]

What happens when two people in a marriage perceive that the relationship is dying or dead? Some choose to stay in it for religious or moral reasons. Other couples stay together "for the sake of the children." Some stay married because they cannot face the criticism of friends and parents. Many couples who can no longer find any joy in being together terminate the marriage in one of four ways: annulment, desertion, legal separation, or divorce. In this chapter we shall also discuss involuntary termination of a marriage through the death of one of the partners.

ANNULMENT

Annulments account for about 3.5 per cent of all marital terminations. This procedure means that legally there has never been a valid marriage between the two people. Neither has acquired marital rights and, therefore, there is a return to the situation as it existed before the wedding ceremony occurred. However, the social meaning is different from the legal meaning. Legally there is nothing to end. Socially, however, the marriage had a beginning—when the couple began to live together—and it has an ending—when they part.

The grounds for annulment are based on fraud. That is, there is some legal reason why the marriage should never have taken place at all, such as unrevealed bigamy, insanity, being underage, duress —any type of gross misrepresentation on the part of either of the pair which a court will recognize as an essential part of the marriage contract.

DESERTION

Desertion is an informal means of terminating a marriage. It can also serve as the basis for divorce proceedings by the deserted spouse. However, desertion does not end the legal obligations, only the social ones. It is difficult to know the frequency of desertion because public records are incomplete. Baber estimated that about 100,000 desertions occur per year, approximately one to every four divorces.[3] Others, such as Kephart, consider Baber's estimate conservative and postulate that the ratio of desertion to divorce is more likely one to one.[4]

Desertion is apparently a more masculine than feminine thing to do. Moreover, there is a high degree of recidivism, repetition of the act. Baber's findings suggest that the male typically deserts for the first time during the first ten years of marriage, when he is approximately thirty-three years of age.[5] Kephart's research uncovered a relationship between desertion and alcoholism.[6]

Desertion has been described as the "poor man's divorce," because divorce is expensive and lower-class people cannot afford the legal fees. Kephart, however, dispelled this myth. Almost half of the desertions he studied among whites were by members of the upper segment of the occupational hierarchy (skilled labor and above).[7] The table below shows that at every occupational level, the percentages of divorce and desertion are very similar. We can also see that both percentages increase as we go down the social-class scale, except for the very lowest occupational level, where the rates go down again. Most investigators explain the lowered rates among unskilled workers on the basis of their ignorance of the possibility of terminating marriages, legally or illegally, religious beliefs, or inertia.

MALE DESERTERS AND DIVORCÉS, BY OCCUPATION—
FIRST MARRIAGES, PHILADELPHIA, 1950

Occupational Category	Divorce Sample (N = 939)	Desertion Cases (N = 922)	Divorce Minus Desertion (Per cent Difference)
Professionals	4.9%	3.1%	+1.8
Proprietors	4.4	8.7	−4.3
Clerical and sales	20.4	14.8	+5.6
Skilled	20.0	21.6	−1.6
Semi-skilled	38.6	37.0	+1.6
Labor-Service	11.7	14.8	−3.1

SOURCE: William M. Kephart, "Occupational Level and Marital Disruption," *American Sociological Review* (August 1955), p. 462.

Race is another variable often believed to be associated with desertion. Kephart studied this variable also and found that when social class is held constant, there is very little difference between whites and blacks in rates of desertion. Thus, social class is a more powerful influence than race in determining who will desert. According to Bell, "This would indicate that the man's failure in the economic role sometimes leads to his rejecting his family roles. In other words, for some men, success in the occupational role may be a necessary precondition to maintaining family roles."[8]

In another study, Monahan and Kephart examined the relationship between desertion and religion.[9] Among whites, they found that Catholics are over-represented in proportion to their number in the population by about 40 per cent, Jews are under-represented by about 40 per cent, and Protestants are under-represented by 25 per cent. These researchers explain these findings by noting that the religious dogma of the Catholic Church prohibits divorce; thus, most Catholics are forced to desert if they wish to end a marriage. Moreover, Catholics are over-represented in the lower classes, and these classes have higher divorce and desertion rates. Jews, on the other hand, have a strong norm for the stability of the family and, in addition, are disproportionately represented in the upper socio-economic strata.

To summarize what is known about desertion, we can say first that it is predominantly male behavior, with a high percentage of recidivism. Desertion is not a poor man's divorce, in spite of popular belief. Although the desertion rates are higher as we go down the social hierarchy, the divorce rates are correspondingly higher also, so that we find that divorce and desertion rates are approximately the same regardless of social class.

The research indicates that children are more likely to be present in desertion than in divorce. But the figures are not to be taken at face value. Bell[10] suggests the following reasons for such findings: (1) A woman with children is more likely to seek public assistance when her husband deserts than a childless woman in the same predicament. This means that deserted women with children more often come to public attention, not necessarily that such women are more apt to be deserted. (2) Because of the high rate of recidivism among male deserters, the couple probably continue to have children. (3) Marriages that terminate in desertion are generally longer in duration than marriages that terminate in divorce, thus increasing the probability of large families. About 30 per cent of all divorces occur within less than four years of marriage and more than 50 per cent occur within less than eight years.[11] Desertion, on the other hand, tends to occur some time around the tenth year. (4) Finally, Bell believes that the fact that there are children probably exacerbates the male's feelings of inadequacy or his desire to avoid responsibility. In other words, children may be a precipitating factor in desertion.

Legal Separation

Separation means that a marriage is socially but not legally ended. The couple are required to live apart; they may not have sexual access to each other; and they cannot marry anyone else. At the same time, the husband is expected to continue his financial responsibilities. Separation, then, is a limited or partial divorce.

Many states have no grounds for legal separation—the status simply does not exist. In those states in which it does exist, grounds for separation vary and are frequently rather arbitrary. The most commonly allowed grounds are desertion and cruelty. Some states do not include adultery as ground for separation, even though they include it as a ground for divorce. This means that it may be legal to get a divorce on grounds that are not legal for separation!

Legal separation is not a popular means of terminating marriage in this country; it accounts for only 2 per cent of all terminations. Nevertheless, it can be useful. It can provide a period of time before divorce, during which couples may reconsider and reconcile. It can provide Catholics, who are forbidden to divorce, with a way out of marriage. Still, legal separation is rare, and there is evidence suggesting that it is becoming rarer as divorce laws become more flexible and more liberal.

There are, of course, many couples who separate without recourse to legal proceedings. Informal separation should not be confused with desertion. In the former situation, each spouse knows the whereabouts of the other; there is some accord about monetary matters and possessions; and they have separated by mutual consent. Such separations may be of long or short duration. They may lead to divorce or to reconciliation. They may be permanent or temporary. They may represent just a preliminary stage in the process of divorce.

Divorce

There is no known society in the world that does not in some way allow for divorce. In ancient times Hebrew husbands could obtain a divorce essentially by announcing, "I divorce thee." Divorce was a personal matter; neither the church nor the state manifested any concern. This was true not only for the Hebrews but also for the Greeks, the Romans, and the early Teutonic tribes.

Divorce was the husband's prerogative in patriarchal societies, and barrenness and adultery on the part of the female were the two most common grounds. However, the husband was typically required to return the bride-price or dowry, if he divorced his wife for any other reason, and this often acted as a deterrent. Thus, although it was relatively easy to get rid of a wife, divorce was not a usual event because the cost extracted by the bride's kinsmen could be very high. It was not until the time of the Romans that women could divorce their husbands at all; Roman matrons became famous for the ease with which they shed their mates and acquired new ones.

When the Christians came to power, they reacted against what they regarded as immoral behavior and decadence in the Roman Empire. Celibacy was most desirable, but if one did marry, faithfulness was expected. Divorce was permitted if one wished to live a celibate life or if one's spouse had committed adultery; there were no other grounds.

At the Council of Trent in the sixteenth century, the canon law regarding marriage and marital dissolution was clarified. Marriage was considered a permanent relationship, dissolvable only by death. However, a separation might be granted if one's spouse were guilty of adultery, heresy, or cruelty. An annulment could be obtained if one was deserted by a non-believing spouse or in the event that the spouse had committed incest or bigamy.

The Reformation brought about some change in the divorce situation. Protestant churches permitted divorce on grounds of adultery or desertion, cruelty, or refusal to engage in sexual relations.

The Puritans brought their anti-church feelings with them to the new world, and this meant that they allowed absolute divorce, which the Church of England forbade. Furthermore, the Puritans moved control over marriage and divorce out of the jurisdiction of the church and into the province of the state, which granted divorce through the state legislatures, primarily on the grounds of desertion and adultery. By the beginning of the nineteenth century, divorce was under the control of civil courts. Nevertheless, the legislatures continued to define the grounds for divorce.

Divorce today in the United States can be defined as the legal termination of a marriage, allowing both parties the right to live separate from each other and to marry again if either should choose to do so. The marriage is both legally and socially terminated, although in most instances the man is required to continue to support his children until they are of age and his wife until she remarries.

There are several ways of looking at divorce rates. Any way, however, reveals that, next to Egypt, the United States has the highest divorce rate in the world, and it is climbing. At the beginning of this century approximately one in every eight marriages ended in divorce. Today, approximately one in four ends in divorce. Between 1890 and 1971, the ratio of divorces to marriages increased dramatically from about 1:17 to about 1:3; the actual figures were 33,000 divorces to 570,000 marriages in 1890, and 768,000 divorces to 2,196,000 marriages in 1971.[12] "Divorce has been increasing since 1962 [after a peak year in 1946], but provisional data indicate that increases in both number and rate became more pronounced in 1968 and 1969."[13] The number of divorces has increased more rapidly than our total population and our married population. Statisticians attribute this increase in the number of divorces in part to the increase in the married population, particularly among young people, who have a higher probability of divorce than older people; and in part to changes in the size and age distribution of the population.[14] The median age at divorce for both men and women declined from 1963 to 1967, as did the median length of marriage, from 7.5 to 7.1 years.

The laws covering divorce are slightly less than chaotic. We have no over-all federal regulations, and the laws vary greatly in all fifty states and the District of Columbia. Some of these laws are clearly archaic. For example, if a couple should agree that they both prefer to be divorced from each other and that their marriage is a failure —they could be refused a divorce in court, on the ground of collusion. Collusion is defined as any agreement between two or more people by which they try to obtain a result—in this case divorce—by an imposition on the court.[14] Yet this is frequently the case. Often two people agree they are incompatible; yet incompatibility is cause for divorce in only one state. Therefore, the parties are obliged to find a legal cause for divorce and claim that it applies to their case. This makes our laws a farce because collusion is more often than not prominent in divorce. The reason for the prohibition of collusion is that our laws are based largely on the notion that divorce is an adversary procedure. This means that one of the spouses must be "innocent" and the other "guilty."

Three possible factors come into play, any of which can lead to the refusal of divorce. One is called *condonation*. If a wife sues her husband for divorce on the ground of adultery but acknowledges in court that she forgives him or shows forgiveness by her actions (such as having sexual relations with him), the divorce may be refused because one cannot forgive an offense that is the basis for divorce. A second factor is called *recrimination*. Again, let us imagine the woman using adultery as ground for divorce. If her husband admits that he has engaged in sexual activity with another woman but at the same time charges that his wife also committed adultery, no divorce would be granted. Recrimination means that there are two guilty people, not one innocent and one guilty; therefore, neither has the right to relief. At this writing, the notion of recrimination is being dropped by several states which are adopting a "no fault" procedure. Finally, there is *connivance*. The same wife is still suing her husband for divorce on ground of adultery. This time, however, she informs the court that she herself is rather disinterested in sex and therefore agreed that her husband should seek sexual satisfaction outside the marriage. Again, the judge would not grant the divorce because if someone consents to any kind of behavior, he cannot claim to be injured by it. Therefore, there is no injured party, and no divorce is possible.

It should be clear to the reader that our divorce laws are in great need of revision. Grounds for divorce are at present unrealistic and do not reflect anything more than the inventive ability of the parties concerned and their lawyers. We now have legal reasons for divorce and "real" reasons for divorce, and rarely do the twain meet. One popular, wastepaper-basket legal ground for divorce is cruelty, which has come to mean anything and nothing. Another popular reason is adultery, which is an acceptable ground in every state in the union. But these legal grounds for divorce are frequently totally unrelated to the "real" reasons. One study of lawyers found that the most common real reasons were financial difficulties, unprovable infidelity, alcoholism, and general incompatibility, in that order.[15]

CHILDREN OF DIVORCE

It has been estimated that there are about one million children under eighteen years of age living with a divorced parent.[16] Approximately 40 per cent of divorcing couples have no children, 40 per cent have one or two, and 20 per cent have three or more. These children, of course, cause the greatest amount of concern, both personal and social, in divorce. Almost everyone, social scientist and layman alike, has believed that divorce has negative effects on children. American norms hold that parents must place their parental roles ahead of their marital roles, at least until the children are old enough so that a divorce will not be too destructive. The questions are, then: Are children better off in homes in which the parents are unhappy together, or is it better for the children to live with just one, happy or unhappy, divorced parent? Are unhappy spouses good parents? Can they set aside their personal problems to give love and attention to their children?

Several sociologists have investigated these questions, and the findings are generally in agreement: Children from divorced homes show no more psychological damage than children in intact unhappy homes.[17] There is no doubt that in the event of divorce the child must make readjustments in his relations with both parents, especially the absent one, who is usually the father. This may mean seeing less of the father, in less homelike surroundings, and less spontaneously. However, many fathers who live with their wives are hardly visible to their children and are not very influential. There is little doubt that some divorced parents use their children as pawns to hurt each other, but children may be used in the same way in unbroken homes.

In most situations of divorce, however, there are problems that must be solved. Generally, because she retains custody of the children, the mother continues in the parental role—albeit the role often requires expansion. The father plays a smaller part in his children's lives after a divorce, especially if the mother remarries. (We will discuss this in more detail when we discuss remarriage, in Chapter 8.)

ALIMONY AND CHILD SUPPORT

In almost every state a husband is required to support his former wife, usually until she remarries, but occasionally for a stated number of years. The amount of alimony awarded is based upon the husband's present income, the couple's previous standard of living, the duration of the marriage, the wife's ability to be self-supporting, and the separation agreement made between the parties. In theory, alimony should make it possible for the wife to maintain the standard of living she enjoyed during her marriage. In fact, the amount generally falls far short of that goal. Infrequently, instead of alimony the husband is required to make a cash settlement at the time of the divorce.

Alimony is distinct from child support. Alimony is paid to the wife in almost all cases and almost always ends when she remarries or becomes self-supporting. Child support continues until the child is of legal age—eighteen or twenty-one, depending on the jurisdiction. Fathers are almost never excused from supporting their children. Like alimony, child support is usually inadequate.

SOCIAL FACTORS IN DIVORCE

Most of the evidence suggests that blacks have higher divorce rates than whites at all income, occupational, and educational levels.[18] However, racial data on divorce tend to be inadequate. As Kephart suggested, social class is a powerful intervening variable.

It is expected that black divorce rates will rise even higher as blacks make increasing strides toward social and financial equality. There are more black lawyers, and they stress divorce as the legal way to end marriage when desired. Moreover, as blacks move into the mainstream, they will be better able to afford the cost of divorce.

Protestants are more likely to divorce than either Jews or Catholics. Only 4 per cent of all Jews divorce, and yet they are the religious group most accepting of divorce. Catholics, as expected, are the most strongly opposed. Few Jews divorce for the same reasons few are involved in desertion: because they value family stability and are more likely to be in the upper socio-economic strata.[19]

Low divorce rates are clearly relate to religiosity. The more religious the Jew, the less likely he is to divorce.[20] Divorce rates are highest among interreligious marriages and people with no religious affiliation at all. It has also been found that previously married people are more likely to marry outside their religion than those who have never been married before. "It may be," says Bell, "that people who get a divorce are by definition less restrictive in their views and as a result may be more willing to have a mixed marriage. In other words, both divorce and marrying outside one's religion are mild forms of social deviancy that may go together."[21]

Apparently there is a relationship between youthful marriage and divorce. At the same time, those who marry young tend to have less education than those who delay marriage. Thus, the combination of youth and low educational level seems to encourage divorce. Glick suggests that if a woman marries before she is eighteen, she is three times more likely to be divorced than her sisters who marry between the ages of twenty-two and twenty-four.[22]

Divorce rates are lower in rural areas than in urban areas. Furthermore, divorce rates differ by region of the country, with the West having the highest rates and the Northeast the lowest. Reiss claims that this difference cannot be accounted for by migratory divorce patterns—that is, by people leaving their home state to get a divorce in one with more flexible laws.[23] He believes that our patterns of settlement are a better explanation. The East was settled first and therefore has a more stabilized pattern of social life than a state like California, which is growing rapidly.

We noted earlier (p. 169) the inverse correlation between social class (using the husband's occupation as a measure) and divorce. This is contrary to the popular notion that the upper classes are forever running to divorce courts.

Goode says that it is not the obvious factors like high education and income that lead to the relatively low divorce rates among the professional, proprietary, and clerical groups.[24] Rather, it is a style of life: stable employment, few economic problems, time for leisure and interaction, later marriage. It is not social class *per se,* then, that determines the probability of divorce so much as it is the kind of life one is likely to lead if one is a member of a certain social class.

DIVORCE THEORIES

There are many explanations for divorce rates, most of which tend to explain either too much or not enough. We will review five of the best-known ones: industrial growth theory, kinship theory, resources-demands theory, friendship theory, and love.

Industrial Growth Theory

We can trace this theory back to Engels and to Durkheim. Engels believed that monogamy is instrumental in subjugating women because the male and the female stand in the same relationship as the owner of the means of production and the worker. Just as he supported the idea that there can be full equality among human beings only when all work is of equal social value, so he believed that there could be equality between the sexes only when man's work and woman's work became unidentifiable as such.

Engels argued that as industrialization increased, women would leave the home to work in the factory because their labor would be needed by the society. Child rearing would become a community concern and responsibility. With women doing the same kind of work as men, their relationship would improve because no longer would there be one group in power and another powerless. In short, Engels posited that as industrialization grows, marriage will become more stable.

Durkheim also addressed himself to the linkage between industrial development and marriage and family patterns. As industry grows, families become smaller, and personal ties replace economic and moral ties. These interpersonal ties bind the members of the family even closer as they increasingly require a refuge from the impersonality of the world of work.

By the twentieth century many sociologists were presenting opposing theories, but based on the same variables as those suggested by Engels and Durkheim. Unlike Engels and Durkheim, however, they had reliable data and were able to see the steady rise in the divorce rate. They blamed industrialization and urban growth for this phenomenon. In 1945, Burgess and Locke offered their famous theory of family change.[25] Their basic point was that industrial growth leads to a change from an institutional-type family to a companionship-type family. The former type is rooted in notions of permanence and responsibility; the latter, in ideas of ego satisfaction, with divorce as the escape hatch. The institutional family works together as one unit and is pressured by the community to avoid divorce. The companionship family, on the other hand, does not form one work unit. City living, because it offers diversity, opportunity, and anonymity, tends to splinter the family.

Burgess and Locke believed that industrialization causes increased divorce rates by creating new pressures in family life during a transitional period. However, they also believed that people will adjust to city life and that eventually a better form of the family will emerge.

Thus the industrial growth theory explains changes in divorce rates by postulating that the family will need to modify its goals, values, power bases, etc., as industrialization dominates social life. During the transition, the rates will rise; after its completion, they will decrease.

Kinship Theory

Anthropologists have been searching for a single theory to account for divorce rates all over the world. The kinship theory was originally posited by Max Gluckman, who suggested that divorce patterns are part of a society's kinship pattern.[26]

In patrilineal societies, kinship is traced through the male line and divorce is rare. The wife actually bears children in order to provide her husband's family with kinsmen. Thus, legitimacy and illegitimacy become extremely important. In matrilineal societies, where kinship is traced through the female line, divorce rates increase. The wife has children for her own kindred; therefore, paternity is unimportant. In our society, which is bilateral, meaning that a person traces his descent from both sides of his family, mother and father, divorce rates may be either high or low. Farber supports this notion by pointing out that bilaterality is useful in modern society because it makes little issue of kinship; therefore there are no strong taboos against divorce.[27]

This theory has been severely criticized on two grounds. One is that many societies in the Human Relations Area Files simply do not fit the theory. Second, divorce rates in a society can change without any accompanying change in the kinship system. The United States is a prime example. Obviously, we cannot use one variable—in this case, the kinship system—to explain change in another variable—the divorce rate—if the first one does not itself change. In addition, even if the kinship systems did change with the divorce rates, this would not prove that kinship systems caused the rate change.

Resources-Demands Theory

This theory states that each marriage has inner resources and external demands made upon it. When there is a favorable balance between the resources and the demands, the marriage will succeed. When the divorce rate rises in a society, something has tipped the balance between the resources and the demands.

Resources refers to any personal, material, or social qualities a couple may have that help them in coping with demands. For example, if one or both brought a great deal of money into the marriage, if they have counseling help available, if one or both has a high level of intelligence and education, these factors may help them to deal with outside pressures. *Demands* are anything that impede the couple's happiness or make it difficult to function in the marriage. One example is poor health; others are alcoholism, promiscuity, joblessness, or ignorance.

Benson has constructed a list of eight trends in our society, of which he believes that three will become resources.[28] One is more education for more people. Research has always shown that marital success is associated with high education. Second, greater wealth per capita is also empirically related to marital success. Third, although the correlation between health and marital adjustment has not been researched, it is reasonable to suppose that better health care and longer life expectancy will contribute to marital resources.

Benson sees three of his eight trends as demands. One is social diversity, which means that heterogeneous groups will be thrown into greater and greater contact with each other as cities grow larger. Most evidence shows that heterogeneity is associated with divorce. The second trend likely to become a demand is the decline of traditional controls. This means that people will have greater freedom, including the freedom to dissolve unhappy marriages. Third, increased geographic mobility, which Benson says can be a resource because it increases job opportunities, is more likely to become a demand because it increases opportunities to meet new people who may become marriage partners.

The remaining two trends Benson sees as imponderables. One is the rising status of women. On the one hand, the liberation of women may mean that they will enjoy more companionable marriage with their husbands, thus keeping marriages intact. On the other hand, the wife will have less need to stay in any marriage for security, either emotional or financial. The other trend is increased knowledge of interpersonal relations. Benson sees this as a possible resource or demand. If one member of the couple learns about himself, he will have more understanding of his own behavior and motives and thus may become easier to live with. On the other hand, he may also have greater understanding of his mate and may begin to interpret his actions. "When couples start analyzing each other with the concepts of modern psychology, they sometimes unleash forces beyond their control."[29]

Benson notes also that there is one other factor that stands between the resource and the demand aspects of marriage. This is easier divorce. Thus, he thinks the theory should be called: Resources-accessibility of divorce-demands theory. The balance between resources and demands remains crucial, but the availability of divorce is a critical intervening factor. Divorce, when readily available, then can become a sensitive index to changing marital patterns.

Friendship Theory

It has been noted by many sociologists that urban life tends to make people anonymous, thereby loosening social controls. However, some couples have more friends than others, and some have more friends in common. Ackerman feels that marital success is more likely when the couple tends to have shared friendships than when it has separate friendships because there is then more social control.[30] In other words, while we know that homogamy is more conducive to successful marriage than heterogamy, Ackerman suggests that homogamy must extend beyond social-background characteristics into homogamous friendships. The probability of divorce is influenced by the couple's network of affiliations. Conjunctive affiliations, meaning that the couple share almost all their friendships, make divorce less likely. Disjunctive affiliations, meaning that they have separate friendship circles, make divorce more likely.

It seems to me that this theory is weak. Obviously, city life encourages heterogeneity in marriage and in friendship groups. However, why should diversity make divorce more likely? One could reverse Ackerman's interpretation and say that as each spouse brings new and different people into the social orbit of the marriage, there could be greater variation, novelty, and interest, thus enlivening the relationship. They could widen each other's horizons in this way, whereas having the same friends could lead to boredom. In addition, friends, whether shared or not, can still offer social control. The question remains an open one.

Love and Industrialization

Reiss believes that love is an important variable to consider in divorce.[31] In societies that stress love as the only reason for marriage, people are more likely to become disillusioned later and to seek a way out.

Love is the only acceptable basis for marriage in our society. But for love to endure, the two people must grow at a similar pace and in the same direction. With longer life spans, increased opportunity for mobility and change (both external and internal), and more and more choices, it seems unrealistic to assume that most couples who are "in love" at age twenty will grow together, keep the same values, and continue to have the same desires and goals for sixty years. When people lived shorter lives, there was less time for boredom and less need for variety in life experience. Fewer people lived long enough to be married for twenty-five years. Golden wedding anniversaries were relatively unheard of. Now we marry in our early twenties and may live well into our eighties. Sixty years is a long time with one mate.

Just to complicate matters, there are more options open to us today. In the past, when people married they continued to live in the same town or even on the same street where they had been born. Now we are more mobile. Companies transfer their employees more readily. Rapid transportation systems allow us to live a greater distance from our place of work. There is more money available for travel, clothes, and entertainment. We are able to make more contact with more people in a shorter period of time. Technology grants us more leisure. The result of all this is that we have more choices than before. In short, we have more experience with variations, and the consequences are that we begin to desire more new experiences—even in the area of marriage. All this places strain on modern marriages.

At the current status of our technology, the odds are against love's enduring " 'til death us do part." Too many other things may part a couple before death gets an opportunity. Not only may the available variety tempt the partners to seek change, but also as we live longer and in more varied ways during each life-span, our needs and goals may change, so that we will demand different characteristics and personality traits in our mates over time.

Furthermore, there is reason to assume that our technology will continue to expand and our life-spans will continue to lengthen. Very soon we will be forced to acknowledge that permanent marital happiness is almost impossible to achieve, that marriage cannot endure forever, and that as we reach new stages of development we will need to seek new partners who have attained that plateau at the same time. Then, perhaps, we can face divorce without guilt, embarrassment, or shock.

As I suggested earlier, freedom of choice in marriage accelerated during the nineteenth century as our society became more industrialized and urbanized. Reiss feels that urban growth means greater autonomy in mate selection, which, in turn, increases the emphasis on love. Love is more easily lost than a sense of responsibility and duty, so that divorce is more likely to follow.

Compared with a culture wherein parents make the choice of mate, they [modern American young people] are more likely to divorce if the interpersonal relationship is of poor quality. In cultures where mate choice is more parentally controlled, I would expect the lack of love to lead not so much to divorce as to adultery, separation, or other compensatory activities that would still allow the marital union to remain technically intact. The more one is culturally taught to seek love as the basis for marriage, the more likely it is that one will entirely break the marriage and go seek another love when the original love relationship deteriorates.[32]

Widowhood

Widowhood is different from the other types of marital terminations we have discussed because it is involuntary, while the others, for at least one partner, are voluntary, and because the widowed tend to be older: the average age of widows is fifty. One quarter of all men and nearly one half of all women are widowed by the time they are sixty-five years old. The chance of both partners remaining alive declines with each passing year. Unlike any of the other possible endings for marriage, widowhood provides recognizable statuses, widow and widower, with reasonably clear rights and obligations, defining behavior.

However, as the structure and the functions of the family in America change, widowed people are finding themselves confronted with new problems. Lopata points out that in the past, surviving spouses generally went to live with adult married children or other relatives.[33] Today, however, they frequently live alone. Another problem for people whose mates die, and also, of course, for those who are divorced, is that our society is structured around the pair. There is very little room for the single person. But those who have never married have an easier time of it than widowed people because they have structured their lives around other single people or around their occupations. Widows and widowers are suddenly ejected out of the couple world, with which they have long familiarity, and into a world with which they have had no experience.

Widows and widowers are not in exactly the same statuses, and generally the female role is more difficult in many respects. One reason for this is that marriage is the primary status for a woman, and the loss of it means a much greater gap in her life. Men, as I have said, are defined primarily by occupation. Upon the death of a spouse, women lose their basic role; men retain theirs. Another reason is that widowers are more likely to remarry than widows because people are more likely to encourage them to do so and because older men have a wider choice of possible spouses than older women. Third, elderly widows are not accustomed to being alone in the social world and therefore, out of fear, tend to restrict their social activities and stay at home, where they feel less threatened. Finally, a widow is likely to have more severe financial problems than a widower, because her income stops when her husband dies, because she is inexperienced in handling money, or because she is unemployed or unemployable. Rosow found that almost one quarter of the widows he studied had no income whatsoever, nearly three quarters had less than $1,000 per year, and only one tenth had over $2,000 per year.[34]

The financial aspect is very important because it permeates or causes problems in other areas of the widow's life. Money intervenes in the widow's relationships with her children. She may become financially dependent on them at a time in their life when they can least afford to help her because they are rearing their own children. It may be necessary for a widow to seek public assistance.

It is, of course, true that many widows live with their adult children. But most would prefer to live alone if they could afford to do so and if their health permitted it. At this time, however, there is a gradual increase in the number who do live alone.[35]

Widowers also have a poor time of it. Most widows' problems are basically financial; widowers are generally better off financially, but they suffer from other kinds of problems. The suicide rate for widows between sixty-five and seventy-five gradually drops while it increases for widowers in the same age period. Widowers in general are less healthy than widows and less capable of taking care of their routine needs. Moreover, women more easily adjust to living in their children's homes or in nursing homes. There are also more widows in the world than widowers, and therefore women are more likely to have friends among their peers than men are, although there is less probability of remarriage for them. Besides, women are better socialized in integrative skills than men and can form and maintain friendships more easily.

Thus the skills that women acquire during their marital years are more useful when they are no longer part of a couple than those men acquire. Men are held together on the basis of their occupations and because widowed men are generally retired, the basic bond they have with other men is broken. This problem is more closely related to age than marital state.

One more complication for men should be noted. Retirement usually means freedom, but it also means loss of power, loss of purpose, and loss of some status, prestige, sense of self-worth, and self-respect. Widowhood, on the other hand, denotes no such loss. Blood and Wolfe showed that the husband's power in the home is highest during the years of youth and child rearing; then it gradually diminishes through the life cycle, finally dropping very sharply when the man retires.[36]

Widowhood has a very different social meaning from divorce. It is assumed that the marriage would have continued if death had not intervened. The widowed person, then, is not seen as a failure. No matter how unhappy the marriage may actually have been, the bereaved survivor receives sympathy and social support to a greater extent than the divorced person does. Nevertheless, widowhood is a sad status in our society. Almost inevitably it carries with it problems of ill health, insufficient money, unemployment, and strained social relations with one's children and one's friends for both men and women.

The worst problem, however, is loneliness.[37] Widowed people are in two unacceptable categories: they are single in a married society, and they are old in a young society. Furthermore, as we said, they are often poor, ill, and unemployable, three more social categories that receive little approval. Our society hides our elderly widows and widowers and tends to avoid their company because they remind us of what may happen to us some day. The result for them is devastating isolation and loneliness.

MARITAL TERMINATIONS IN THE FUTURE

To speak of changes in the ways we will terminate marriage requires acceptance of my previous prediction that marriage itself, in both its structure and its functions, will undergo radical change by the year 2000. Before I turn to that, however, let us look at how other sociologists view marital termination in the future, assuming that there will be no radical changes in the basic structure and functions of marriage as it is today. The first three options I described—annulment, legal separation, and desertion—are not susceptible to prediction, first, because the rates are very low and have changed very little over time and, further, because the rates and percentages are not reliable, since proper records are not generally maintained. We will discuss, then, the future of divorce and widowhood only.

Widowhood

Very few family sociologists have discussed the probable future trends of widowhood. Parke and Glick suggest that as a result of a probable change in our sex ratio during the marriageable years, the gap in age between husband and wife will narrow.[38] This would mean that people would live together longer and that there would be fewer widows and widowers in the population.

I predict, therefore, that there will be fewer widowed people in our society by 2000. A great deal of our technology and our increasing psychological and sociological knowledge are being brought to bear to make this prediction a reality.

Divorce

Many sociologists have tried to analyze the meaning of divorce trends, and their interpretations differ. Benson is one who believes that the rate will accelerate because incompatibility is becoming a morally and legally acceptable reason for divorce.[39] Benson explains that as we continue to stress the importance of ego satisfaction in a marital relationship, and as our divorce laws continue to become more flexible, permanent availability will become the norm.

Reiss apparently agrees with Benson. "If love-based marriage promotes high divorce rates and if urban industrial growth promotes love-based marriage, then it follows that divorce rates will increase as a society increases its urban industrial development."[40]

Christensen and Johnsen also predict that divorce rates will rise, although they are more tentative in arriving at this conclusion.[41]

These writers note worldwide interest and concern over a population explosion, which they feel has had a significant impact on the family in the United States. The population revolution has forced us to perfect contraceptive devices and dispense them widely. This, in turn, means smaller families, which could have the consequence, among others, of reduced restrictions on divorce. Of course, reducing the restrictions on divorce does not necessarily mean that there will be more divorce, but that seems to be the implication.

Toffler also sees divorce as on the rise.[42] He feels that people move around more, thus increasing the number of relationships they have and decreasing the duration of each relationship. In the past, people classified relations among family members, especially between husbands and wives, as long term. Now, according to Toffler, this is changing, and we will soon be entering marriage with the expectation that it will not last for a lifetime—probably not longer than a few years. This is in accord with Benson's belief that permanent availability will be the norm.

Nye places values centrally in his discussion of the future of marriage. He identifies instrumental values as "the desirability which becomes attached to an object, experience, or event because the property has become identified as necessary or effective in producing an outcome desired by the individual or the society."[43] Intrinsic values are those "objects, events, and experiences that are valued for their own sake without reference to still other consequences which flow from them."[44] Nye posits that instrumental values will become primary in marriage and that there will be many latent consequences flowing from this orientation, all of which can readily lead to an increase in the divorce rate. He lists increased equality for women, the transfer of child-care responsibilities to agents other than the mother, a declining birth rate, and an increased marriage age for females. If these things come to pass, Nye predicts that we will have more divorce.

I have given a few examples of sociologists who believe that more people will be divorced in the future. There are many who disagree strongly with this viewpoint. Parke and Glick, for example, note that there has been a steady decrease in the number of teenage marriages and a general rise in our standard of living.[45] Since youth and low income have always been correlated with poor marital adjustment, these facts suggest that marriage will become more stable and the divorce rate will go down.

Mogey offers another reason to believe that family stability will increase in the future.[46] He hypothesizes that fathers will become increasingly involved in family life, and that as the father role is redefined in terms of greater visibility, the marital bond will strengthen. Mogey made this prediction in 1957, before either the women's liberation movement or the youth movement began to advocate greater participation by men in family life. His forecast is proving remarkably accurate.

Hobart, like Nye, sees the concept of value as dominant in any analysis of the family in the future. He argues that we are currently engaged in a value conflict between things and people. "As a society we tend to love things and use people, rather than the reverse."[47] This value conflict is a major source of family instability. Hobart describes the modern family as a loosely knit group in process of deterioration because the members are confused and alienated. Most significant, he thinks that the family is rapidly losing the important functions of companionship and socialization. Hobart suggests, however, that we are about to experience a value revolution, and that the family that emerges will have a less explicit structure than the current family, the members will be more individuated, and each will value the others for their intrinsic worth. In the end, Hobart opts for the preservation of our marriage institution and predicts that if we can overcome the value conflict, marriage will become more stable than ever. He sees a new basis for a deeper commitment and a "renewed emphasis on *being* rather than on *doing*."[48]

Edwards engaged in a polemic with Hobart, challenging the primacy of the role of values. Instead, Edwards believes that our weakened family ties are the result of our strengthened orientation to our economic institution. In other words, our society is so preoccupied with the desire for new material benefits that this attitude "permeates virtually all social relationships, including that between husband and wife and the progeny."[49] Our pragmatic attitude invades marriage as it invades every area of life. Edwards sees this as beneficial to the family institution because marriages are now "more likely to be based on reason rather than the impulses of habit."[50]

Burchinal has made a very thoughtful contribution to the literature on the future direction of marital dissolution.[51] First he notes that rural and urban family and marriage patterns are converging. The two types of family are now similar in size (moderate), decision-making patterns, levels of education, fertility rates, and kinship networks. Burchinal expects that divorce rates either will remain constant or will decrease slowly, for several reasons, including developing socialization patterns that stress competence in interpersonal relations, greater freedom of choice in mate selection, greater sexual equality and flexibility in male and female roles, increased concern with sexual pleasure for both men and women, less rigid and puritanical attitudes toward premarital sex, more joy in child rearing, higher standards of living in general, new vigor in extended-kin relations, professionalization of marital and parental roles, governmental programs which help the family, and emergent norms of marital success based on interpersonal satisfaction.

In other words, Burchinal sees the companionship marriage as superior to the traditional type. "At present, it seems that the voluntary commitment to marriage based upon companionship and mutual development . . . is a stronger bond for marriage than functional economic interdependence and the social and legal sanctions which held traditional families together."[52]

How can I summarize the expectations of family sociologists? Obviously they are divided in their opinions on divorce rates of the future; yet the difference of opinion may actually be more superficial than first appearances indicate. There is, first of all, considerable agreement on what the trends are; the disagreement arises as to their meaning.

What are these trends? First, industrialization and urban growth will continue, and both of these will probably lead to less social control and more freedom in mate selection and in sexual activities. Second, technology will continue to perfect contraceptive methods, to raise the standard of living, to lengthen our lives, and to improve our health. Third, equality between the sexes will increase, meaning smaller families, shared child care, and more working mothers. Fourth, reasons for marriage are changing. People are no longer marrying for utilitarian reasons but, rather, are seeking mates for the satisfaction of ego-needs, and such goals in marriage are being accepted more by the society.

These trends can be interpreted to mean that divorce rates will rise; on the other hand, I can take the same trends and interpret them to mean that the rate will go down. Industrialization, urban growth, and technological development all mean that people will become more independent, better educated, and freer in their outlooks on life. Such characteristics must mean changing values, especially when it comes to marriage. We will contract parental marriage only because we truly believe that marriage will make our lives happier, and for no other reason. We will marry later and take time to choose carefully. We will no longer marry because of financial and social pressures. Thus, when we do marry, we will do so with the expectation that the relationship will last, at least through the child-rearing years—the period that most concerns society.

It is easy to turn this argument around and say that this same freedom from outside pressure and the new emphasis on personal gratification could also be conducive to quick divorce. However, I believe that when the reasons for marriage change and education enables us to consider our actions more clearly, there will be less need to rectify unnecessary mistakes because we will make fewer of them. We will be less likely to marry for the wrong reasons.

Now let us consider what changes will occur in the divorce rates if marriage can be restructured in several ways, as I suggested in Chapter 5. To review, for a moment, I predicted that four types of marriages would be institutionalized in the United States. Premarriage would be the marriage of young people, a licensed union permitting them to live together and cohabit but not to have children. Parental marriage would license people to have families. Serial monogamy would be acceptable after the responsibility of child rearing had been discharged. Polygyny would be the form of marriage for later life, to relieve the loneliness and financial problems of old age.

We can expect a high divorce rate, perhaps as high as 50 to 75 per cent of all marriages, among those in the premarriage arrangement. However, this need not be seen as detrimental to anyone because there can be no societal repercussions. These marriages will carry no postmarital responsibilities for either the woman or the man. There would be no children from these marriages; therefore, there would be no questions of child support, custody, or visitation. All property would be equally divided; there would be no alimony.

In short, such marriages could easily be dissolved with little harm to the society or to the individual.

Because parental marriage would require prior satisfaction of many conditions—that is, proof of emotional and financial stability —we could expect that during these childbearing and child-rearing years the divorce rate would be very low. Laws would be stringent, and negative social sanctions would attach to divorce during this part of the life cycle. Society would expect that individuals entering parental marriage would be fully prepared to face and resolve the problems inherent in it and that they would not be likely to fail.

I predict that, during the third period of married life, divorce would be institutionalized and simple. This is the time for serial monogamy, and people would almost be expected to have short-term relationships. It may seem surprising that I do not expect a high divorce rate during this period, despite the permissiveness. Most of these people will be in their forties; they will probably have had at least two mates already. It is likely that they will not wish to disrupt their lives so frequently as society will permit. As Linder says, most people are lazy and find it distasteful to disorganize their lives if their present relationship is remotely bearable.[53] Thus, I predict only a moderately high divorce rate (perhaps between 25 and 30 per cent of all serial marriages) during the serial-monogamy period, with most people divorcing once, if at all.

I would also predict an extremely low divorce rate during the last part of the marriage cycle, polygyny. The older people involved in these relationships are unlikely to want any disruption in their lives. They will be seeking peace, comfort, companionship, and financial and emotional security. I suggest that divorce after sixty-five in polygynous marriage would be very rare.

To summarize, it is expected that, even if the form of marriage does not change, divorce rates will drop because people will marry with less social pressure and, therefore, for more mature and personal reasons. Because they will have married more sensibly, the probabilities are that they will stay married.

If pluralistic types of marriage become institutionalized in our society, I would expect an extremely high premarriage divorce rate, a very low parental-marriage divorce rate, a moderately high serial-monogamy rate, and an almost nonexistent polygynous-marriage divorce rate. All this, I suggest, bodes well for our society because the two periods in life when society is most likely to be required to intervene will have the lowest rates of divorce. There will be fewer children involved in divorce who would need state help, and fewer old people who also would need state support. Premarital and serial-monogamy divorces would not be at all costly for the society.

NOTES

1. Peter C. Pineo, "Disenchantment in the Later Years of Marriage," *Marriage and Family Living* 23 (1961): 3–11.
2. Robert O. Blood, Jr., *Love Match and Arranged Marriage: A Tokyo-Detroit Comparison* (New York: Free Press, 1967).
3. Ray E. Baber, *Marriage and the Family* (New York: McGraw-Hill, 1953), pp. 493–494.
4. William M. Kephart, "Occupational Level and Marital Disruption," *American Sociological Review* 20 (1955): 460.
5. Baber, *op. cit.,* pp. 494–495.
6. William M. Kephart, "Drinking and Marital Disruption," *Quarterly Journal of Studies on Alcohol* (March 1954): 71.
7. Kephart, 1955, *op. cit.,* p. 461.
8. Robert R. Bell, *Marriage and Family Interaction,* 3d. ed. (Homewood, Ill.: Dorsey, 1971), p. 489.
9. Thomas P. Monahan and William M. Kephart, "Divorce and Desertion by Religious and Mixed Religious Groups," *American Journal of Sociology* 59 (1954).
10. Bell, *op. cit.,* p. 490.
11. Hugh Carter and Alexander Plateris, "Trends in Divorce and Family Disruption," *Health, Education, and Welfare Indicators* (September, 1963).
12. *World Almanac* (New York: Newspaper Enterprise, 1973), p. 952.
13. U.S. Department of Health, Education, and Welfare, *Monthly Vital Statistics Report* 18:12 (March 1970): 3.
14. Helen I. Clarke, *Social Legislation* (New York: Appleton-Century-Crofts, 1957), p. 128.
15. Harry C. Harmsworth and Mhyra S. Minnis, "Non-Statutory Courses of Divorce: The Lawyer's Point of View," *Marriage and Family Living* 17 (1955): 316–321.
16. Bell, *op. cit.,* p. 524.
17. Judson T. Landis, "The Trauma of Children When Parents Divorce," *Marriage and Family Living* 22 (1960): 7–13; and F. Ivan Nye, "Child Adjustment in Broken and in Unhappy Unbroken Homes," *Marriage and Family Living* 19 (1957):356–361.
18. William J. Goode, *After Divorce* (New York: Free Press, 1956); and Richard J. Udry, "Marital Instability by Race, Sex, Education, and

194   MARRIAGE AND ITS ALTERNATIVES

Occupation Using 1960 Census Data," *American Journal of Sociology* 72 (1966): 203–209.
19. Leonard Benson, *The Family Bond* (New York: Random House, 1971), pp. 287–288.
20. Calvin Goldscheider and Sidney Goldstein, "Generational Changes in Jewish Family Structure," *Journal of Marriage and the Family* 29 (1967): 269.
21. Bell, *op. cit.,* p. 504.
22. Paul C. Glick, *American Families* (New York: John Wiley, 1957).
23. Ira L. Reiss, *The Family System in America* (New York: Holt, Rinehart, and Winston, 1971), p. 284.
24. William J. Goode, *op. cit.,* p. 46.
25. Ernest W. Burgess and Harvey J. Locke, *The Family* (New York: American Book, 1945).
26. Max Gluckman, "Kinship and Marriage Among the Lozi of Northern Rhodesia and the Zulu of Natal," in *African Systems of Kinship and Marriage,* eds. A. R. Radcliffe-Brown and Daryll Forde (London: Oxford University Press, 1950), pp. 166–206.
27. Bernard Farber, *Kinship and Family Organization* (New York: John Wiley, 1966).
28. Benson, *op. cit.,* pp. 308–311.
29. *Ibid.,* p. 310.
30. Charles Ackerman, "Affiliations: Structural Determinants of Differential Divorce Rates," *American Journal of Sociology* 69 (1963): 13–20.
31. Reiss, *op. cit.*
32. *Ibid.*
33. Helena Z. Lopata, "Loneliness: Forms and Components," *Social Problems* 17 (1969): 249.
34. Irving Rosow, "And Then We Were Old," *Trans-action* 2 (1965): 21–26.
35. John C. Belcher, "The One-Person Household: A Consequence of the Isolated Nuclear Family," *Journal of Marriage and the Family* 29 (1967): 535.
36. Robert O. Blood, Jr., and Donald M. Wolfe, *Husbands and Wives* (New York: Free Press, 1960).
37. Lopata, *op. cit.,* p. 250.
38. Robert Parke, Jr. and Paul C. Glick, "Prospective Changes in Marriage and the Family," *Journal of Marriage and the Family* 29 (May, 1967): 249–256.
39. Benson, *op. cit.,* p. 285.
40. Reiss, *op. cit.,* p. 287.
41. Harold T. Christensen and Kathryn P. Johnsen, *Marriage and the Family,* 3d ed. (New York: Ronald Press, 1971), p. 495.
42. Alvin Toffler, *Future Shock* (New York: Random House, 1970).
43. F. Ivan Nye, "Values, Family, and a Changing Society," in *The Family and Change,* ed. John N. Edwards (New York: Alfred A. Knopf, 1969), p. 313.
44. *Ibid.,* p. 314.
45. Parke and Glick, *op. cit.*
46. John Mogey, "A Century of Declining Paternal Authority," *Marriage and Family Living* 19 (1957): 234–239.

47. Charles W. Hobart, "Commitment, Value Conflict and the Future of the American Family," in Edwards, ed., *op. cit.,* p. 330.
48. *Ibid.,* p. 335.
49. John N. Edwards, "The Future of the Family Revisited," in Edwards, ed., *op. cit.,* p. 245.
50. *Ibid.,* p. 350.
51. Lee G. Burchinal, "The Rural Family of the Future," in Edwards, ed., *op. cit.,* pp. 409–445.
52. *Ibid.,* p. 417.
53. Staffan Burenstam Linder, *The Harried Leisure Class* (New York: Columbia University Press, 1969).

8 Remarriage

Remarriage is neither a new nor a peculiarly American phenomenon. Almost every known society has some mechanism that makes remarriage possible, although frequently it is not equally available to everyone.

The ancient Hebrews placed several restrictions on remarriage for women. A woman was allowed to remarry if her husband had divorced her, unless she had been divorced for adultery. However, if her second husband were to divorce her or leave her a widow, she could not remarry her first husband because she was considered to have been defiled. Finally, a divorced woman was forbidden to marry a priest, which clearly indicates that she occupied a status beneath that of single women and was regarded as unfit to be a priest's wife.

In traditional China, divorced or widowed men could readily remarry, but divorce was not common, and remarriage for divorced women was rare because most Chinese men did not want a woman who had been discarded by another man. Even widowed women did not often remarry. In fact, a widow's husband's family could prevent her remarriage if they did not approve of it. Since she could not take any property with her into a remarriage, because it remained in her first husband's family, a widow was not an especially desirable bride.

Remarriage was common among the settlers of Colonial America. Colonial life was difficult and short. Many women died in childbirth because they were likely to have too many children too close together and under unsanitary conditions. Men died young also because of inadequate housing and food, and because of exposure to harsh weather. Remarriage generally followed death quickly because individuals could not survive without a spouse. Thus, remarriage has always been an accepted institution in the United States, although it was encouraged only between widowed people. Well into the twentieth century, American culture rejected remarried couples if one or both of the partners had been divorced. Clergymen were disinclined to perform such remarriage ceremonies; laws were intended to discourage them also. However, as the divorce rates rose after World War I, so did the remarriage rates. At the present time, the vast majority of remarriages occur between divorced people.

Today the practice of remarriage is rapidly becoming more prevalent. Almost one of every eight currently married persons has been married before; one in every five marriages is a remarriage for at least one of the spouses. According to census data, between 1960 and 1966, about half of the divorced men had remarried by the end of the second year of divorce. Not until the early part of the fifth year did half of the men remarry during the decade 1950 to 1959. For women, about half remarried before the end of the third year during the period 1960 to 1966, compared to half who remarried by the end of the fifth year between 1950 and 1959.[1] Among the widowed, half of the men and one quarter of the women remarried within the same period.[2]

SOCIAL FACTORS IN REMARRIAGE

The remarriage rate is higher among blacks than among whites. One reason is that blacks have higher divorce and death rates. It is known that in any society with high divorce and death rates, there is a concomitant high remarriage rate. Glick found that 18.6 per cent of black women were living with their husbands in a second or subsequent marriage compared to 9.3 per cent of white women.[3] We can expect, however, that as more black families enter the middle class, their remarriage patterns will become more like the national average.

Obviously those entering second marriages are older than those who are marrying for the first time. The median age at first marriage is 22.8 for males and 20.3 for females compared to 38.3 and 34.0, respectively, for those in second marriages.[4] Besides being older than first-time brides and grooms, spouses in second marriages have a greater age differential. In 1959, the median age difference was 2.5 years for first marriages and 4.4 years for second marriages.[5]

Bowerman found that when previously married people remarried, the second mate was younger if he or she was single than if he or she had also been married before.[6] But if the second mate was widowed, he or she would be older than a second mate who had been divorced. Bowerman also found that the older the remarrying man, the greater the probability that he would marry a woman many years his junior. On the other hand, when older women remarry, they choose men close to their own age.

Remarriage rates are higher among poorly educated women than among those with a college education.[7] We already know that the more education a woman has, the less likely she is to marry even the first time. The reverse is probably true for men. Educated women have a relatively small pool of eligibles from which to choose, while educated men are highly desirable as marriage partners and can probably select from among women in their own or a lower educational group.

Lenski found that Catholics remarry after divorce much less frequently than Protestants.[8] This is surprising because Catholics are more committed to family life. Lenski's explanation is that Catholics, especially if they are religious, are probably under greater social pressure to make the first marriage successful and hence probably experience more guilt if they remarry after divorce.

CHOICE OF A SECOND MATE

Approximately nine out of ten people who have never been married before marry another single person. Approximately half of all divorced people who remarry choose people who are also divorced, 40 per cent marry single people, and 10 per cent marry widows or widowers. Those whose marriages were terminated by death tend to marry people whose first mates also died. In short, people tend to marry others like themselves. We practice homogamy in the second marriage as well as in the first. The divorced mostly marry the divorced, single people marry single people, and widowers marry widows.

Bell offers a typology to explain why some divorced people do not remarry.[9] The first group he calls *the bitter.* These people equate any marriage with the unsatisfactory one they have experienced. "Marriage is a rejected relationship based on hostility to the opposite sex in the marriage role."[10] The second group is called *the frightened,* because these persons view themselves as marital failures and are unwilling to risk failure twice. The third group Bell refers to as *the overdemanding.* Such people seek perfection in the second mate and have a need to be absolutely sure that the characteristics of the first spouse will not be present in the second one. The result, of course, is an inability to find anyone who can fulfill the requirements. The fourth group is composed of *the rejected,* those people who simply never get a second chance to marry because they possess social or psychological traits that make them undesirable as marriage partners. Examples would be an older woman or a low-income man. The final category is *the adjusted.* Such individuals prefer the divorced status and choose to occupy it. They differ from the rejected because they opt for the divorced role, while the rejected often have little choice or opportunity.

Yet many Americans have several spouses during their lifetimes, one after another. Divorced people tend to marry more than single or widowed people. In a given year, for example, for every 1,000 single women between the ages of twenty-five and twenty-nine, 140 will marry. On the other hand, 319 of every 1,000 divorced women in that age range will remarry. Approximately the same percentages hold for men. For both sexes the differentials between the marriage rates for the two marital statuses widen over time. Samuel Johnson once remarked, "Remarriage is the triumph of hope over experience," and apparently most divorced people are hopeful, because their remarriage rate is extremely high. This indicates, for one thing, that divorced people do not reject marriage *per se,* only one particular mate. These people want to be married, and they have the characteristics that are attractive to the opposite sex. Further-more, they are accustomed to being part of a couple, and they probably find it uncomfortable to be alone. Most are used to reg-ular sexual relations, and single life deters this. Also, many di-vorced men and women are likely to have young children and want to provide them with surrogate parents. Divorced people generally have a shorter "mourning" period than the widowed because often the emotional disinterest existed long before the legal divorce oc-curred. Because they are likely to be young, divorced people are strongly motivated to remarry. Most important, remarriage offers an opportunity to erase the stigma of divorce. The remarried "prove" that they have not failed in a role in which most people succeed, or at least appear to succeed. Although we have no statis-tics to prove it, many apparently select the second spouse before they get a divorce.

PROBLEMS IN REMARRIAGE

In addition to marrying at different rates and for different rea-sons, divorced and widowed people face different problems in re-marriage. Let us discuss the problems of the widowed first.

In the chapter on mate selection we discussed the myth in our culture that there is one, and only one, great love for each person. Because of this myth, widowed people are often conflicted and con-fused when faced with the possibility of remarriage. This may, in part, explain the lower remarriage rate among the widowed as com-pared to those who are divorced. Widowed people who remarry often rationalize their ambiguous feelings by seeing the relationship with the second mate as "different"—i.e., more mature—reserving the "romantic love" for the first spouse.

Bernard points to several areas that are likely to cause problems in a remarriage when at least one of the partners has been wid-owed.[11] One is the tendency of widowed people to idealize their first spouses. If this has not prevented them from remarrying alto-gether, it can cause problems if the two spouses are unrealistically compared. Second, the new spouse of a widowed person knows that the first marriage was not terminated voluntarily, which implies that he or she is really a second choice. Third, long-standing friends or relatives may see the new spouse as an intruder or a usurper, and they may be less than friendly. Fourth, there is often a "left-over" set of in-laws with whom to contend. The family of the deceased spouse may resent the remarriage and may cause unpleasantness, especially if young children are involved.

Yet most remarriages involving a widowed man or woman appear to be successful. Bernard feels that this is because the widowed remarry cautiously and slowly. They have rational reasons to marry and do not have unrealistically romantic expectations. "Older people may have less exact standards; they may be willing to settle for less than when they were younger. The contrast between the loneliness of life without a spouse and the companionship and security of married status may tip the scales in favor of marriage, even if it is not a success by any other measure."[12]

The status of widowed people in our society is a respectable one, but divorced persons seek to escape from a limbo in which a society like ours tends to place them. Therefore they may more anxiously seek readmission into the social network through remarriage.

There are some very serious adjustments to be made by the divorced when they remarry that widowed individuals frequently do not face. There are usually financial problems because of alimony payments to a former wife or the loss of alimony from a former husband. There is a greater probability that young children are involved, which has several implications. The divorced spouses may try to create difficulties between the couple through the children. Moreover, stepchildren who visit at regular intervals and those who live with the couple pose potential adjustment problems. Finally, we must apply W. I. Thomas's famous statement: "If people define situations as real they are real in their consequences." Americans have defined remarriage as difficult, and this may prove to be a self-fulfilling prophecy. Divorce is a stigmatized status, and the process of divorce leaves scars. Those who experience it often feel that they are failures or that they are somehow inadequate because they have been unsuccessful in a role that most people perform. In addition, the community is often skeptical about the divorced person's ability to succeed the second time around. These attitudes of uncertainty and doubt frequently define the situation for the remarrying divorced and may be very destructive for the new relationship unless all concerned can redefine it in terms of probable success.

Using divorce rates as a criterion, remarriages between divorced people seem to be somewhat less successful than remarriages between widowed people. This brings up the concept of "divorce-proneness," which certain sociologists use to mean that people in the divorced group have social or psychological characteristics that make them likely candidates for second, third, or even fourth divorces.

There is a great deal of evidence to refute this characterization of the divorced. For one thing, only a tiny percentage of Americans divorce more than once. "One in four marriages ends in divorce; two out of three divorced persons remarry; more than nine out of ten of the remarried stay married."[13] Actually, only 6 per cent of all marriages in any given year involve a person marrying for at least the third time; 74 per cent of all marriages at any point in time are first marriages, and 20 per cent contain at least one person who has been married once before.[14]

Nevertheless, we cannot deny the statistics: remarriages between divorced people are more apt to end in divorce than remarriages between widowed people or first marriages. It does not seem accurate to conclude that some people have a tendency to divorce because of character flaws. There are situational factors that could be detrimental to remarried divorced people. We have already noted the fact that divorced people tend to marry sooner than widowed people in order to regain an acceptable social position. In addition, divorcées tend to be younger and to have younger children than widows, which may create the pressure for a more rapid marriage. Then, too, as Morton Hunt points out, those who have experienced divorce are less likely to tolerate a second poor marriage because they know that being divorced can be bearable.[15] They have been through it and survived. They know that they will survive again.

In trying to understand which marriage is likely to be happier, the first or the second, sociologists may have been comparing the wrong things. Instead of comparing divorce rates, they should be asking subjects to evaluate the relative happiness of their own two marriages. We would guess that when divorced people do stay together in the second relationship, they are as happy as, or happier than, those who stay together in a first marriage.

Goode has approached this problem properly.

> Granted that the divorced who remarry are somewhat more prone to divorce than those who marry for the first time; nevertheless, the only comparison that makes sense to those divorced people is between their second marriage and *their own first marriage.* Our divorcées are not, after all, asserting that their second marriages are better than marriages of *others* who are first married. They are only claiming that their second marriages are "happier" than their *own first* marriages.[16]

In summary, the term "divorce-prone" is pejorative and unnecessary. It is true that divorce rates are somewhat higher for second marriages than for first, but this does not necessarily indicate that second marriages are less happy than first ones. In fact, it may be that second marriages are happier. Remarried divorced people face unusual problems—self-doubt, communal skepticism, extra financial burdens, and extraordinary dyadic adjustment—yet most of them rate their remarriages "very happy" and most of them stay married in spite of the fact that they fear divorce less than those who have never experienced it.

Children in Remarriage

We might reasonably expect that childless divorced or widowed women would be more likely to remarry than women with children because most men would presumably be hesitant about taking on the burdens and responsibilities of someone else's children. On the other hand, we could just as reasonably anticipate that divorced mothers would be more eager to marry again than women without children in order to provide a home and a father figure for their children.

Data indicate that mothers are somewhat less likely to remarry than women who have no children. However, when age is held constant, having or not having children from a previous marriage loses significance. Furthermore, it appears that when there are more children, the chances of remarriage are greater than when there are few.[17]

Generally, remarriage with children involves the children's biological mother and a new father. This is an advantage to the children because the female parent is usually the more significant one, and as the children make the necessary adjustments, they have the support of the parent on whom they are more emotionally dependent.

Children are frequently happier in remarried families than in unhappy intact homes.[18] We know that for children the husband-wife relationship is the most influential of all dyadic relations and is the one most likely to govern other intrafamilial relations.[19] Thus the marital relationship is an important determinant of the parental relationship; when parents are unhappy with each other, they are often poor parents. If the remarried parents are satisfied with each other, the children are likely to benefit.

It is estimated that some seven million children live with a stepparent; yet there has been very little empirical research on this relationship.[20] Bowerman and Irish found that the situation is easier if the stepchildren are either very young or grown-up.[21] They also found that when divorce preceded the remarriage, the children formed better relationships with their stepparent than when death preceded it. These investigators explain their finding by saying that for the child of a divorce, the stepparent appears when they are younger and sooner after the marital break-up.

In a more recent study, just the opposite was found. If the previous marriage had been terminated by death rather than by divorce, successful step-relations were more likely to obtain. The author explains this by saying that the stepparent does not have a living biological parent to compete with. The data from this study also suggest that younger stepmothers (those under forty) are more successful than older ones; that Protestants form better relationships with their stepchildren than any other religious group; that stepfathers who had never been married before did better than divorced or widowed stepfathers; and, conversely, that previously unmarried stepmothers were least successful in dealing with stepchildren.[22]

The same study found that social class was a minor influence, but there was some indication that the higher the class, the better the stepparent-stepchild relationship. Of much greater significance was the advent of a new child in the family. When the remarried couple had a child of their own, the relations between the stepparent and the stepchild were decidedly better. Most important, the stepfather was much more successful in general than the female stepparent. This was expected because the female role vis-à-vis the children is the more active one, which makes the stepmother more vulnerable in her relations with her husband's children.[23] Bowerman and Irish also found the role of the stepmother more difficult. They believe that this is because society is more likely to give assistance and social acceptance to the male stepparent.[24] Furthermore, the myth in our culture denigrates the stepmother—folklore has it that she is cruel and heartless.

Some research indicates that stepparents and stepchildren do not get along well. Margaret Mead offers a possible reason. She suggests that in our family system the child develops an overdependence on the parents. This results in a demand that the parents act as the only source of security for the child. "Each American child learns early and in terror that his whole security depends on that single set of parents. . . . Our children are not prepared to trust anyone but their own parents. . . . We have never made adequate social provision for the security and identity of the children if that marriage is broken."[25] The result, Mead points out, is an inability to commit oneself to a stepparent in a manner that will permit a meaningful relationship.

Bohannan feels that our kinship terms are inadequate.[26] "Stepparent" was a useful term when death was the usual precursor of remarriage because the stepparent was a replacement. But a stepparent after divorce is an additional parent, not a replacement. Stepparents are not real in American culture. The norm is either to ignore the relationship or to take special care to avoid any appearance of difference between parent and stepparent. Our culture does not provide us with norms to show the difference, nor do we have norms for behavior and expectations. Thus, Bohannan tells us, the creation of a stepparent-stepchild relationship is difficult in our society.

Several investigators disagree. Nye found little evidence to support the notion that there are special difficulties between stepparents and stepchildren.[27] His data show that although there are more adjustment problems in reconstituted families than in intact families, the greatest adjustment is needed in unhappy primary families. Goode found that a majority of his remarried mothers thought their children's lives had improved when they remarried.[28] Burchinal's study also refutes the commonly held belief that divorce and remarriage have detrimental effects on the children.[29]

Bernard reported on a study of graduate students who were stepchildren and revealed that none of them differed from the general college population in stability, self-sufficiency, or dominance.[30] The comments of her subjects concerning the love, help, friendship, and understanding their stepparents had provided documented the distortion of the stepparent stereotype.

Thus, we can see that there is considerable disagreement among sociologists as to the quality of the stepparent-stepchildren relationship. Work is just beginning in this area as we become aware of the frequency of remarriage, particularly remarriage involving children.

REMARRIAGE IN THE FUTURE

If divorce disorganizes marriage, remarriage seems to reorganize it. Indeed, our only institutionalized response to divorce seems to be remarriage. Overwhelmingly, most people who remarry today have been divorced, not widowed—a complete reversal from the beginning of the century, when 90 per cent of all remarriages included at least one widowed mate. Thus, in discussing the future of remarriage, it is well to concentrate on remarriage among our divorced population. First I will offer some predictions based on the assumption that the suggested system of multiple-structured marriage will not develop.

There is nothing in the literature that sheds light on remarriage rates in the future. However, if trends are indicative, we can expect the rates of remarriage to rise as more people divorce. Furthermore, divorced people are remarrying much sooner than they did before. The implication is that, over time, more will remarry. And since death is less often the reason for marital termination, and since divorced people remarry more often and sooner than widowed people, we have additional reason to expect the rates to rise.

One final statistical indication that remarriage rates are getting higher: In 1968, there were approximately 600,000 divorces and 500,000 new marriages including at least one divorced person. This could mean that people are coming to consider divorce simply as a temporary break in their marital lives. This fact bolsters Goode's argument that high divorce rates do not imply social disorganization, especially not when half of all the divorced remarry within three years of divorce.[31] In fact, our marital system actually seems to have greater influence than ever.

Finally, our low age at the time of marriage plus our increasing longevity make remarriage a stronger probability than it was in the past. In short, we have more social approval, more opportunity, and more time in which to remarry.

Let us now discuss the probable rate of remarriage were our society to institutionalize premarriage, parental marriage, serial monogamy, and polygyny. Probably the remarriage rate would be greatly accelerated, since very few people would remain married to their first premarriage mate. However, such a situation would not be destructive to society since, as I mentioned in the last chapter, divorce and remarriage during parental marriage and polygynous marriage would be rare. These are the two stages in the life cycle when divorce and remarriage demand a high price from the society because often it must assume care of children and of elderly people. There is much less societal responsibility during the premarriage and serial monogamy periods. Thus, the greater part of the burden on society would be relieved.

In short, I predict that, regardless of the number or kind of accepted marriage forms, our remarriage rates will accelerate. I also predict that this will be in no way harmful to our society; indeed, it will probably be beneficial.

NOTES

1. *Probabilities of Marriage, Divorce, and Remarriage*, P-23, no. 32 (Washington, D.C.: Government Printing Office, 1970).
2. Jessie Bernard, *Remarriage* (New York: Dryden, 1956), p. 64.
3. Paul C. Glick, *American Families* (New York: John Wiley, 1957), p. 729.
4. U.S. Department of Health, Education, and Welfare, Public Health Service, "Marriage and Divorce Statistics," *Vital Statistics of the United*

States 1959, sec. 2 (Washington, D.C.: National Office of Vital Statistics, 1959), p. 9.

5. *Ibid.,* p. 7.
6. Charles E. Bowerman, "Age Relationships at Marriage, by Marital Status, and Age at Marriage," *Marriage and Family Living* 18 (1956): 231–233.
7. Leonard Benson, *The Family Bond* (New York: Random House, 1971): 313.
8. Gerhard Lenski, *The Religious Factor* (Garden City, New York: Doubleday, 1961).
9. Robert R. Bell, *Marriage and Family Interaction,* 3d ed. (Homewood, Ill.: Dorsey, 1971), pp. 527–529.
10. *Ibid.,* p. 527.
11. Bernard, *op. cit.,* p. 199.
12. *Ibid.,* p. 279.
13. Ben J. Wattenberg and Richard M. Scammon, *This U.S.A.* (Garden City, New York: Doubleday, 1965), p. 36.
14. U.S. Department of Health, Education, and Welfare, National Center for Health Statistics, *Divorce Statistics Analysis: United States 1963,* Series 21, no. 13 (Washington, D.C.: Government Printing Office, 1963).
15. Morton Hunt, *The World of the Formerly Married* (New York: McGraw-Hill, 1966), pp. 278–279.
16. William J. Goode, *Women in Divorce* (New York: Free Press, 1956).
17. William F. Kendel, *The Family in Perspective,* 2d ed. (New York: Appleton-Century-Crofts, 1966), p. 331.
18. F. Ivan Nye, "Child Adjustment in Broken and in Unhappy Unbroken Homes," *Marriage and Family Living* 19 (1957): 356–361.
19. Bert N. Adams and Thomas Weirath, *Readings on the Sociology of the Family* (Chicago: Markham, 1971), p. 257; and Lucile Duberman, "Becoming a Family: A Study of Reconstituted Families" (unpublished Ph.D. diss., Case Western Reserve University, 1973).
20. Charles E. Bowerman and Donald P. Irish, "Some Relationships of Stepchildren to Their Parents," *Marriage and Family Living* 24 (1962): 113–121.
21. *Ibid.,* p. 118.
22. Duberman, *op. cit.*
23. *Ibid.*
24. Bowerman and Irish, *op. cit.*
25. Margaret Mead, "Anomalies in American Postdivorce Relationships," in *Divorce and After,* ed. Paul Bohannan (Garden City, New York: Doubleday, 1970), p. 102.
26. Paul Bohannan, *Divorce and After* (Garden City, New York: Doubleday, 1970), pp. 29–56.
27. F. Ivan Nye, *op. cit.*
28. Goode, *op. cit.,* pp. 307–309.
29. Lee G. Burchinal, "Characteristics of Adolescents from Unbroken, Broken, and Reconstituted Families," *Journal of Marriage and the Family* 26 (1964): 44–50.
30. Bernard, *op. cit.,* pp. 306–311.
31. Goode, *op. cit.*

9 Woman's Role

Technology has revolutionized our culture. Yet in and of itself it cannot make our world happier or more satisfying or richer or more fulfilling. Certainly it has made work easier in the labor market for men and in the home for women. It has increased our lifespans, improved our health and appearance, made our clothes and homes more attractive, comfortable, and durable, made our foods taste better, allowed us to control our birth rates, and enlarged our leisure world. But, as Ogburn said, a change in our material world is inadequate unless it is accompanied by a change in our nonmaterial world—in our values, attitudes, beliefs, and goals.[1]

Our technology is capable of producing a world in which men and women occupy equal social statuses and are accorded the same prestige because it has largely eliminated the importance of physical strength. But until now, there have been insufficient changes in our attitudes to implement the possibilities. The women's liberation movement, probably the most important social movement of this century, is capable of removing the culture lag by bringing our ideas into line with our technology. Full equality between the sexes was not possible before the advent of the post-industrial society. But now that necessary condition has been satisfied.

THE WOMEN'S LIBERATION MOVEMENT

Until the end of the eighteenth century, women were totally subordinate to men. Women were permitted no formal higher education; they had no vote; they had few legal rights. Completely un-equipped to support themselves, they were dependent on men for economic security. The young girl went from her father's house and protection to her husband's house and protection. When her husband died, she was supported by her son.

The American and French revolutions promoted an egalitarian atmosphere in the world. This spirit, combined with the sociological changes brought about by the Industrial Revolution, encouraged women in the early part of the nineteenth century to begin their fight for civil rights. From that time until the present, women have made great progress. They now have the right to vote. They are allowed to enroll in universities. Many are professionals in occupations that were formerly the exclusive province of men. Socialization processes are changing as well. Little girls are being encouraged to be physically freer—to run, to climb trees, to get dirty. Adolescence is now marked by greater social and sexual freedom. Adult male and female relationships are changing also. Women's sexual rights are being acknowledged. Women are no longer passive sex partners; they have become assertive in their sexual demands. Fathers are playing larger roles in family life; they are becoming more than just disciplinarians and breadwinners.

More and more women are in the labor force. The Bureau of Labor Statistics reported that in 1962, some twenty-four million women worked, comprising one third of all workers. Today 36 per cent of all women work, and 56 per cent of these are married women living with their husbands. Thus, women are becoming economically more important in the society and in the home; as they do so, they gain power.

Nevertheless, women have still not gained full equality with men. They still are not wholly welcome in the world of work—the factories, business, the professions. They still do not receive equal compensation for equal work. The Labor Department's Women's Bureau reported that not only are salaries of women workers lower than those of men but also the gap between them is widening. The 1970 full-time, year-round wage or salary income figures put white men at a median of $9,373 followed by minority men at $6,598. Next came white women at $5,490, and finally, at the bottom, minority women at $4,674.[2] Women are still considered commanders-in-chief of the household and the children, regardless of how important the positions they hold are or the amount of money they earn.

Conversely, men have still not gained full equality with women. They are still not permitted to show emotion or weakness. They still cannot have complete, open relationships with their children. Most of all, they do not have the choice that women have among a career, parenthood, and a combination of both. Men are expected to combine the occupational and marital roles; women may have both or either.

The women's liberation movement, if we can date it at all, may be said to have begun with the publication of Betty Friedan's *The Feminine Mystique* in 1963.[3] Friedan stressed women's need for freedom from housework and urged her readers to give up the delusions of the feminine mystique—the myth that, for a woman, "it is easier to live through someone else than to become completely yourself"—and to "realize that neither her husband, nor her children, nor the things in her house, nor sex, nor being like all the other women, can give her a self."[4] Once a woman recognizes that, Friedan argued, the solution to the problem of liberation will be simple.

Friedan's book disturbed the complacency of the women who had moved to the suburbs "for the sake of the children," where they rarely saw their husbands, where they were isolated with their children and other women, and where they were presumed to be content as wives and mothers. Freudian psychoanalysis had promoted the notion that if these women were frustrated, they had a personal problem. No one suggested that the problem could be societal. Each woman had to work out for herself why being wife and mother was simply not enough. Generally, the problem remained insoluble, and women learned to smother their unhappiness and discontent.

In 1966 the National Organization of Women (NOW) was formed by Betty Friedan and a group of like-thinking women. The purpose of the organization was to bring women into the mainstream of American society and to see that they acquired the rights and obligations that would give them equality with men. The members are predominantly middle-aged, many of them professional, upper-middle-class women, who work for abortion-law

repeal, the establishment of day-care centers for people of all incomes, equal opportunities for women in the labor market, and
equal pay for equal work.

A second branch of the women's liberation movement is composed of younger, more radical women, who emerged primarily
out of the black civil rights movement. These women left the black
movement when they realized that they were being relegated to secondary statuses—helper, typist, sandwich maker—for the men who
were in control. Typical of the attitudes that caused their withdrawal from the black movement is the famous remark by Stokeley
Carmichael, "The best position for women in the movement is
prone."

These young women then founded the more militant groups
within the women's movement, such as Redstockings, the Female
Liberation Front, and the Women's International Terrorist Conspiracy from Hell (WITCH). Revolution is the goal of these
groups. They want a complete change in the structure of our society and our interpersonal relationships, notably marriage. Some
urge abolishment of any form of the institution whatsoever. They
view our traditional conjugal-marriage system as destructive to
women. They argue that marriage enslaves women, forcing them
to perform tasks that are mindless and demeaning, without dignity
or compensation. In short, they feel that marriage guarantees that
women will always be in a subordinate position to men.

Some of these militant groups suggest that women refuse to have
any sexual relations with men at all, in or out of marriage. Such
women resent any reference to women in terms of sexuality or femininity and offer lesbianism or celibacy as substitutes for heterosexuality.

Other radical women would like to see females give up having
and rearing children. They point to Freud's famous edict "Anat-
omy is destiny" as the myth that has prevented women from seeking and satisfying their true potential. If women must have children
(and they have not as yet proposed this as a male obligation), then
surely the children should be the responsibility of the state.

In short, the women's liberation movement includes many kinds
of women and organizations, with varying ideologies and degrees
of radicalism. However, most agree that there should be several

basic changes in society. One is equality for women at work, at universities, and in the home. A second is the establishment of universal day-care centers. Third, they object to the mass media's treatment of women as sex objects instead of as human beings. Fourth, they would like to see our socialization practices altered so that children are not trained from infancy to believe that males are superior to females. Women in the liberation movement would prefer to have children grow up believing that all human beings are equal and that, except for different biological processes and functions, there is little difference between men and women that is not socially induced.

THE CHANGING ROLE OF WOMEN

Several sociologists have addressed themselves to the impact of the women's liberation movement on the family of the future. Bell notes that many women, especially older women, are opposed to the movement; indeed, some work actively against it.[5] These women are threatened because the creed of the movement suggests that their whole lives have been wasted, and now it is too late or they are too frightened to change. Bell predicts, then, that there will be increasing hostility and resistance from the majority of women who are housekeepers, wives, and mothers only. Nevertheless, although he does not specify in what ways, Bell says, "It seems clear that this movement is going to have far-reaching effects on marriage and family roles in the United States."[6]

Linda Gordon suggests that although the women's liberation movement has the potential of encouraging young women to give up marriage and having babies completely, this would be destructive; the institution of the family is useful and should be retained.[7] What really needs to be changed, she argues, and what can be changed effectively, is the division of labor within the family so that men, women, and children can all benefit.

Reiss notes that there are already many signs of increasing male-female equality.[8] For one thing, women are more involved in the labor market, although they still do not have complete access to the higher-paying, more prestigious jobs. Nonetheless, increasing participation in the world of work has already increased the woman's power in the family.

Improved contraception techniques also increase woman's power in the family because now she can decide if and when she will have children, and having them will not incapacitate her as it has in the past. Furthermore, day-care centers mean that women no longer have to rear their children full time if they prefer not to do so. In short, Reiss says, we have a de-emphasis on woman as mother and a new emphasis on woman as worker, earner, and power-wielder.

But Reiss feels that even with increased power, "full equality is not possible as long as the female and male roles are radically different in the family and occupational systems."[9] As long as women are primarily housewives, they cannot have equality because power in our society is related to occupation, and the occupation of housewife is not highly ranked. What is needed, this author states, is a radical change, which can be accomplished only if men and women fully share in household roles. Reiss does not anticipate that men will ever cooperate to this extent; therefore, women must push for, and rely on, day-care centers and increased help from the government and the private sector for child care. In addition, he thinks, as Bell does, that some women will sabotage other women in this effort by preferring the low-prestige homemaking status. "The block to full equality of the sexes does not lie in their biological differences. Rather it consists of the evaluation many people make of the costs and benefits of such a change. Thus, I foresee in the next few decades a partial rather than a radical victory in the search for sexual equality."[10]

Janet Zollinger Giele goes beyond what others are saying. Giele feels that without doubt important changes have already occurred and will continue.[11] She poses the questions: Why is a new consciousness rising that criticizes women's status and the relationship between the sexes? What are the forces in the larger society that are attacking traditional sex roles? This author feels that a process has been going on so that "a crossover is possible in many aspects of role performance that were formerly linked to sex. Consequently, a shared consciousness is possible in which men and women can perceive more clearly each other's problems and satisfactions, and as a result identify with each other."[12]

Giele thinks that changes in four major institutional areas have been influential in arousing a shared consciousness about sex roles. The first is the change in our moral code, so that the boundaries are becoming blurred between what is proper for youth and adults, the single and the married, and men and women. Sexuality is now acceptable outside of marriage and apart from its reproductive function, provided that it occurs within a framework of affection. The first change, then, is that sexual activity is now equally available to youth as well as adults; to single, divorced, and widowed as well as married people; and to women as well as men.

Giele sees a change in our attitudes toward the family. From the 1920s through the 1950s, the child-rearing function was dominated by the nuclear family, particularly by mothers who were seen as "experts." Now we are gradually recognizing the importance of the father role; further, we are switching from the notion of a child-centered home to one that acknowledges the psychological needs of the parents.

The third change is in the relationship between the family and the government. Whereas in the 1930s, because of the Depression, governmental concern centered on the financial needs of children, now there is governmental interest in freeing parents, especially women, to work and to realize themselves.

The fourth change is related to the third one. There is official recognition that all the members of the nuclear family may benefit if the mother works instead of "devoting" herself to her home and children. With this in mind, the government is moving toward the distribution of contraceptive information and devices, legalized abortion, day-care centers, and universal family allowances.

Giele concludes that as these changes become solidified, men and women will move into each other's orbits. Women will understand the intricacies of the work world; men, the intricacies of housework and child rearing. They will thus develop a joint consciousness. Giele believes that these changes are already occurring to a very large extent. "If people can be shown that [the] liberation of men and women is not a wild idea, but an extension of reasonable principles they have already accepted, and in fact *lived,* then it is only a matter of time until we shall see further change of remarkable proportions."[13]

In combination with our unbelievable technological growth, the women's liberation movement may radically alter our society. It should help us to rethink our traditional attitudes toward men's roles, women's roles, the family, sexual behavior, courtship, and divorce, as well as work, war, education, leisure—life itself. It can mean only greater happiness, freedom, and satisfaction for all people in the century to come.

NOTES

1. W. F. Ogburn, *Social Change* (New York: Dell, 1966).
2. *New York Times,* 28 December 1972, p. 34.
3. Betty Friedan, *The Feminine Mystique* (New York: Dell, 1963).
4. *Ibid.,* p. 326.
5. See, e.g., Midge Decter, *The New Chastity and Other Arguments Against Women's Liberation* (New York: Coward, McCann, and Geoghegan, 1972); and Esther Vilar, *The Manipulated Man* (New York: Farrar, Straus, and Giroux, 1973).
6. Robert R. Bell, *Marriage and Family Interaction,* 3d ed. (Homewood, Ill.: Dorsey, 1971).
7. Linda Gordon, "Functions of the Family," in *Voices From Women's Liberation,* ed. Leslie B. Tanner (New York: New American Library, 1970), pp. 181–188.
8. Ira L. Reiss, *The Family System in America* (New York: Holt, Rinehart and Winston, 1971), p. 403.
9. *Ibid.*
10. *Ibid.,* p. 405.
11. Janet Zollinger Giele, "Changes in the Modern Family: Their Impact on Sex Roles," in *The Women's Movement,* eds. Helen Wortis and Clara Rabinowitz (New York: John Wiley, 1972), pp. 65–77.
12. *Ibid.,* p. 68.
13. *Ibid.,* p. 76.

Bibliography

ACKERMAN, CHARLES. 1965. "Affiliations: Structural Determinants of Differential Divorce Rates," *American Journal of Sociology,* 69 (July), pp. 13–20.

ADAMS, BERT N. 1964. "Structural Factors Affecting Parental Aid to Married Children," *Journal of Marriage and the Family,* 26 (August).

———. 1968. *Kinship in an Urban Setting.* Chicago: Markham.

ADAMS, BERT N., and THOMAS WEIRATH. 1971. *Readings on the Sociology of the Family.* Chicago: Markham.

ADAMS, CLIFFORD R. 1950. "Evaluating Marriage Prediction Tests," *Marriage and Family Living,* 12, pp. 55–56.

ADAMS, MARGARET. 1972. "The Single Woman in Today's Society: A Reappraisal," in Helen Wortis and Clara Rabinowitz (eds.), *The Women's Movement.* New York: Wiley.

ALPENFELS, ETHEL J. 1970. "Progressive Monogamy: An Alternate Pattern?" in Herbert A. Otto (ed.), *The Family in Search of a Future.* New York: Appleton-Century-Crofts.

BABER, RAY E. 1953. *Marriage and the Family.* New York: McGraw-Hill.

BACH, GEORGE R., and PETER WYDEN. 1969. *The Intimate Enemy.* New York: Morrow.

BARNETT, LARRY D. 1962. "Research in Interreligious Dating and Marriage," *Marriage and Family Living,* 24, pp. 191–94.

———. 1963. "Interracial Marriage in California," *Marriage and Family Living,* 25 (November), pp. 424–27.

BEIGEL, HUGO C. 1961. "Illegitimacy," in Albert Ellis and Albert Abarbanel (eds.), *The Encyclopedia of Sexual Behavior.* New York: Hawthorn.

BELCHER, JOHN C. 1967. "The One-Person Household: A Consequence of the Isolated Nuclear Family," *Journal of Marriage and the Family,* 29 (August), pp. 534–40.

BELL, ROBERT R. 1966. *Premarital Sex in a Changing Society.* Englewood Cliffs, N.J.: Prentice-Hall.

———. 1971. *Social Deviance.* Homewood, Ill.: Dorsey.

———. 1971. *Marriage and Family Interaction,* 3d ed. Homewood, Ill.: Dorsey.

BELL, ROBERT R., and JAY B. CHASKES. 1970. "Premarital Sexual Experience Among Coeds, 1958 and 1968," *Journal of Marriage and the Family* 32 (February), pp. 81–84.

BENSON, LEONARD. 1971. *The Family Bond.* New York: Random House.

BERNARD, JESSIE. 1956. *Remarriage.* New York: Dryden.

———. 1966. "Notes on Educational Homogamy in Negro-White and White-Negro Marriage, 1960," *Journal of Marriage and the Family,* 28 (August), pp. 274–76.

BLAZER, JOHN A. 1963. "Complementary Needs and Marital Happiness," *Marriage and Family Living,* 25 (February), pp. 89–95.

BLOOD, ROBERT O., JR. 1967. *Love Match and Arranged Marriage: A Tokyo-Detroit Comparison.* New York: Free Press.

———. 1969. *Marriage.* 2d ed. New York: Free Press.

———. 1972. *The Family.* New York: Free Press.

BLOOD, ROBERT O., JR., and DONALD M. WOLFE. 1960. *Husbands and Wives.* Glencoe, Ill.: Free Press.

BOHANNAN, PAUL. 1970. *Divorce and After.* Garden City, N.Y.: Doubleday.

BOWERMAN, CHARLES E. 1956. "Age Relationships at Marriage, By Marital Status, and Age at Marriage," *Marriage and Family Living,* 18, pp. 231–33.

BOWERMAN, CHARLES E., and BARBARA R. DAY. 1956. "A Test of the Theory of Complementary Needs as Applied to Couples During Courtship," *American Sociological Review,* 21, pp. 602–5.

BOWERMAN, CHARLES E., and DONALD P. IRISH. 1962. "Some Relationships of Stepchildren to Their Parents," *Marriage and Family Living,* 24 (May), pp. 113–21.

BRIM, O. G., JR. 1958. "Family Structure and Sex Role Learning by Children: A Further Analysis of Helen Koch's Data," *Sociometry,* 21, pp. 1–16.

———. 1966. "Socialization Through the Life Cycle," in O. G. Brim, Jr., and S. Wheeler, eds., *Socialization After Childhood.* New York: Wiley.

BUCKINGHAM, J. S. 1867. *The Eastern and Western States of America,* 2 vols. London: Fisher.

BURCHINAL, LEE G. 1964. "Characteristics of Adolescents from Unbroken, Broken, and Reconstituted Families," *Journal of Marriage and the Family,* 26 (February), pp. 44–50.

———. 1969. "The Rural Family of the Future," in John N. Edwards (ed.), *The Family and Change.* New York: Knopf.

BURGESS, ERNEST W. 1926. "The Family as a Unity of Interacting Personalities," *The Family*, 7 (March), pp. 3–6.

BURGESS, ERNEST W., and HARVEY J. LOCKE. 1945. *The Family: From Institution to Companionship*. New York: American.

BURGESS, ERNEST W., HARVEY J. LOCKE, and MARY MARGARET THOMAS. 1963. *The Family: From Institution to Companionship*, 3d ed. New York: American.

BURGESS, ERNEST W., and PAUL WALLIN. 1953. *Engagement and Marriage*. Philadelphia: Lippincott.

BURKS, JAYNE B. 1973. "The Delphi Study," unpublished Ph.D. dissertation. St. Louis: Fontbonne College.

CAMMER, LEONARD. 1971. "Are Most People Dissatisfied with Their Sexual Life?" *Sexual Behavior* (December), p. 55.

CAMPBELL, ARTHUR A. 1968. "Population Dynamics and Family Planning," *Journal of Marriage and the Family*, 30 (May), pp. 202–6.

CAPLOW, THEODORE. 1968. *Two Against One: Coalitions in Triads*. Englewood Cliffs, N.J.: Prentice-Hall.

CARTER, HUGH, and ALEXANDER PLATERIS. 1963. "Trends in Divorce and Family Disruption," *Health, Education, and Welfare Indicators* (September).

CHILMAN, CATHERINE S. 1968. "Child-Rearing and Family Relationship Patterns of the Very Poor," in Marvin B. Sussman (ed.), *Sourcebook in Marriage and the Family*, 3d ed. Boston: Houghton Mifflin.

———. 1968. "Fertility and Poverty in the United States: Some Implications for Family-Planning Programs, Evaluations, and Research," *Journal of Marriage and the Family*, 30 (May), pp. 207–27.

CHRISTENSEN, HAROLD T. 1968. "Children in the Family: Relationship of Number and Spacing to Marital Success," *Journal of Marriage and the Family* 30 (May), pp. 283–89.

——— (ed.). 1964. *Handbook of Marriage and the Family*. Chicago: Rand McNally.

CHRISTENSEN, HAROLD T., and CHRISTINA F. GREGG. 1970. "Changing Sex Norms in America and Scandinavia," *Journal of Marriage and the Family*, 32 (November), pp. 616–27.

CHRISTENSEN, HAROLD T., and KATHRYN P. JOHNSON. 1971. *Marriage and the Family*, 3d ed. New York: Ronald.

CLARKE, HELEN I. 1957. *Social Legislation*. New York: Appleton-Century-Crofts.

COGSWELL, BETTY E., and MARVIN B. SUSSMAN. 1972. "Changing Family and Marriage Forms: Complications for Human Service System," *Family Coordinator*, 21:4, pp. 505–16.

CONSTANTINE, LARRY, and JOAN CONSTANTINE. 1970. "Where Is Marriage Going?" *The Futurist*, 4:2, pp. 44–46.

COOLEY, C. H. 1909. *Social Organization*. New York: Scribner's.

COOMBS, ROBERT H. 1962. "Reinforcement of Values in the Parental Home as a Factor in Mate Selection," *Marriage and Family Living,* 24, pp. 155–57.

CRAIN, ALAN J., and CAROLINE S. STAMN. 1965. "Intermittent Absence of Fathers and Children's Perceptions of Parents," *Journal of Marriage and the Family,* 27 (August), pp. 344–47.

CUBER, JOHN F. 1972. "How New Ideas About Sex Are Changing Our Lives," in Joann S. Delora and Jack R. Delora (eds.), *Intimate Life Styles.* Pacific Palisades, Calif.: Goodyear.

CUBER, JOHN F., and PEGGY B. HARROFF. 1968. *Sex and the Significant Americans.* Baltimore: Penguin.

CUMMING, ELAINE. 1963. "Further Thoughts on the Theory of Disengagement," *International Social Science Bulletin* (UNESCO), 15, pp. 377–93.

CUMMING, ELAINE, LOIS R. DEAN, DAVID S. NEWELL, and ISABEL MC-CAFFREY. 1960. "Disengagement: A Tentative Theory of Aging," *Sociometry* 23, pp. 23–25.

CUMMING, ELAINE, and WILLIAM E. HENRY. 1961. *Growing Old: The Process of Disengagement.* New York: Basic Books.

DAGER, EDWARD Z. 1964. "Socialization and Personality Development in the Child," in Harold T. Christensen (ed.), *Handbook of Marriage and the Family.* Chicago: Rand McNally.

DAVIS, ALLISON, and ROBERT J. HAVIGHURST. 1947. *Father of the Man.* Boston: Houghton Mifflin.

DAVIS, K. B. 1929. *Factors in the Sex Life of 2,200 Women.* New York: Harper.

DAVIS, KINGSLEY. 1949. *Human Society.* New York: Macmillan.

DECTER, MIDGE. 1972. *The New Chastity and Other Arguments Against Women's Liberation.* New York: Coward, McCann, and Geoghegan.

DeFLEUR, M. L., and F. R. WESTIE. 1960. "Changes in Interpersonal Perception as a Means of Reducing Cognitive Dissonance," *Journal of Abnormal and Social Psychology,* 61, pp. 402–10.

DEUTSCHER, IRWIN. 1964. "The Quality of Postparental Life: Definitions of the Situation," *Journal of Marriage and the Family,* 26, pp. 52–59.

DUBERMAN, LUCILE. 1973. "Becoming a Family: A Study of Reconstituted Families," unpublished Ph.D. dissertation. Cleveland: Case Western Reserve University.

DYER, EVERETT D. 1963. "Parenthood as Crisis: A Restudy," *Marriage and Family Living* 25 (May), pp. 196–201.

EDWARDS, JOHN N. 1967. "The Future of the Family Revisited," *Journal of Marriage and the Family,* 29:3, pp. 505–11.

———. 1969. *The Family and Change.* New York: Knopf.

EHRMANN, WINSTON. 1959. *Premarital Dating Behavior.* New York: Holt.

ELDER, GLEN H., JR. 1969. "Appearance and Education in Marriage Mobility," *American Sociological Review*, 34.

ELLIS, ALBERT. 1970. "Healthy and Disturbed Reasons for Having Extramarital Relations," in Gerhard Neubeck (ed.), *Extramarital Relations*. Englewood Cliffs, N.J.: Prentice-Hall.

FARBER, BERNARD. 1964. *Family: Organization and Interaction*. San Francisco: Chandler.

————. 1966. *Kinship and Family Organization*. New York: Wiley.

FARRIS, EDMOND J. 1955. "Male Fertility," in Marvin B. Sussman (ed.), *Sourcebook in Marriage and the Family*. Boston: Houghton Mifflin.

FELDMAN, HAROLD. 1967. "Development of the Husband-Wife Relationship: A Research Report," in Gerald R. Leslie, *The Family in Social Context*. New York: Oxford University Press.

FOLSOM, JOSEPH K. 1943. *The Family and Democratic Society*. New York: Wiley.

FORD, CLELLAN S., and FRANK A. BEACH. 1952. *Patterns of Sexual Behavior*. New York: Harper.

FREEDMAN, RONALD, PASCAL K. WHELPTON, and ARTHUR A. CAMPBELL. 1959. *Family Planning, Sterility, and Population Growth*. New York: McGraw-Hill.

FRIEDAN, BETTY. 1963. *The Feminine Mystique*. New York: Dell.

FULLERTON, GAIL PUTNEY. 1972. *Survival in Marriage*. New York: Holt.

GALLUP, GEORGE. 1962. "The Woman's Mind: America's Young Mothers," *Ladies' Home Journal* (March).

GARIGUE, PHILIP. 1961. "French Canadian Kinship and Urban Life," *American Anthropologist*, 63, pp. 498–507.

GEBBARD, PAUL H., WARDELL B. POMEROY, CLYDE E. MARTIN, and CORNELIA V. CHRISTENSON. 1958. *Pregnancy, Birth and Abortion*. New York: Harper.

GIELE, JANET ZOLLINGER. 1972. "Changes in the Modern Family: Their Impact on Sex Roles," in Helen Wortis and Clara Rabinowitz (eds.), *The Women's Movement*. New York: Wiley.

GLASSER, PAUL H., and LOIS N. GLASSER. 1962. "Role Reversal and Conflict Between Aged Parents and Their Children," *Marriage and Family Living*, 24 (February), pp. 46–51.

GLICK, PAUL C. 1957. *American Families*. New York: Wiley.

————. 1969. "Bachelors and Spinsters," in Jeffrey K. Hadden and Marie L. Borgatta (eds.), *Marriage and the Family*. Itasca, Ill.: Peacock.

GLUCKMAN, MAX. 1950. "Kinship and Marriage Among the Lozi of Northern Rhodesia and the Zulu of Natal," in A. R. Radcliffe-Brown and Daryll Forde (eds.), *African Systems of Kinship and Marriage*. London: Oxford University Press.

GOFFMAN, ERVING. 1961. *Asylums*. Garden City, N.Y.: Anchor Books.

GOLDBERG, PHILIP. 1972. "Are Women Prejudiced Against Women?" in Constantina Safilios-Rothschild (ed.), *Toward a Sociology of Women*. Lexington, Mass.: Xerox College.

GOLDSCHEIDER, CALVIN, and SIDNEY GOLDSTEIN. 1967. "Generational Changes in Jewish Family Structure," *Journal of Marriage and the Family*, 29 (May), pp. 267–76.

GOODE, WILLIAM J. 1956. *Women and Divorce*. New York: Free Press.

————. 1959. "The Sociology of the Family," in Robert K. Merton, Leonard Broom, and Leonard J. Cottrell (eds.), *Sociology Today*. New York: Basic Books.

————. 1959. "The Theoretical Importance of Love," *American Sociological Review*, 24 (February), pp. 38–47.

————. 1963. *World Revolutions and Family Patterns*. New York: Free Press.

GORDON, LINDA. 1970. "Functions of the Family," in Leslie B. Tanner (ed.), *Voices From Women's Liberation*. New York: New American Library.

GORDON, M., and M. C. BERNSTEIN. 1969. "Mate Choice and Domestic Life in the Nineteenth Century Marriage Manual," unpublished manuscript. University of Connecticut.

GOUGH, E. KATHLEEN. 1955. "The Nayars and the Definition of Marriage," *Journal of the Royal Anthropological Institute*, 85, pp. 45–80.

GREENE, GAIL. 1972. "A Vote Against Motherhood: A Wife Challenges the Importance of Childbearing," in Constantina Safilios-Rothschild (ed.), *Toward a Sociology of Women*. Lexington, Mass.: Xerox College.

GREENWALD, HAROLD. 1970. "Marriage as a Non-Legal Voluntary Association," in Herbert A. Otto (ed.), *The Family in Search of a Future*. New York: Appleton-Century-Crofts.

GRUNWALD, HENRY A. 1964. *Sex in America*. New York: Bantam Books.

GURIN, HAROLD, JOSEPH VEROFF, and SHEILA FELD. 1960. *Americans View Their Mental Health*. New York: Basic Books.

GUTTMACHER, ALAN F. 1957. "Abortions," in Morris Fishbein and Ruby Jo R. Kennedy (eds.), *Modern Marriage and Family Living*. New York: Oxford University Press.

HAMILTON, G. V. 1929. *A Research in Marriage*. New York: Boni.

HARMSWORTH, HARRY C., and MHYRA S. MINNIS. 1955. "Non-Statutory Courses of Divorce: The Lawyer's Point of View," *Marriage and Family Living*, 17, pp. 316–21.

HEER, DAVID. 1965. "Negro-White Marriage in the United States," *New Society*, 6, pp. 7–9.

HEISS, JEROLD S. 1960. "Premarital Characteristics of the Religiously

Intermarried in an Urban Area," *American Sociological Review,* 25 (February), pp. 53–54.

HEISS, JEROLD S., and MICHAEL GORDON. 1964. "Need Patterns and the Mutual Satisfaction of Dating and Engaged Couples," *Journal of Marriage and the Family,* 26 (August), pp. 337–39.

HILL, REUBEN. 1964. "The American Family of the Future," *Journal of Marriage and the Family,* 26 (February), pp. 20–28.

HOBART, CHARLES W. 1969. "Commitment, Value Conflict and the Future of the American Family," in John N. Edwards (ed.), *The Family and Change.* New York: Knopf.

HOBBS, DANIEL F., JR. 1965. "Parenthood as Crisis: A Third Study," *Marriage and Family Living,* 27 (August), pp. 367–72.

HUNT, MORTON. 1962. *Her Infinite Variety.* New York: Harper.

————. 1966. *The World of the Formerly Married.* New York: Mc-Graw-Hill.

IRISH, DONALD P. 1964. "Sibling Interaction: A Neglected Aspect in Family Life Research," *Social Forces,* 42, pp. 279–88.

JOHANNIS, THEODORE B., JR. 1959. "Married College Students and Their Honeymoons," *Family Life Coordinator,* 7, pp. 39–40.

JOHNSON, MICHAEL P. 1969. "Courtship and Commitment: A Study of Cohabitation on a University Campus," unpublished M.A. thesis. Iowa City: University of Iowa.

JONES, ERNEST. 1955. *The Life and Work of Sigmund Freud,* vol. II. New York: Basic Books.

JONES, HAROLD. 1960. "Adolescence in Our Society," in Jerome M. Seidman (ed.), *The Adolescent.* New York: Holt-Dryden.

JOUVENEL, BERTRAND DE. 1967. *The Art of Conjecture.* Trans. by Nikita Lary. New York: Basic Books.

KAGAN, JEROME. 1964. "Acquisition and Significance of Sex Typing and Sex Role Identity," in Martin L. Hoffman and Lois W. Hoffman (eds.), *Review of Child Development Research,* vol. I. New York: Russell Sage Foundation.

KALLMAN, F. I. 1952. "Comparative Twin Study of the Genetic Aspects of Male Homosexuality," *Journal of Nervous and Mental Diseases,* 115, pp. 283–98.

————. 1952. "Twin and Sibship Study of Overt Male Homosexuality," *American Journal of Human Genetics,* 4, pp. 136–46.

KANIN, EUGENE J., KAREN R. DAVIDSON, and SONIA R. SCHECK. 1970. "A Research Note on Male-Female Differentials in the Experience of Heterosexual Love," *Journal of Sex Research* (February), pp. 64–72.

KARDINER, ABRAM. 1961. "Bringing Up Children in Russia," *Saturday Review* (August 26).

KASSEL, VICTOR. 1966. "Polygyny After Sixty," *Geriatrics,* 21.

KELLY, JANIS. 1972. "Sisterlove: An Exploration of the Need for Homosexual Experience," *Family Coordinator,* 21:4, pp. 473–75.

KENDEL, WILLIAM F. 1966. *The Family in Perspective,* 2d ed. New York: Appleton-Century-Crofts.

KEPHART, WILLIAM M. 1954. "Drinking and Marital Disruption," *Quarterly Journal of Studies on Alcohol* (March), pp. 63–73.

————. 1955. "Occupational Level and Marital Disruption," *American Sociological Review,* 20 (August), pp. 456–65.

KERCKHOFF, ALAN C., and KEITH E. DAVIS. 1962. "Value Consensus and Need Complementarity in Mate Selection," *American Sociological Review,* 27, pp. 295–303.

KINSEY, ALFRED C., WARDELL B. POMEROY, and CLYDE E. MARTIN. 1948. *Sexual Behavior in the Human Male.* Philadelphia: Saunders.

KINSEY, ALFRED C., WARDELL B. POMEROY, CLYDE E. MARTIN, and PAUL H. GEBBARD. 1953. *Sexual Behavior in the Human Female.* Philadelphia: Saunders.

KIRKENDALL, LESTER A., and ROGER W. LIBBY. 1972. "Interpersonal Relationships: Crux of the Sexual Renaissance," in Joann S. Delora and Jack R. Delora (eds.), *Intimate Life Styles.* Pacific Palisades, Calif.: Goodyear.

KIRKPATRICK, CLIFFORD. 1963. *The Family as Process and Institution.* New York: Ronald.

KOHN, MELVIN L. 1969. *Class and Conformity.* Homewood, Ill.: Dorsey.

KUBIE, L. S. 1956. "Psychoanalysis and Marriage: Practical and Theoretical Issues," in V. E. Eisenstein (ed.), *Neurotic Interaction in Marriage.* New York: Basic Books.

KUHN, MENFORD H. 1955. "How Mates Are Sorted," in Howard Becker and Reuben Hill (eds.), *Family, Marriage, and Parenthood.* Boston: Heath.

KUNZ, PHILIP R., and MERLIN B. BRINKERHOFF. 1969. "Differential Childlessness by Color: The Destruction of a Cultural Belief," *Journal of Marriage and the Family,* 31 (November), pp. 713–19.

LANDIS, JUDSON T. 1960. "The Trauma of Children When Parents Divorce," *Marriage and Family Living,* 22 (February), pp. 7–13.

LANDIS, JUDSON T., and MARY G. LANDIS. 1953. *Building a Successful Marriage.* New York: Prentice-Hall.

LANGNER, THOMAS L., and STANLEY T. MICHAEL. 1963. *Life Stress and Mental Illness.* New York: Free Press.

LEDERER, WILLIAM J., and DON D. JACKSON. 1968. *The Mirages of Marriage.* New York: Norton.

LEMASTERS, E. E. 1957. "Parenthood as Crisis," *Marriage and Family Living,* 19, pp. 352–55.

LENSKI, GERHARD. 1961. *The Religious Factor.* Garden City, N.Y.: Doubleday.

LEPIERE, R. T. 1934. "Attitudes vs. Action," *Social Forces,* 13.

LESLIE, GERALD R. 1967. *The Family in Social Context.* New York: Oxford University Press.

LESLIE, GERALD R., and ARTHUR H. RICHARDSON. 1956. "Family Versus Campus Influences in Relation to Mate Selection," *Social Problems*, 4, pp. 117–21.

LEVENTHAL, GERALD S. 1970. "Influence of Brothers and Sisters on Sex-Role Behavior," *Journal of Personality and Social Psychology*, 16:3, pp. 452–65.

LEVETT, CARL. 1970. "A Parental Presence in Future Family Models," in Herbert A. Otto (ed.), *The Family in Search of a Future*. New York: Appleton-Century-Crofts.

LINDER, STAFFAN BURENSTAM. 1969. *The Harried Leisure Class*. New York: Columbia University Press.

LITWAK, EUGENE. 1960. "Occupational Mobility and Extended Family Cohesion," *American Sociological Review*, 25, pp. 9–21.

LOPATA, HELENA Z. 1969. "Loneliness: Forms and Components," *Social Problems*, 17.

LOWENTHAL, MARJORIE FISK, and CLAYTON HAVEN. 1968. "Interaction and Adoption: Intimacy as a Critical Variable," *American Sociological Review*, 33, pp. 20–30.

LYNN, DAVID B. 1966. "The Process of Learning Parental and Sex-Role Identification," *Journal of Marriage and the Family*, 28 (November), pp. 466–70.

LYNN, DAVID B., and WILLIAM L. SAWREY. 1958. "The Effects of Father-Absence on Norwegian Boys and Girls," *Journal of Abnormal and Social Psychology*, 59, pp. 258–62.

MALINOWSKI, BRONISLAW. 1964. "The Principle of Legitimacy," in Rose L. Coser (ed.), *The Family: Its Structure and Functions*. New York: St. Martin's Press.

MASTERS, WILLIAM H., and VIRGINIA E. JOHNSON. 1966. *Human Sexual Response*. Boston: Little, Brown.

——. 1970. *Human Sexual Inadequacy*. Boston: Little, Brown.

MEAD, GEORGE H. 1934. *Mind, Self, and Society*. Chicago: University of Chicago Press.

MEAD, MARGARET. 1966. "Marriage in Two Steps," *Redbook* (July), pp. 48–49, 84–85.

——. 1970. "Anomalies in American Postdivorce Relationships," in Paul Bohannan (ed.), *Divorce and After*. Garden City, N.Y.: Doubleday.

MEAD, MARGARET, and FRANCES B. KAPLAN (eds.). 1965. *American Women: The Report of the President's Commission on the Status of Women*. New York: Scribner's.

MENCHER, JOAN P. 1965. "The Nayars of South Malabar," in M. F. Nimkoff (ed.). *Comparative Social Systems*. Boston: Houghton Mifflin.

MERTON, ROBERT K. 1957. *Social Theory and Social Structure*. New York: Free Press.

MINARD, R. D. 1952. "Race Relations in the Pocahontas Coal Field," *Journal of Social Issues,* 8, pp. 29–44.

MOGEY, JOHN. 1957. "A Century of Declining Paternal Authority," *Marriage and Family Living,* 19, pp. 234–39.

MONAHAN, THOMAS P., and WILLIAM M. KEPHART. 1954. "Divorce and Desertion by Religious and Mixed Religious Groups," *American Journal of Sociology,* 59 (March).

MONEY, J. 1961. "Sex Hormones and Other Variables in Human Eroticism," in W. C. Young (ed.), *Sex and Internal Secretions,* vol. II. Baltimore: Williams and Wilkins.

MONEY, J., J. L. HAMPSON, and J. G. HAMPSON. 1955. "An Examination of Some Basic Sexual Concepts: The Evidence of Human Hermaphroditism," *Bulletin of the Johns Hopkins Hospital,* 97, pp. 301–19.

MOSS, J. JOAN, and MARIAN MYERS MACNAB. 1961. "Young Families," *Journal of Home Economics,* 53 (December), pp. 829–34.

MURDOCK, GEORGE PETER. 1949. *Social Structure.* New York: Free Press.

MYERS, LONNY, and HUNTER LEGGITT. 1972. "A New View of Adultery," *Sexual Behavior* (February), pp. 52–62.

National Center for Health Statistics. 1972. *Monthly Vital Statistics Report,* 1, p. 9.

NEUGARTEN, BERNICE L., and KAROL K. WEINSTEIN. 1964. "The Changing American Grandparent," *Journal of Marriage and the Family,* 26 (May), pp. 199–205.

New York Times, October 19, 1971, p. 1.

———, December 5, 1972, p. 1.

———, December 28, 1972, p. 34.

———, February 18, 1973; Section E., p. 4.

Newsweek, "Campus '65," March 22, 1965.

NIMKOFF, M. F. (ed.). 1965. *Comparative Family Systems.* Boston: Houghton Mifflin.

NORTON, ELEANOR HOLMES. 1972. *Women's Role in Contemporary Society: The Report of the New York City Commission on Human Rights, September 21-25, 1970.* New York: Avon Books.

NYE, F. IVAN. 1957. "Child Adjustment in Broken and in Unhappy Unbroken Homes," *Marriage and Family Living,* 19, pp. 356–61.

———. 1969. "Values, Family, and a Changing Society," in John N. Edwards (ed.), *The Family and Change.* New York: Knopf.

NYE, F. IVAN, and LOIS W. HOFFMAN (eds.). 1963. *The Employed Mother in America.* Skokie, Ill.: Rand McNally.

OGBURN, W. F. 1966. *Social Change.* New York: Dell.

OGBURN, W. F., and M. F. NIMKOFF. 1955. *Technology and the Changing Family.* Boston: Houghton Mifflin.

OGBURN, W. F., and CLARK TIBBITTS. 1934. "The Family and Its Functions," Report of the President's Research Committee on Social Trends, in *Recent Social Trends in the United States*. New York: McGraw-Hill.

OLSON, DAVID H. 1972. "Marriage of the Future: Revolutionary or Evolutionary Change?" *Family Coordinator*, 21:4, pp. 383–93.

ORLEANS, MYRON, and FLORENCE WOLFSON. 1970. "Future of the Family," *The Futurist*, 4:2, pp. 48–49.

OSOFSKY, JOY, and HOWARD OSOFSKY. 1972. "Androgyny as a Life Style," *Family Coordinator*, 21:4, pp. 411–18.

PACKARD, VANCE. 1968. *The Sexual Wilderness*. New York: McKay.

PARKE, ROBERT, JR., and PAUL C. GLICK. 1967. "Prospective Changes in Marriage and the Family," *Journal of Marriage and the Family*, 29 (May), pp. 249–56.

PARRY, JOSEPH B., and ERDWIN H. PFUHL. 1963. "Adjustment of Children in 'Sole' and 'Remarriage' Homes," *Marriage and Family Living*, 25, pp. 221–23.

PARSONS, TALCOTT. 1959. "The Social Structure of the Family," in Ruth N. Anschen (ed.), *The Family: Its Function and Destiny*. New York: Harper.

PARSONS, TALCOTT, et al. 1955. *Family, Socialization, and Interaction Process*. New York: Free Press.

PAVELA, TODD H. 1964. "An Exploratory Study of Negro-White Intermarriage in Indiana," *Journal of Marriage and the Family*, 26 (May), pp. 209-11.

PHERSON, R. 1954. "Bilateral Kin Groups as a Structural Type," *Journal of East Asiatic Studies* (University of Manila), 3, pp. 199–202.

PINEO, PETER C. 1961. "Disenchantment in the Later Years of Marriage," *Marriage and Family Living*, 23, pp. 3–11.

POFFENBERGER, THOMAS. 1960. "Individual Choice in Adolescent Premarital Sex Behavior," *Marriage and Family Living*, 22 (November), pp. 324–30.

Population Reference Bureau. 1963. "Marriage and the American Woman," *Population Profile*, Washington, D.C.: U.S. Government Printing Office, June.

PRICE, SHARON. 1971. "Are Most People Dissatisfied with Their Sexual Life?" *Sexual Behavior* (December), p. 52.

RABIN, A. I. 1957. "Personality Maturity of Kibbutz and Non-Kibbutz Children as Reflected in Rorschach Findings," *American Journal of Orthopsychiatry*, 27, pp. 48–53.

———. 1958. "Infants and Children Under Conditions of Intermittent Mothering in the Kibbutz," *American Journal of Orthopsychiatry*, 28, pp. 577–84.

———. 1959. "Attitudes of Kibbutz Children to Parents and Families," *American Journal of Orthopsychiatry*, 29, pp. 172–79.

RAINWATER, LEE. 1964. "Marital Sexuality in Four Cultures of Poverty," *Journal of Marriage and the Family,* 26 (November), pp. 457–66.

―――. 1965. *Family Design: Marital Sexuality, Family Size, and Contraception.* Chicago: Aldine.

RAPOPORT, RHONA, and ROBERT N. RAPOPORT. 1964. "New Light on the Honeymoon," *Human Relations,* 17, pp. 33–56.

―――. 1965. "Work and Family in Contemporary Society," *American Sociological Review,* 30, pp. 381–94.

REISS, IRA L. 1960. *Premarital Sexual Standards in America.* Glencoe, Ill.: Free Press.

―――. 1965. "The Universality of the Family: A Conceptual Analysis," *Journal of Marriage and the Family,* 27 (November), pp. 443–53.

―――. 1971. *The Family System in America.* New York: Holt.

―――. 1972. "How and Why Americans' Sex Standards Are Changing," in Joann S. Delora and Jack R. Delora (eds.), *Intimate Life Styles.* Pacific Palisades, Calif.: Goodyear.

REISS, PAUL J. 1962. "The Extended Kinship System: Correlates of and Attitudes on Frequency of Interaction," *Marriage and Family Living,* 24 (February), pp. 33–39.

ROKEACH, MILTON. 1969. "Definition of Attitude," in Edgar F. Borgatta (ed.), *Social Psychology.* Chicago: Rand McNally.

ROLLINS, BETTY. 1971. "Motherhood: Who Needs It?" in Arlene S. Skolnick and Jerome H. Skolnick (eds.), *Family in Transition.* Boston: Little, Brown.

ROLLINS, BOYD C., and HAROLD FELDMAN. 1970. "Marital Satisfaction Over the Family Life Cycle," *Journal of Marriage and the Family,* 32 (February), pp. 25–28.

ROSE, ARNOLD M. 1955. "Factors Associated with the Life Satisfactions of Middle-Class, Middle-Aged Persons," *Marriage and Family Living,* 17, pp. 15–19.

―――. 1964. "A Current Theoretical Issue in Social Gerontology," *The Gerontologist,* 4, pp. 46–50.

ROSENBERG, B. G., and BRIAN SUTTON-SMITH. 1972. *Sex and Identity.* New York: Holt.

ROSOW, IRVING. 1957. "Issue in the Concept of Need-Complementarity," *Sociometry,* 20, pp. 216–33.

―――. 1965. "And Then We Were Old," *Trans-action,* 2, pp. 21–26.

ROY, RUSTUM, and DELLA ROY. 1970. "Is Monogamy Outdated?" *The Humanist,* pp. 19–26.

RUBIN, ISADORE. 1965. *Sexual Life After Sixty.* New York: New Amsterdam Library.

SAFILIOS-ROTHSCHILD, CONSTANTINA. 1969. "Family Sociology or Wives' Sociology? A Cross-Cultural Examination of Decision-Making," *Journal of Marriage and the Family,* 31:2, pp. 290–301.

SATIR, VIRGINIA. 1970. "Marriage as a Human-Actualizing Contract," in Herbert A. Otto (ed.), *The Family in Search of a Future*. New York: Appleton-Century-Crofts.

SCANZONI, JOHN. 1972. *Sexual Bargaining*. Englewood Cliffs, N.J.: Prentice-Hall.

SCHELLENBERG, JAMES A. 1960. "Homogamy in Personal Values and the Field of Eligibles," *Social Forces*, 39, pp. 157–62.

SCHELLENBERG, JAMES A., and LAWRENCE S. BEE. 1960. "A Reexamination of the Theory of Complementary Needs in Mate Selection," *Marriage and Family Living*, 22, pp. 227–32.

SCHLEGEL, W. S. 1962. "Die Konstitutionsbiologischen Grundlagen der Homosexualität," *Zeitschrift für Menschliche Vereinbarung: Konstitutionslehre*, 36, pp. 341–64.

SCHNEIDER, DAVID M. 1968. *American Kinship: A Cultural Account*. Englewood Cliffs, N.J.: Prentice-Hall.

SIMON, WILLIAM, and JOHN GAGNON. 1972. "Sex, Marriage, and Social Class," in Saul D. Feldman and Gerald W. Thielbar (eds.), *Life Styles: Diversity in American Society*. Boston: Little, Brown.

SIMPSON, GEORGE E., and J. MILTON YINGER. 1958. *Racial and Cultural Minorities*. New York: Harper.

SKINNER, B. F. 1948. *Walden II*. New York: Macmillan.

SOMERVILLE, ROSE M. 1972. "The Future of Family Relationships in the Middle and Older Years: Clues in Fiction," *Family Coordinator*, 21:4, pp. 487–98.

SPIRO, M. E. 1954. "Is the Family Universal?" *American Anthropologist*, 56, pp. 839–46.

———. 1958. *Children of the Kibbutz*. Cambridge, Mass.: Harvard University Press.

SPREY, JETSE. 1971. "Are Most People Dissatisfied with Their Sexual Life?" *Sexual Behavior* (December), pp. 52–53.

———. 1972. "Extramarital Relations," *Sexual Behavior* (August).

STEFFENSMEIR, DARRELL. 1966. "Male and Female Attitudes Toward Homosexuality," unpublished M.A. thesis. Iowa City: University of Iowa.

STRAUSS, A. 1946. "The Ideal and the Chosen Mate," *American Journal of Sociology*, 52, pp. 204–8.

STREIB, GORDON. 1969. "Disengagement: Scientific Theory or Sociological Interpretation?" Paper read at Southern Sociological Association meetings in New Orleans (April 12).

SUSSMAN, MARVIN B. 1953. "The Help Patterns in the Middle Class Family," *American Sociological Review*, 17 (February), pp. 22–28.

———. 1955. "Activity Patterns of Post Parental Couples and Their Relationship to Family Continuity," *Marriage and Family Living*, 17, pp. 338–41.

———. 1970. "A Family Policy," original version presented at Groves Conference of Marriage and the Family, Winston-Salem, N.C.

————. 1970. "Family Systems in the 1970's: Analysis, Politics, Programs," *Annals of American Academy of Political and Social Science*, 396, pp. 40–56.

————. 1971. "Changing Families in a Changing Society," *Report of Forum 14: 1970 White House Conference on Children.* Washington, D.C.: U.S. Government Printing Office.

SUSSMAN, MARVIN B., and LEE BURCHINAL. 1962. "Kin Family Network: Unheralded Structure in Current Conceptualizations of Family Functioning," *Marriage and Family Living,* 24 (August), pp. 231–40.

SUSSMAN, MARVIN B., and BETTY E. COGSWELL. 1972. "The Meaning of Variant and Experimental Marriage Styles and Family Forms in the 1970's," *Family Coordinator* 21:4, pp. 375–81.

SUTTON-SMITH, B., and B. G. ROSENBERG. 1965. "Age Changes in the Effects of Ordinal Position on Sex-Role Identification," *Journal of Genetic Psychology,* 107, pp. 61–73.

SWITZER, ALAN L. 1966. "Some Factors Related to In-Law Difficulty and Conflict," unpublished M.S. thesis. West LaFayette, Ind.: Purdue University.

TERMAN, L. M. 1938. *Psychological Factors in Marital Happiness.* New York: McGraw-Hill.

THEODORE, ATHENA. 1971. *The Professional Woman.* Cambridge, Mass.: Schenkman.

THOMPSON, WAYNE E., and GORDON F. STREIB. 1961. "Meaningful Activity in a Family Context," in Robert W. Kleemeier (ed.), *Aging and Leisure.* New York: Oxford University Press.

TOFFLER, ALVIN. 1970. *Future Shock.* New York: Random House.

TOWNSEND, PETER. 1968. "The Emergence of the Four-Generation Family in Industrial Society," in Bernice L. Neugarten (ed.), *Middle Age and Aging.* Chicago: University of Chicago Press.

TRAIN, ARTHUR. 1931. *Puritan's Progress.* New York: Scribner's.

UDRY, RICHARD J. 1966. "Marital Instability by Race, Sex, Education, and Occupation Using 1960 Census Data," *American Journal of Sociology,* 72 (September), pp. 203–9.

U.S. Department of Commerce, Bureau of the Census. 1960. *Current Population Reports, Series P-25.* Washington, D.C.: U.S. Government Printing Office.

————. 1963. "Marriage and the American Woman," *Population Profile.* Washington, D.C.: Population Reference Bureau (June).

————. 1963. *United States Census of Population: 1960.* Final Report PC (2)-4A. Washington, D.C.: U.S. Government Printing Office.

————. 1964. *Statistical Abstracts of the United States: 1964.* Washington, D.C.: U.S. Government Printing Office.

————. 1970. *Probabilities of Marriage, Divorce, and Remarriage,* P-23, No. 32. Washington, D.C.: U.S. Government Printing Office.

————. 1971. *Statistical Abstracts of the United States: 1971.* Washington, D.C.: U.S. Government Printing Office.

U.S. Department of Health, Education, and Welfare, National Center for Health Statistics. 1963. *Divorce Statistics Analysis: United States 1963,* Series 21, no. 13. Washington, D.C.: U.S. Government Printing Office.

U.S. Department of Health, Education, and Welfare, Public Health Service. 1959. "Marriage and Divorce Statistics," *Vital Statistics of the United States: 1959,* section 2. Washington, D.C.: National Office of Vital Statistics, p. 9.

UPDIKE, JOHN. 1969. "Van Loves Ada, Ada Loves Van," *New Yorker* (August 2), pp. 67–75.

VAN GENNEP, ARNOLD. 1960. *The Rites of Passage.* Trans. by Monika B. Vizedom and Gabrielle L. Caffee. Chicago: University of Chicago Press.

VERNON, GLENN A., and JACK A. BROADWAY. 1959. "Attitudes Toward Artificial Insemination and Some Variables Associated Therewith," *Marriage and Family Living,* 21, pp. 43–47.

VILAR, ESTHER. 1973. *The Manipulated Man.* New York: Farrar, Straus, and Giroux.

VINCENT, CLARK. 1961. *Unmarried Mothers.* Glencoe, Ill.: Free Press.

WATTENBERG, BEN J., and RICHARD M. SCAMMON. 1965. *This U.S.A.* Garden City, N.Y.: Doubleday.

WEINBERG, S. KIRSON. 1955. *Incest Behavior.* New York: Citadel.

WHELPTON, PASCAL K., ARTHUR A. CAMPBELL, and JOHN E. PATTERSON. 1966. *Fertility and Family Planning in the United States.* Princeton: Princeton University Press.

WINCH, ROBERT F. 1952. *The Modern Family.* New York: Henry Holt.

————. 1958. *Mate Selection.* New York: Harper.

————. 1963. *The Modern Family,* 2d ed. New York: Holt.

————. 1967. "Another Look at the Theory of Complementary Needs in Mate Selection," *Journal of Marriage and the Family,* 29, pp. 756–62.

WITTMAN, CARL. 1972. "A Gay Manifesto," in Joann S. Delora and Jack R. Delora (eds.), *Intimate Life Styles.* Pacific Palisades, Calif.: Goodyear.

World Almanac. 1973. New York: Newspaper Enterprise.

YARROW, MARIAN, *et al.* 1962. "Childrearing in Families of Working and Nonworking Mothers," *Sociometry,* 25, pp. 122–40.

YOUNG, MICHAEL, and PETER WILLMOTT. 1964. *Family and Kinship in East London.* Baltimore: Penguin.

ZELDITCH, MORRIS. 1964. "Family, Marriage, and Kinship," in R. E. L. Faris (ed.), *Handbook of Modern Sociology.* Chicago: Rand McNally.

Index